W9-DGL-679

SCHOLARSHIP IN WOMEN'S HISTORY: REDISCOVERED AND NEW

Editor

GERDA LERNER

A CARLSON PUBLISHING SERIES

For a complete listing of the titles in this series,
please see the back of this book.

Status of Women in Georgia, 1783-1860

Eleanor Miot Boatwright

CARLSON
Publishing Inc

BROOKLYN, NEW YORK, 1994

Please see the end of this volume for a listing of all the titles in the Carlson Publishing Series *Scholarship in Women's History: Rediscovered and New*, edited by Gerda Lerner, of which this is Volume 2.

The *Preface* to this book is a revised version of a portion of Anne Firor Scott's essay "A Different View of Southern History," originally published on pages 47-54 of *Unheard Voices: The First Historians of Southern Women*, edited by Anne Firor Scott (University of Virginia Press, 1993). It is Copyrighted by the Rector and Visitors of the University of Virginia and published here by permission.

Library of Congress Cataloging-in-Publication Data

Boatwright, Eleanor Miot, 1895-
   Status of women in Georgia, 1783-1860 / by Eleanor Miot
Boatwright ; preface by Anne Firor Scott ; introduction by
Kathleen Brown.
     p. cm. — (Scholarship in women's history : v. 2)
   Includes bibliographical references and index.
   ISBN 0-926019-63-5
   1. Women—Georgia—History. 2. Women—Georgia—Social conditions.
I. Title. II. Series: Scholarship in Women's History ; 2.
HQ1438.G4B63   1994
305.42'09758—dc20   94-16767

Typographic design: Julian Waters

Typeface: Bitstream ITC Galliard

Jacket and Case design: Alison Lew

Index prepared by Scholars Editorial Services, Inc., Madison, Wisconsin.

Printed on acid-free, 250-year-life paper.

Manufactured in the United States of America.

Contents

Editor's Introduction
to the Series

An important aspect of the development of modern scholarship in Women's History has been the recovery of lost, forgotten or neglected sources. In the 1960s, when the practitioners of Women's History were so few as to be virtually invisible to the general profession, one of the commonly heard answers to the question, why is there nothing about women in your text? was that, unfortunately, women until the most recent past, had to be counted among the illiterate and had therefore not left many sources. It was common then to refer to women as among the "anonymous"—a group that included members of minority racial and ethnic groups of both sexes, most working-class people, colonials, Native Americans and women. In short, most of the populations of the past. These ignorant and erroneous answers satisfied only those who wished to stifle discussion, but they did make the issue of "sources" an urgent concern to practitioners of Women's History.

To historians who had done work in primary sources regarding women, it was obvious that the alleged dearth of sources did not exist, but it was true that the sources were not readily available. In archives and finding guides, women disappeared under the names of male family members. The voluminous records of their organizational work were disorganized, uncatalogued, and not infrequently rotting in file boxes in basement storage rooms. Since few if any researchers were interested in them, there seemed to be little purpose in making them accessible or even maintaining them. There were no archival projects to preserve the primary sources of American women comparable to the well-supported archival projects concerning Presidents and male political leaders. There were only a few and quite partial bibliographies of American women, while the encyclopedic reference works, such as the *DAB* (*Dictionary of American Biography*) or similar sources traditionally neglected to include all but a small number of women notables.

When the three-volume *Notable American Women: 1607—1950: A Biographical Dictionary* appeared in 1971, (to be followed by a fourth volume in 1980), it marked an important contribution to sources on women.[1] This comprehensive scholarly work consisted of 1,801 entries, with a biographical essay and a bibliography of works by and about each woman under discussion. It readily became obvious to even the casual user of these volumes how few modern biographies of these notable women existed, despite the availability of sources.

The real breakthrough regarding "sources" was made by a "grand manuscript search," begun in 1971, which aimed to survey historical archives in every state and identify their holdings pertaining to women. This project was started by a small committee—Clarke Chambers, Carl Degler, Janet James, Anne Firor Scott and myself. After a mail questionnaire survey of 11,000 repositories in every state, to which more than 7,000 repositories responded, it was clear that the sources on women were far wider and deeper than anyone had suspected. Ultimately, the survey resulted in a two-volume reference tool, Andrea Hinding, ed., *Women's History Sources: A Guide to Archives and Manuscript Collections in the United States*.[2]

The project proved that there were unused and neglected sources of Women's History to be found literally in every archive in the country. Participation in the survey convinced many archivists to reorganize and reclassify their holdings, so that materials about women could be more readily identified.

The arguments about "illiterate women" and absence of sources are no longer heard, but the problem of having accessible sources for Women's History continued. Even after archives and libraries reorganized and reclassified their source holding on the subject, most of the pertinent materials were not available in print. Many of the early developers of Women's History worked on source collections, reprint edition projects and, of course, bibliographies. The rapid and quite spectacular expansion of the field brought with it such great demand for sources that publishers at last responded. The past twenty years have seen a virtual flood of publications in Women's History, so that the previous dearth of material seems almost inconceivable to today's students.

For myself, having put a good many years of my professional life into the development of "source books" and bibliographies, it did not seem particularly urgent to continue the effort under the present conditions. But I was awakened to the fact that there might still be a problem of neglected and forgotten sources in Women's History as a result of a conference, which Kathryn Sklar and I organized in 1988. The Wingspread Conference "Graduate Training in U.S. Women's History" brought together 63 representatives of 57 institutions of higher education who each represented a graduate program in Women's History. As part of our preparation for the conference, we asked each person invited to list all the dissertations in Women's History she had directed or was then directing. The result was staggering: it appeared that there were 99 completed dissertations and 236 then underway. This was by no means the entire national output, since we surveyed only the 63 participants at the conference and did not survey the many faculty persons not represented, who had directed such dissertations. The questions arose—What happened to all these dissertations? Why did so many of them not get published?

When Ralph Carlson approached me at about that time with the idea of publishing "lost sources" in Women's History, I was more ready than I would have been without benefit of the Wingspread survey to believe that, indeed, there still were some such neglected sources out there, and to undertake such a project.

We used the dissertation list from the Wingspread Conference as a starting point. A researcher then went through all the reference works listing dissertations in history and other fields in the English language from 1870 to the present. Among these she identified 1,235 titles in what we now call Women's History. We then cross-checked these titles against the electronic catalog of the Library of Congress, which represents every book owned by the LC (or to define it differently, every book copyrighted and published in the U.S.). This cross-check revealed that of the 1,235 dissertations, 314 had been published, which is more than 25 percent. That represents an unusually high publication ratio, which may be a reflection of the growth and quality of the field.

A further selection based on abstracts of the 921 unpublished dissertations narrowed the field to 101. Of these we could not locate 33 authors or the authors were not interested in publication. Out of the 68 remaining dissertations we selected the eleven we considered best in both scholarship and writing. These are first-rate books that should have been published earlier and that for one reason or another fell between the cracks.

Why did they not get published earlier? In the case of the Boatwright manuscript, an unusually brilliant Master's thesis done in 1939, undoubtedly the neglect of Women's History at that time made the topic seem unsuitable for publication. Similar considerations may have worked against publication of several other earlier dissertations. In other cases, lack of mentorship and inexperience discouraged the writers from pursuing publication in the face of one or two rejections of their manuscripts. Several of the most valuable books in the series required considerable rewriting under editorial supervision, which, apparently, had not earlier been available to the authors. There are also several authors who became members of what we call "the lost generation," historians getting their degrees in the 1980s when there were few jobs available. This group of historians, which disproportionately consisted of women, retooled and went into different fields. Three of the books in this series are the work of these historians, who needed considerable persuasion to do the necessary revisions and editing. We are pleased to have found their works and to have persisted in the effort of making them available to a wider readership, since they have a distinct contribution to make.

The books in this series cover a wide range of topics. Two of them are detailed studies in the status of women, one in Georgia, 1783-1860, the other in Russia in the early 1900s. Two are valuable additions to the literature on the anti-woman's suffrage campaigns in the U.S. Of the four books dealing with the history of women's organizations, three are detailed regional studies and one is a comparative history of the British and American Women's Trade Union League. Finally, the three biographical studies of eighteenth- and nineteenth-century women offer either new information or new interpretations of their subjects.

Eleanor Miot Boatwright, *Status of Women in Georgia, 1783—1860*, was discovered by Professor Anne Firor Scott in the Duke University archives and represents, in her words "a buried treasure." An M.A. thesis written by a high school teacher in Augusta, Georgia, its level of scholarship and the depth of its research are of the quality expected of a dissertation. The author has drawn on a vast range of primary sources, including legal sources that were then commonly used for social history, to document and analyze the social customs, class differences, work and religion of white women in Georgia. While her treatment of race relations reflects the limitations of scholarship on that subject in the 1930s, she gives careful attention to the impact of race relations on white women. Her analysis of the linkage made by Southern male apologists for slavery between the subordination ("protection") of women and the subordination of slaves (also rationalized as their "protection") is particularly insightful. The work has much information to offer the contemporary scholar and can be compared in its scholarship and its general approach to the work of Julia Spruill and Elizabeth Massey. When it is evaluated in comparison with other social histories of its period, its research methodology and interpretative focus on women are truly remarkable.

Anne Bobroff-Hajal's, *Working Women in Russia Under the Hunger Tsar: Political Activism and Daily Life*, is a fascinating, excellently researched study of a topic on which there is virtually no material available in the English language. Focusing on women industrial workers in Russia's Central Industrial Region, most of them employed in textile production, Bobroff studied their daily lives and family patterns, their gender socialization, their working and living conditions and their political activism during the Revolution: in political organizations, in food riots and in street fighting. The fact that these women and their families lived mostly in factory barracks will be of added interest to labor historians, who may wish to compare their lives and activities with other similarly situated groups in the U.S. and England. Drawing on a rich mixture of folkloric sources, local newspapers, oral histories, workers' memoirs and ethnographic material, Bobroff presents a convincing and intimate picture of working-class life before the Russian Revolution. Bobroff finds that the particularly strong mother-child bonding of Russian women workers, to which they were indoctrinated from childhood on, undermined their ability to form coherent political groups capable of maintaining their identity over a long period of time. Her thesis, excellently supported and well argued, may undermine some commonly held beliefs on this subject. It should prove of interest to all scholars working on gender socialization and to others working on labor culture, working-class activism, and class consciousness.

Rosemary Keller, *Patriotism and the Female Sex: Abigail Adams and the American Revolution*, is a sophisticated, well-documented interpretation of Abigail Adams's intellectual and political development, set firmly within the historical context. Compared with other Abigail Adams biographies, this work is outstanding in treating her seriously as an agent in history and as an independent intellectual. Abigail Adams emerges from this study as a woman going as far as it was possible to go within the limits of the gender conventions of her time and struggling valiantly, through influencing her husband, to extend these gender conventions. This is an accomplishment quite sufficient for one woman's life time. Professor Keller's sensitive biography makes a real contribution to colonial and women's history.

Elizabeth Ann Bartlett, *Liberty, Equality, Sorority: The Origins and Integrity of Feminist Thought: Frances Wright, Sarah Grimké and Margaret Fuller*, is another work of intellectual history. It attempts to define a common "feminism" emerging from the thought of these important nineteenth-century thinkers and concludes that feminism, in order to sustain itself, must balance the tensions between the concepts of liberty, equality, and sorority. The lucid, well-researched discussions of each woman's life and work should appeal to the general reader and make this book a valuable addition to courses in intellectual history and women's history and literature.

Mary Grant, *Private Woman, Public Person: An Account of the Life of Julia Ward Howe from 1819 to 1868*, is a sensitive, feminist study of Howe's life and thought up to the turning point in 1868, when she decided to dedicate her life to public activism in behalf of women. By carefully analyzing Howe's private letters and journals, the author uncovers a freer, more powerful and creative writer beneath the formal *persona* of the author of "The Battle Hymn of the Republic" than we have hitherto known. She also discusses in detail Howe's fascinating, never published, unfinished novel, "Eva and Raphael," which features a number of then taboo subjects, such as rape, madness and an androgynous character. This well-written biography reveals new aspects and dimensions of Julia Ward Howe's life and work.

Jane Jerome Camhi, *Women Against Women: American Anti-Suffragism, 1880-1920*, and Thomas J. Jablonsky, *The Home, Heaven, and Mother Party: Female Anti-Suffragists in America, 1868-1920*, are complementary studies that should be indispensable for any serious student or scholar of woman suffrage. They are, in fact, the only extant book-length studies of anti-suffragism. This important movement has until now been accessible to modern readers only through the somewhat biased lens of contemporary suffragists' observations. They consistently underestimated its scope and significance and did not engage with its basic paradox, that it was a movement by women against women.

Jane Camhi's comprehensive study of nationwide anti-woman's suffrage movements makes this paradox a central theme. Camhi analyses the "antis' " ideas and ideology and offers some thought-provoking theories about the competing and contradictory positions women took in regard to formal political power. Her insightful profile of a noted anti-suffragist, Ida Tarbell, is an additional contribution this fine book makes to the historical literature.

Thomas Jablonsky's study is focused more narrowly on the organizational history of the rise and fall of the movement. The book is based on extensive research in the organizational records of the anti-suffragists on a state and national level, the records of Congressional hearings, biographical works and the manuscripts of leaders. Jablonsky takes the "antis" seriously and disproves the suffragists' argument that they were merely pawns of male interest groups. He offers a sympathetic, but critical evaluation of their ideas. His detailed attention to organizational efforts in states other than the major battle-grounds—Massachusetts, New York and Illinois—make this book a valuable resource for scholars in history, political science and Women's History.

The four remaining books in the series all focus on aspects of women's organizational activities. Taken together, they reveal the amazing energy, creativity, and persistence of women's institution building on the community and local level. They sustain and highlight the thesis that women built the infrastructures of community life, while men held the positions of visible power. Based on research in four distinctly different regions, these studies should prove useful not only for the intrinsic worth of each, but for comparative purposes.

Darlene Roth, *Matronage: Patterns in Women's Organizations, Atlanta, Georgia, 1890-1940*, is a thoroughly researched, gracefully written study of the networks of women's organizations in that city. The author's focus on conservative women's organizations, such as the Daughters of the American Revolution, the Colonial Dames, and the African-American Chatauqua Circle, adds to the significance of the book. The author defines "matronage" as the functions and institutionalization of the networks of social association among women. By focusing on a Southern city in the Progressive era, Roth provides rich comparative material for the study of women's voluntarism. She challenges notions of the lack of organizational involvement by Southern women. She traces the development of women's activities from communal service orientation—the building of war memorials—to advocacy of the claims of women and children and, finally, to advocacy of women's rights. Her comparative approach, based on the study of the records of white and African-American women's organizations and leadership—she studied 508 white and 150 black women—is illuminating and offers new insights. The book should be of interest to readers in Urban and Community History, Southern History, and Women's History.

Robin Miller Jacoby, *The British and American Women's Trade Union Leagues, 1890-1925: A Case Study of Feminism and Class*, is a comparative study of working-class women in Britain and America in the Progressive period. Although parts of this work have appeared as articles in scholarly journals, the work has never before been accessible in its entirety. Jacoby traces the development of Women's Trade Union Leagues in Britain and America, exploring their different trajectories and settings. By focusing on the interaction of women's and labor movements, the author provides rich empirical material. Her analysis of the tensions and overlapping interests of feminism and class consciousness is important to feminist theory. Her discussion of protective labor legislation, as it was debated and acted upon in two different contexts, makes an important contribution to the existing literature. It also addressees issues still topical and hotly debated in the present day. The book will be of interest to labor historians, Women's History specialists, and the general public.

Janice Steinschneider, *An Improved Woman: The Wisconsin Federation of Women's Clubs, 1895-1920*, is a richly documented study based on a multitude of primary sources, which reveals the amazing range of women's activities as community builders and agents of change. Wisconsin clubwomen founded libraries, fostered changes in school curricula and worked to start kindergartens and playgrounds. They helped preserve historic and natural landmarks and organized to improve public health services. They built a sound political base—long before they had the right of suffrage—from which they trained women leaders for whom they then helped to secure public appointments. They worked to gain access for women to university education and employment and, in addition to many other good causes, they worked for world peace. Steinschneider's description and analysis of "women's public sphere" is highly sophisticated. Hers is one of the best studies on the subject and should prove indispensable to all concerned with understanding women's political activities, their construction of a public sphere for women, and their efforts and successes as builders of large coalitions.

Margit Misangyi Watts, *High Tea at Halekulani: Feminist Theory and American Clubwomen*, is a more narrowly focused study of clubwomen's work than are the other three, yet its significance ranges far above that of its subject matter. Watts tells the story of the Outdoor Circle, an upper-class white women's club in Hawaii, from its founding in 1911 on. Its main activities were to make Hawaii beautiful: to plant trees, clean up eyesores, preserve nature and rid the islands of billboards. To achieve these modest goals, the women had to become consummate politicians and lobbyists and learn how to run grassroots boycotts and publicity and educational campaigns, and how to form long-lasting coalitions. Above all, as Watts's fine theoretical analysis shows, they insisted that their female vision, their woman-centered view, become an accepted part of the public discourse. This case study is rich in theoretical implications. Together with the other three studies of women's club activities it offers not only a wealth of practical examples of women's work for social change, but it also shows that such work both resists patriarchal views and practices and redefines them in the interests of women.

Gerda Lerner
Madison, Wisconsin

Preface

by Anne Firor Scott

Whether purposefully or accidentally, Eleanor Miot Boatwright left few traces of her life for those who came after. Perhaps if we could ask her she would say that her legacy is to be found in the lives of thousands of young women who had studied history under her tutelage at the Tubman Girls High School in Augusta, Georgia, many of whom, half a century after her death, still speak with awe and enthusiasm about her teaching, the example she set, and the encouragement she gave them.

Whatever the reason, no papers seem to have survived, and a reasonably assiduous search for biographical data has turned up very few verifiable facts. She was born in Augusta, Georgia, in 1895. Her parents had earlier lost two sons in infancy. Her father, after trying a number of different careers, had a florist shop in North Augusta, South Carolina, by the time she was growing up. She enrolled at the all-female Tubman High School, named for an early Augusta feminist, Emily Tubman, and considered to be one of the best schools in the state, one in which the most ambitious young teachers in Georgia hoped to find jobs. There Boatwright came under the influence of an extraordinary woman named Julia Flisch, who, identifying her as a talented person and adopting her as a protégé, urged her to seek a university education.

This *Preface* is a revised version of a portion of Anne Firor Scott's essay "A Different View of Southern History," originally published on pages 47-54 of *Unheard Voices: The First Historians of Southern Women*, edited by Anne Firor Scott (University of Virginia Press, 1993). It is Copyrighted by the Rector and Visitors of the University of Virginia and published here by permission.

Since the University of Georgia did not admit women, Flisch recommended the University of Tennessee. Boatwright took the advice but later transferred to Teachers College, Columbia University, where she graduated in 1918. Meanwhile her father had died, and her mother had taken over the florist business. There are hints that Eleanor would have liked to stay in the larger world of New York City, but as a dutiful daughter she came home to live with her mother and shortly began teaching at Tubman herself. Since appointments to the school were so much in demand, they usually went to women who had served a successful apprenticeship elsewhere in the state, often to women who had master's degrees from major universities.[1] We can infer that this young woman was already recognized as unusually able, or that Julia Flisch's influence opened the door, or both.[2]

She was early on recognized as a remarkable teacher and as a leader on behalf of women teachers. Julia Flisch remained her mentor on all fronts.[3] Sometime in the 1920s, Flisch led a strike for equal pay for women teachers. Some of her contemporaries, now in their nineties, remember that in the 1930s Boatwright followed suit by organizing a teachers' strike over the issue of equal pay and retirement benefits for women.[4] In the process she helped lay the initial groundwork for the first teacher retirement program for the state of Georgia and was deeply involved in an effort to make sure that women teachers received benefits equal to those provided for men.[5]

A woman who had been her student wrote in 1992:

> Eleanor Boatwright was my first female historian role model. She encouraged me to study and enjoy history during my four years. . . . When I was a Freshman, I asked her for a world history book to study over the summer. . . . She found me a left over text. . . . I remember overhearing my mother talking to Miss B. about how much I studied, and Miss B. saying that I had not used one fifth (or some tiny amount) of my brain power yet. I was amazed. . . . She gave a pop quiz the first five minutes of every class . . . you had to be prepared to survive. I remember it as very interesting and I couldn't wait for the next installment.[6]

In 1934, by then sixteen years beyond the A.B., Boatwright enrolled in Duke University summer school to study history and made the highest grades the university bestowed. After several more summers in residence she presented the thesis published here for the master's degree. It is excellent social history and is better than many Ph.D. dissertations that have passed muster in the intervening years.

She writes with delicate irony and an ever-present sense of humor. Her description of the situation of the first white women in Georgia is typical: "Indians and forests, and unplowed fields; toil, and danger, and unknown lands increased the weight of their chains without materially lengthening them."[7] The chapter on courtship and marriage begins:

> In the State of Georgia prior to the Civil War an unmarried woman stood equal to her brother before the bar, but in her husband she found her legal grave and by his death her resurrection. The code under which she lived was biting with the acid of an old bachelor—St. Paul; and stinging with the vengeance of a henpecked husband—Lord Coke.[8]

Many things she found in the case law and in other documents amused her, but she was not amused by the basic constraints laid upon women by law and social expectation. She made a thorough and sophisticated analysis of the legal disabilities women experienced. In an essay drawn from her thesis she remarks:

> The ceremonial pledge of a man to his bride "with all my worldly goods I thee endow" did not have the legal significance of a valentine. For the civil law saw to it that the new-made husband lost nothing of his own at the altar and took away from it all his bride possessed—perhaps even the ring with which he made his vow.[9]

Along the way she makes many intriguing discoveries. For example, that advertisements for runaway wives were still common in antebellum Georgia. She understood the existence of the "plain folk" better than most southern historians of her generation, and her detailed attention to health and sickness showed that she had learned a good deal from Richard Shryock. She recognizes the gap between law and custom, between image and reality. She confirms earlier evidence that women were politically active, that they were gradually getting control of their own earnings.

She reinforces Guion Johnson's assertions (in *Ante-bellum North Carolina: A Social History*, 1937) about the importance of miscegenation and makes the point that not all interracial sex was restricted to the lower classes. For example, she discovered records of a magistrate in Charleston who had sent away a mulatto girl said to be the daughter of a white woman of a leading family. She also finds a number of cases of slaves who gained their freedom by proving that their mothers had been white. Her data on the debate in Georgia over the definition of "Negro" has an extraordinarily modern ring. It seems quite likely that Johnson and Boatwright were the first white historians of the

South to deal seriously with this set of issues, and almost certainly they were among the first to discuss the possibility that some mulatto children had white mothers.[10]

Using city directories to good effect, Boatwright confirms the findings of Johnson with respect to the widespread development of women's voluntary associations.[11]

In her section on women's work, Boatwright (who says at the beginning of her thesis that it would focus on white women) recognized that census data did not separate black and white. She found many women in business and discovered that the number of women planters was increasing through the antebellum period. Her concentration on white women distorts this section since black women were certainly, as Zora Neale Hurston once put it, the mules of the South. Though Boatwright like most of her white contemporaries was blind to this fact, from the general tone of her thesis one is tempted to believe that if she had lived into the 1960s her outlook would have broadened.

In addition to studying and doing the research for her thesis, a fellow teacher who went to Duke with Boatwright remembers that they had a joyful experience. For a brief time she was away from the responsibilities of caring for her mother and her household, she met interesting people, and above all she was happy doing historical research. Though the state of Georgia promised a $1,000 increment to teachers who finished the master's degree, the doing itself seemed to be her primary motivation.[12] "She wanted," said her friend, "to be a *real* historian."[13]

A handful of surviving letters provide glimpses of her personality. Writing W. K. Boyd in May 1937, she had sought permission to take six semester hours in the summer, adding, "I know your standards are very high, but I work hard."[14] Evidently the fact that Boyd was in what would become his last illness led Charles Sydnor to answer her letter. On May 22 she wrote him, misspelling his name, to say that she hoped for an opportunity to work with him; "since I read your book I have wanted to." She announced her plan to stay for both summer terms, adding, "I have to get something started if I ever do, for: 'At last I am forty and ready to start / Beginning to live;—if I don't fall apart.' "[15] The next surviving letter, dated May 5, 1938, reported that she would return for the summer and asked Sydnor's approval for taking a history course and one in sociology. "I hope you won't put me out for I'm still sticking to my 'Georgia women' tho I sometimes doubt if they are worth all this fidelity." She said she was studying Spanish for her reading examination.[16] Sydnor replied approving her choices and advising her to work with E. Merton

Coulter, who was to visit that summer, or with Richard Shryock, the medical historian. Since she eventually would thank Shryock for his help with her thesis, perhaps she took the latter's course, but she also knew Coulter well enough to write joking letters to him, so she may have studied with both. In 1939 she again sent word that she would be coming: "This is just to forewarn you that my 'Women' and I are headed toward you for this summer . . . so that you may have ample time to organize your resources if you expect to avoid us." Her life had been busy:

> In addition to all the usual complications . . . now there is the state situation which leaves the schools without money. I without any qualifications other than strong lungs am almost continuously being sent somewhere to do something about it, and coming home with only another unpaid expense account.
>
> Sincerely hoping that you are unable to find a successful means of escape, I am Very truly yours,[17]

Sydnor wrote saying he had no wish to avoid her, but that he would only be on deck for the first term. She came, and the thesis was signed July 15, 1939.

By the following year she was seeking Sydnor's advice as to whether her study could be turned into a book. She herself thought the material good and hoped it might interest a university press, but she wanted an expert opinion. Sydnor replied in a long, careful letter in which he said that she did indeed have something worth publishing, that her thesis was a superior one both in research and in thoughtfulness. He then suggested that if it was to be published there were some things that needed work: for example, there were a number of unsubstantiated generalizations. Although he said clearly that he thought the thesis, in whole or in part, deserved publication, she, as insecure graduate students are wont to do, gave his letter a pessimistic interpretation. Her summary of what he had said was "my thesis is not good enough, but too good not to be better. Perhaps some time something creditable may evolve out of the primeval ooze between those covers. Right now I don't feel that my back will ever be equal to the task."[18] Some weeks later he replied, explaining that he had broken his elbow in the meantime, saying that she had misunderstood and reiterated: "Your work does have very real merit and with some polishing ought to be published." He said he had only given her the advice he would have given himself in like circumstances.[19]

In March she thanked him for a copy of his essay "The Southerner and the Laws" and inquired about his broken arm. She reported discussing publication of her thesis with Robert P. Brooks, an economics professor at the University of Georgia who apparently at that time ran the University of Georgia Press. Brooks had given her work high marks but told her the press had no money; only authors who could afford to pay the costs were being published. She went on to say that she was "green eyed" over the success of some of her contemporaries, and that she had sent a finished copy to Richard Shryock (who by that time had moved to the University of Pennsylvania) hoping for some suggestions as to possible publishers.

Nothing came of her efforts to interest people in the possibility of turning the thesis into a book, and by January 1941 she had apparently decided to settle for publishing the much abbreviated version quoted earlier. She wrote Coulter, who was editor of the *Georgia Historical Quarterly,* that she had finally reduced the essay to the required length. After some discussion of forms of citation she went on: "I thought you said I could be a member of the Georgia Historical Society. What happened? Did I get black-balled? Don't mind telling me. I'm used to it. My best friend did as much to me in a bridge club recently. She said I was all right if I wasn't playing bridge. I was quite cheered up. I knew how I was when I was playing bridge, but I didn't know how I was when I wasn't." Coulter hastened to reassure her that she would be welcome in the historical society, and in her next letter she thanked him and told him of an "old lady" in Augusta who had some plantation records. She thought he might extract the records by a typical southern combination of flattery and references to kinfolks. She added, "Miss Sarah knows about you and admires your work, or at least admires your reputation, for I doubt how much reading she had been able to do for the past several years."[20]

The publication of her article proceeded apace, and in her last surviving letter to Coulter, Boatwright was again apologetic, this time for the fact that he had found errors in her footnotes. She commiserated with him about the budget cuts being instituted by Governor Eugene Talmadge. She enclosed an early history of the Augusta Presbyterian Church and an 1883 catalog of the Lucy Cobb Institute, which she thought he might like to have.

While all this was going on she was teaching full-time and playing an active role in the life of her school. She taught a Sunday school class. She continued to agitate for equal pay for women teachers and to work for an improved retirement system. Twice the young women at Tubman dedicated their yearbook to Eleanor Boatwright. They also gave her name to the Future

Teachers club. The former pupil quoted earlier described her at that time as "always smiling, easy going, chuckling, and good natured. . . . She sat on a stool when she taught, right in front of her pull-down maps and always pointing at them when she was teaching." Colleagues remember the joyful atmosphere of her classroom and that she was a person to whom other people went with their problems. Survivors speak fondly of her to this day.

Yet something about her life was not joyful. For years she had cared for an ailing mother and borne heavy financial burdens for the whole family, which included her sister and a niece. She seems to have suffered considerably from arthritis. Her closest friend remembers that sometimes she was subject to depression. In early 1950 her eighty-four-year-old mother died; in October, Boatwright took her own life.

Her coworkers and her students were stunned. One friend remembered that Boatwright had long supported the right of people to commit suicide. There were speculations that her life had taken a turn for the worse when Tubman merged with the Richmond Academy (male) and she was remanded to a dreadful room on the fourth floor where, in addition to requiring her to climb four flights of stairs (a problem for a person with severe arthritis), there was too much noise from the music room next door for decent teaching. The male faculty were not, so memories say, very welcoming to the women from Tubman who were, on the whole, better educated than they. Half a century later one can only speculate that a situation such as her friends describe might have come to symbolize all the disappointed ambitions of a woman whose dream was to "be a real historian." Whatever her reason, her death was a great waste—the loss not only of a gifted teacher, but of a promising scholar.

Duke University
April 1994

Introduction

by Kathleen Brown

Eleanor Miot Boatwright's 1940 master's thesis presages much of the work on the southern lady and planter families that has appeared since the 1970s resurgence of women's history. Written in the grand style of Julia Cherry Spruill, Boatwright's study of white women in Georgia between the Revolution and the Civil War incorporates a wealth of primary evidence from legal documents, planter manuscripts, and literary sources. Although the reader occasionally glimpses the changes accompanying the escalating sectional conflict, historical transformation is subsumed to thematic discussions of education, courtship and marriage, legal and political status, manners and customs, and slavery.

Assessing white women's activities in all of these arenas, Boatwright concludes that "status" was a complex product of many factors that varied with a woman's class. Unrecognized in political life and hampered by their loss of property rights after marriage, Georgia's white women nonetheless found their freedoms depended less on legal statutes than upon individual circumstances such as a spouse's personality, his recourse to the letter of the law, public opinion, and their own efforts at self-assertion. In the case of divorce, for example, Boatwright looks beyond official prohibitions to discover a rising divorce rate during the nineteenth century. Although opportunities to divorce remained limited, many unhappy couples took advantage of contradictions and ambiguities in the law to obtain separations by legislative decree. Like the incidence of divorce, property ownership by married women also occasionally defied legal strictures that rendered wealth to husbands.

Georgia's white women also encountered a mixed array of intellectual progress and constraint. Until the 1850s, Boatwright argues, the curriculum at southern girls' schools generally kept pace with that of their northern sisters, offering limited instruction in reading, writing, modern languages and genteel accomplishments such as painting and embroidery. As sectional conflict intensified, male pundits discouraged young women of means from traveling north to institutions where advanced courses of study and antislavery sentiment had gained currency. Plans to develop female colleges in Georgia, moreover, suffered setbacks as critics linked female intellectual accomplishment with the much-despised northern effort to end slavery. By mid-century, southern regionalism's dependence upon the intellectual subordination of white women had stunted the promise of educational reform in the state.

Boatwright's treatment of the mistress-slave relationship as but one part of planter women's lives, an approach that contrasts sharply with more recent studies of southern women, is the key to her comprehensive discussion of female status. Her discussion of slavery focuses mainly upon its relationship to patriarchal power and southern regionalism. Proslavery ideologues lashed out against the women's rights ideas circulating among abolitionists during the 1840s and 1850s. Lucretia Mott and Elizabeth Cady Stanton's previous involvement in abolition sealed the fate of the women's rights cause in the eyes of southern regionalists, provoking withering attacks upon reforms ranging from bloomers to female equality. The association of women's rights with abolitionism, moreover, molded southern defenses of slavery. White southern women, proslavery ideologues contended, enjoyed the reverence of their men and a release from exhausting labor as a consequence of slavery. Defenses of the institution thus became inextricably linked with arguments for perpetuating the subordination of women. The latter, Boatwright claims, "was fitted into the concept of a stratified society and became an inalienable part of the defense of slavery." She also notes how such an argument elided the existence of non-elite white women, observing that "the philosophers of this ideal state continued to romanticize women of the upper classes and to forget those of the lower" (p. 123).

Boatwright never forgets these women of the southern yeomanry, nor is she guilty of romanticizing the lives of southern ladies. Throughout her study, she carefully distinguishes between the material conditions, labor and customs of southern elites and those of middle class "crackers" (p. 67). Log cabins, camp meetings, and the work of non-slaveholding women weigh as heavily in her study as the elegant homes, recreations and managerial routines of plantation mistresses. Boatwright is no less democratic in her discussion of interracial sexual unions, acknowledging that "miscegenation was not unknown among white women, and such affairs were not always restricted to the lower classes" (p. 88).

Boatwright's candid and prescient commentary on the links among southern regionalism, white women's subordination, and slavery placed her in the vanguard of southern historians during the 1940s. A scattered and largely disconnected handful of intrepid female scholars were attempting similar regional studies of white women in the southern states. Like Boatwright, few of these women enjoyed the support of professional colleagues who shared their research interests. Many passed through graduate school without learning of their predecessors, relying instead upon male mentors for encouragement. Boatwright's achievement lies in her ability to define her own research priorities, meticulously comb the archives, and bring subtle, nuanced interpretation to the primary sources. Her study is well-documented and remarkably free of the "received wisdom" that passed for the professional history of women during the 1940s, an accomplishment that merits our admiration.

Yet if Boatwright's prescience and intellectual fortitude inspire our praise, her acceptance of prevailing attitudes about slave women and men and the poorest substratum of white society nevertheless provoke our discomfort. A historian of women before her time, Boatwright remained a product of white southern society when addressing questions of race and class. Although *Status of Women in Georgia* presages contemporary studies of slaveholding women, compelling us to view our recent achievements with humility, its shortcomings remind us of the progress of women's history as a field not only since the 1940s, but indeed, since the early 1980s.

"Women" to Boatwright means white women exclusively, a myopia she shared with most white intellectuals during the 1940s and for many decades thereafter. Her organization of the manuscript reflects this unexamined usage of the term. The discussion of slavery is contained in two chapters, neither of which ventures to explore white women's complicity in the perpetuation of the institution. And while Boatwright's candor on most other topics is refreshing and fruitful, when she writes about slaves her ideas are shopworn. Such is the case in Chapter Six when she contends that slaves were for the most part incompetent and unskilled laborers who constituted a tremendous burden to their white mistresses (p. 91-92). Boatwright similarly ignores the Cherokee removal taking place in Georgia during the period considered in her study. "Women" did not include Indian women, a group whose expulsion from the state and changing status among their own people would have complicated Boatwright's discussions of women's political and civil rights.

Boatwright demonstrates more self-awareness about class stereotypes, but her discussion of southern midwives and the poor white people they served reveals the limits of her ability to challenge contemporary opinions. She describes midwives as "ignorant" (p. 78) and their clients as "slovenly and inert" (p. 89). Unlike the bulk of her research on women of the planter and yeoman classes, Boatwright's analysis of poor women relied upon undigested platitudes about the reasons for poverty and the characteristics of the impoverished.

Using the racist, elitist, and ethnocentric rhetoric popular among historians of her day, Boatwright quietly distinguishes herself from her historical subjects, thereby lessening her own marginality within the profession. Writing about women as a member of a male-dominated profession, Boatwright would never belong to the academic mainstream, but her recapitulation of the profession's middle-class and ethnocentric values allow her to construct her own identity as educated and industrious. It is doubtful that Boatwright was aware of her own complicity in the discourse of the profession; rather, she seems to have perceived herself as a scholar struggling in the margins of academia, unsure to the end of her life about the success of her work. We can acknowledge this dilemma sympathetically, on its own terms, even as we evaluate her treatment of African-American, Indian, and poor white women critically, according to our own standards.

Fifty years after it was written, *Status of Women in Georgia* remains worthy of our attention both for its contribution to women's history and for its flaws. Boatwright's careful assessment of the evidence of white women's status will provide many scholars with a starting point for their own research on antebellum class relations, family life, education, and regionalism in the South. Her neglect of Indian removal and her occasionally offensive commentary about slave women and men and poor white people, meanwhile, will undoubtedly make her readers uncomfortable. In the tension generated by the contradictions in her work, readers may gain some insight into the struggles of a southern white woman seeking acceptance and membership in a profession whose sacred cows she was attempting to slaughter.

Rutgers University
May 1994

A Note on Editing Policy

This book was originally written as an M.A. thesis at Duke University in 1940. Eleanor Boatwright did not revise it for publication before her death in 1950. The conventions of writing history have changed over the last fifty years, as they will over the next fifty. Rather than trying to make Eleanor Boatwright sound like our contemporary, we have retained her style. (For example, we have left her word "negro" [with a lower case "n"], rather than changing it to African-American.) We have corrected obvious typographical mistakes and errors in grammar and punctuation in her manuscript. We have added a few explanatory phrases in brackets [   ]. Otherwise this book is published as it was written.

Ralph Carlson
Carlson Publishing, Inc.

Acknowledgments

On the advice of Dr. Charles S. Sydnor, of Duke University, this work was begun and with his forbearance it was finished. Whatever merit the paper may have is due to his counsel and that of Dr. Richard H. Shryock, now of the University of Pennsylvania.

E.M.B.

Status of Women in Georgia, 1783-1860

ONE

The Heritage

The status of white women in Georgia from the establishment of the republic to the Civil War did not vary greatly from that of women in the other southern states, nor, until slavery had set its seal on southern institutions, from that of the other women of America.

Women came to the new world carrying the burdens of the old, and the frontier made slight change in their status. Most of them were from the middle and lower classes, and, except that they found more wood to hue and more water to draw on this side of the Atlantic, they behaved as middle and lower class women behaved in England. Indians, and forests, and unplowed fields; toil, and danger, and unknown lands increased the weight of their chains without materially lengthening them.

Nancy Hart [a legendary Georgia heroine of the American revolution] and her kind were exceptional women to whom the frontier gave unusual opportunities to exhibit their talents. Had the cross-eyed heroine of Georgia lived in London, however, it would, probably, still have been true that "her husband was nobody when she was around."[1]

Women have usually occupied a humble position in early societies. This is generally agreed to be due to the impelling dangers that glorified the sphere of man and demeaned the work of women in the primitive division of labor. If this may be regarded as a general law the American frontier was not conducive to its violation and Georgia furnishes a good example of its enforcement. Established, as the colony was, to promote silk culture, a woman's industry,[2] it might be assumed that Georgia was liberal toward them. The contrary is true. Before the "Anne" weighed anchor women had been denied the right to own property in their new homes.[3]

The charter shows that in founding the colony some dreamed of a haven for others; some of financial reward for themselves; but all expected it to be a citadel to protect South Carolina against the "neighboring savages"[4] of Florida. The trustees visioned the owner of each plot of land as a potential musket bearer, and planned to make it true by establishing a system of *tale*

1

male, which denied women the right to own or inherit property in the colony.[5] This was unpopular and led to almost continuous complaints; to frequent exceptions;[6] and finally to repeal in 1750.[7] Still its phantom survived statehood, for although under the common law of England a man unconditionally controlled his wife's personal property,[8] his power over her real [property] was limited.[9] Yet by Georgia statute of 1789, with a four-year retroactive clause, a woman forfeited both at the altar.[10]

In the eras between Father Adam and General Oglethorpe the forces for the subordination of women found a powerful ally in Christianity, which remained a persistent enemy to the progress of women in the new world. The Church on both sides of the Atlantic, however, failed to recognize the reactionary character of Christian theology on the status of women. On the contrary Hugh Smith, rector of St. Paul's, the aristocratic and conservative Episcopal Church of Augusta, was only repeating accepted doctrine when he said that women were "indebted to the Gospel for personal emancipation and respectability, and . . . knew its diffusion to be the very guardian of their happiness, their purity, and their rights."[11]

This Christian legend, however, was without foundation in fact. In the last three centuries of pagan Rome, women, particularly the upper classes, probably exercised as great political influence and enjoyed as high status as women had ever in the history of the world until the present era. The power of a father to determine the choice of a husband was limited; and a man exercised no control over his wife's person and little over her possessions. A woman had freedom of divorce, and her right to an education, to enter business, to inherit, and to bequeath property was unquestioned.[12]

In 313 A.D., when Constantine saw the cross, women occupied a relatively high position in Christian thought. This, however, added little to pagan practice, and, although the Justinian Code of 530 A.D. was slightly restrictive in regard to women, it reflects the conception of them existing before the conversion.[13] The liberal teachings of Jesus are without significance in a discussion of women under Christianity, for they were ignored by those who followed him. Instead, Old Testament theology, the concepts of oriental fisherman, the celibate writings of St. Paul, together with the extreme asceticism of the early church fathers—particularly Tertullian, with Augustine and Jerome only in a lesser degree—dominated the cultural pattern that Rome wrote into the canon law and England into the common. This is the pattern that Georgia eventually adopted.

The apostles retained the "even as Sarah obeyed Abraham" philosophy of the Jews;[14] continued to remember that "Adam was first formed then Eve"; that "the women being deceived, was in the transgression";[15] and demanded both revenge and sacrifice. Pauline theology stressed the desirability of celibacy;[16] ordered that wives "submit" themselves "unto" their "husbands, as unto the Lord";[17] disapproved of divorce;[18] prohibited remarriage of divorced people;[19] discouraged it for widows, except for the very young, who "have begun to wax wanton against Christ";[20] commanded that women "adorn themselves in modest apparel, with shamefacedness and sobriety,"[21] lest men be lured to destruction; admonished a man to "love his wife even as himself," but commanded a woman to "reverence her husband."[22] Paul ordered women to "keep silence in the churches" and "ask their husbands at home";[23] to "learn with all subjection"; and not to "usurp authority over man." He, however, conceded women salvation through "childbearing, if they continue in faith and charity and holiness with sobriety."[24]

The church fathers followed the philosophy of Paul, which was compatible with their own concept of women.[25] The twelve patriarchs testified they had been shown by the "Angels of God . . . that forever women bear rule over king and beggar alike and from the king they take away his glory, and from the valiant man his strength, and from the beggar even that little which is the stay of his poverty."[26] Tertullian, with an African background, wrote of women: "The sentence of God on this sex of ours lives in this age." And: "You are the devil's gateway. You destroy God's image, Man."[27] He believed that: "Nothing disgraceful is proper for man, who is endowed with reason; much less for woman, to whom it brings shame to reflect on what nature she is."[28] Tertullian felt that "no wise man would ever willingly desire sons" and that "the whimpering brats will make a fine scene combined with the advent of the Judges and sound of the trumpet," which would spoil the splendor of the last Judgment.[29]

The medieval attitude of the church toward women was, at its best, that of old Bishop Marbodious, who pronounced them: "A pleasant evil, at once a honey comb and a poison."[30] The spirit of Paul, which decreed, "the husband is the head of the wife, even as Christ is the head of the church,"[31] was incorporated in the canon law, which, seeing in a woman's hair a God-given "veil and sign of her subjection," forbade that it be cut;[32] and required that brides be "veiled during the ceremony, for this reason, that they may know they are lowly and in subjection to their husbands."[33]

The Reformation did not alter the spirit of the canon law or the religious dogmas concerning women, and Puritanism took away from them most of the little personal liberty the Catholic Church had allowed. This was to prove important in Georgia, for American thought and habit was infused with the theology, ethics, and "bear and spectator" philosophy of Calvin and Knox.

The State as well as the Church played a vital part in determining the status of women in the mother country. The English are a property-loving people, and to protect orderly inheritance legitimate heirs were essential. So the British added the sacredness of legitimacy to the canon law and the results were written into the common law of England,[34] under which John Stuart Mill pronounced the status of a wife to be that of "a personal body servant of a despot."[35] Yet Lord Coke concluded that "the female sex" is a "favorite . . . of the laws of England!"[36]

It has been suggested that: "Chief Justice Coke, having married the rich and beautiful widow of Lord Chancellor Hatton, soon found that though he could lay down the law in the court room and in the law books, Lady Coke lay down the law at home and that without appeal; and that as a result every night when sulking over his defeats he wrote into the English law what he thought married women deserved, so that for three centuries they have paid the penalty of Lady Coke's eloquence."[37]

The code under which Georgia women were to live came into the colony with Oglethorpe. It was made up of the canon laws of Rome, the common laws of England, and was seasoned with the blue laws of Puritanism. This code prevailed throughout the colonial period, and as early as 1777 was adopted into the statutes of Georgia.[38]

TWO

Girls in School

From 1783 to 1860 there were few occupations for which a woman might prepare, and the principal objectives of a Georgia girl's formal education were the "3 R's," social status, and a wedding ring. Masculine taste demanded glamorous gentility flavored with piety, so the school shaped its curriculum toward that end.[1] Toward the latter part of the period there was discontent with the course of study, and efforts were made to find subjects for girls that would "soften while they strengthen."[2] Improvements in academic standards came slowly, however, for girls found "it was almost a reproach to be called literary," and in public opinion, a clever woman was a "perfect horror."[3]

Eugenius A. Nesbit, of Georgia, was an early advocate for substantial education for women. Through the *Southern Ladies' Book*, published first in Macon, then in Savannah, he insisted they must "learn to appreciate the dignity of their position; to know that they have something *to do*; that the end of human life is not merely to attract admiration, and to catch a beau." Nesbit was at a loss to understand why "young ladies seem practically to concede their own inferiority and to devolve upon the other sex all the duties and the honors of society."[4] But "Clara," from Newton County, Georgia, knew the answer:

> If a lady chance to acquire an education . . . she must keep her knowledge a profound secret, if she wishes to mix in society, for should it once get abroad that she is learned . . . introduce any topic of discourse farther than some remark on the party in which she was engaged the preceding evening the title of female pedant . . . blue stocking will be awarded her. . . . This ridicule or at least the dread of it, has . . . been the cause that many a highly gifted female has consented to bury her talent in oblivion that to expose herself to sneers of a fashionable world.[5]

And Dr. Richard Arnold of Savannah reassured his daughter, Ellen, in a Philadelphia school, that he "would not laugh" at her if she took "a fancy to Latin."[6]

5

So women continued to "content themselves with learning to sing and dance, to make a mere pretence of talking French and Italian, which they themselves [usually] did not understand, still less others; to read wretched novels, talk scandal, and flirt and coquette and finally settle down as wives . . . and live over in the persons of their untrained daughters, the same aimless life."[7]

The schools provided the only type of education that was wanted for women of the upper classes for many years,[8] and even elementary education was less valuable to those of the lower classes than to men. The census report showed for Georgia:[9]

Illiterates over 21 years of age:

1850:	Males	16,552
	Females	24,648
1860:	Males	16,900
	Females	26,784

Numbers attending schools:

1850:	Males	42,365
	Females	34,650
1860:	Males	50,552
	Females	44,128

In 1859, Governor Brown made an educational survey of Georgia. His report, based on 102 of the 132 counties in the state, approximately agrees with the proportionate difference between the sexes shown in the census returns.[10]

The educational offering, particularly in the lower branches, was usually poor in quality for both sexes, since "school keeping" was done by anybody who couldn't do anything better.[11] There were some good teachers, many of whom had come from the North;[12] but maiden aunts, "relicts" of improvident husbands, drunken Irishmen, and the flotsam of the frontier, all tried their hand.[13] Elementary education for the well-to-do was acquired at home under the instruction of a governess, tutor, or member of the family;[14] in juvenile schools;[15] or in the elementary departments of the seminaries and academies. While, for those less fortunate, there were the field,[16] Sabbath,[17] charity,[18] and, eventually, the "free schools" financed by the state.[19]

James R. Coombs has left a colorful picture of the schoolmaster at Tarversville, George P. Cooper, renamed "Ginny" for his birthplace:

> He was a man somewhat passed middle age, tall in stature. . . . His outside appearance was seedy. He wore a tall crown black silk hat, with a narrow brim, and such fashion as had been caste off by past generation. His coat was of *Blue Broad Cloth*, surmounted with metal buttons [and his panterloons were of the same material except that] from professional use [they] had become holey . . . and . . . the skill of the tailor had been called into exercise to exemplify that portion of his profession called patchwork . . . [which] was only seen as an outward movement would incline the nether portion of his outside garment from a perpendicular. . . . His features were rather sharp with aquiline nose . . . his hair always cut short and stood all around as a roach . . . his attitude was always erect as though his younger days had been spent nor far from a bean pole.[20]

"Ginny" believed in and inflicted corporal punishment with "a certain elastic billet . . . with book, or with hand," as proved most convenient. He searched "diligently throughout the surface for a soft place whereat and whereon an impression was likely to be produced, and when the soft place was found he thereat and thereon dwelt, and never left the premises until a profitable result was produced and externally visible."[21]

Nor did he confine such activities to boys, for Coombs recalls "one old mother of Isreal" who accosted him in school for punishing her "baby daughter and show marks of violence inflicted." "Ginny" was accustomed to such encounters, for he did not interrupt the speaker until "her breath failed and her tongue became too weary to do further service." He then replied, "she ought to have been trained for a lawyer and remained in full possession of the field no doubt ruminating in real Old Bachelor style in his own mind that he had none such as she to caress, nor none such as she to tame."[22]

At best, these rural schools were uncomfortable. Gabriel T. Mathis, of Clarke County, was "happy in stating" that his was a "very pleasant log house with two very good chimneys so as to render it warm and comfortable in winter." He further informed possible patrons that "very genteel and decent boarding may be had in the neighborhood within a convenient distance."[23] Emily Burke, a Northern teacher in Georgia, in her *Reminiscences of Georgia*, published in 1850, states:

> In the country where the plantations are so large, families are separated at the distance of several miles from each other. Education was formerly confined to

7

those whose wealth enabled them to support private teachers at a great expense. Consequently, many in affluent circumstances made no attempt to educate their children. But now efforts are being made by the planters in various parts of Georgia to collect together in little communities during a portion of the year in order to unite their funds in sustaining select schools and academies.[24]

It is quite common now, too, for children and youths who attend these schools to board at home when they live at no great distance, from four to six miles. I have myself boarded at the distance of four miles from the school room, and would always prefer to do so under the same circumstances, and with the same company of jolly school girls.

Little girls will ride four or five miles every day on horse-back to attend school, and consider it no more of a hardship than children at the North do to walk half a mile for the same purpose. They always set out on their little journey early in the morning, taking their dinner with them, and do not return till the cool of the evening.

The mules and horses that convey them to and from school twice every day soon become accustomed to their tasks, and the childish freaks of their riders, they are as docile and as easily managed as sheep. If a lesson is to be studied a little more before recitation, it can be done just as well on the way to school as anywhere else, for without the least guidance, these faithful animals would take their precious burdens directly to the academy door.[25]

Formal education even in the elementary subjects was a badge of class distinction. Miss Burke maintained that the "great expense that attends an education in the Southern States, has placed it as an impassable barrier between the rich and the poor. It has been true that the wealthy only were educated and this is true now in the country."[26]

Gradually, however, the people of Georgia came to want a democratic plan of education. In 1823 the free school system was established and the state began to assume the responsibility of educating its poor. The little education they had received previously had been dependent on the interest of a few kindly souls. Mr. McWhir, minister and teacher of Savannah, Midway, and Sunbury, was one of these. He was so zealous in his efforts to maintain a charity school that he "brought on a fever of great severity and long continuance"; nevertheless, "the people among whom these schools were established were at first very jealous of the design. They feared it was part of a scheme for making the poor more dependent on the rich." Later, however, they began "to think better" and became "anxious to forward the design."[27]

Illiteracy was so general among the poor that "out of a hundred children" in one community, it was found that only "two could repeat the Lord's prayer."[28] The church became alarmed over this condition, and the Sunday schools, supported by the press,[29] undertook to help with the education of the poor. The Savannah Sabbath School Society decided that its text should be the "Bible and Testament . . . Catechism as may be agreed upon and the spelling book." To these they added "select hymns for children, such as Watt's Divine Songs." The children were divided "according to sexes and capacities," and each placed under "teachers of their own sex." After devotional exercises came the religious lesson, and the remainder of the time was devoted to "spelling, reading, and conversation with children." To maintain discipline, a system of rewards and punishments was inaugurated, as "corporal punishment is unsuited to the Lord's day."[30]

The free schools might have done more effective work if the feeling had not prevailed that they were "synonyms with 'schools for poor people' "; for the class for whom they were designed felt that it was "quite as reputable not to have an education at all as to have it said they were educated at a free school." Miss Burke found that "even teachers shrink from the stigma of teaching in these institutions."[31]

Boys between the ages of seven and eighteen and girls from six to thirteen were admitted to the free schools.[32] Otherwise there was no discrimination against girls in state support for educational purposes. Any child was eligible whose parents paid not more than fifty cents a year in taxes, who was within the age limits, and not advanced beyond the elementary subjects.[33] The justices of the peace were required to "list" the number of these children who attended the poor schools in his district[34] and file the results with the ordinary. On these records the state based its appropriation.

These "lists" show a haphazard distribution of the sexes in the poor schools. Selected at random, but typical of those of Richmond County in 1830, were the reports of A. N. Verdrey, which show twenty boys and twenty-six girls in the poor schools of his district, and that of James A. May, naming twenty-five boys and only nine girls enrolled in his.[35] By 1837 the total number being educated by the poor school funds of Georgia was 3,808. Only forty-three percent of these were girls. This does not signify, however, that boys were the favorites of the state.[36] It seems to mean that elementary education did not have the same social or economic value to the daughters of the poor that it had to their sons.

Free schools that offered adequate advantages to indigent children may have existed,[37] but they were probably few in number as long as they employed such teachers as Fanny Anderson. Her letters to the Ordinary of Richmond County give an idea of what might be expected:

Will you send me something this evening you said yesterday that i could send to day will you please put it in an envellope and seal it up i am not verry well this evening you must come Monday anser this if you please and oblige.[38]

and again:

Will you send me som spelling book and rading books Slats and Copy books and oblige.[39]

Usually, it seems, the sexes were kept separate even in the elementary grades. Miss E. E. Witherspoon thought it advisable to advertise that, in her Juvenile School in Athens, they used different entrances and that the girls would "take exercises in Dr. Hoyt's lot."[40] Even the free schools frequently followed the same rule of segregation,[41] and when they violated it, financial stringency was probably responsible.

Secondary education was almost entirely for the upper classes. In contemporary opinion, northern schools were superior to southern. In spite of the sincerity of its advocates, there seems to have been no academic basis for their claim.[42] In antebellum education, however, subject matter was subordinate to social prestige, and northern institutions were in vogue. They continued to be so until the sectional reaction just prior to the war. Then all things southern became fashionable to the plantation aristocracy and to the "cotton snobs" who imitated them.[43]

However desirable it may have been to be "finished" in northern schools, most Georgia girls got their secondary education in their own state. At the latter part of the period, a few high schools were established for them,[44] but these were half-hearted affairs,[45] whereas the academies and their glorified cousins, the seminaries, were the backbone of secondary education for Georgia girls.

The academies began in 1783 and reached their peak in 1840.[46] From 1830 to 1840 was the time of their greatest growth; their most significant development during that period was the increase in the proportion of girls in the student body. By 1838 it has reached fifty-two percent of the entire academy enrollment for the state.[47] The census reports of 1850 and 1860 showed a total of more boys than girls attending the various schools of the state. This excess must have been piled up in the elementary grades, for girls were in the majority in the secondary schools. The census also showed less illiteracy among men than women. These facts seem to indicate that the elementary school was less valuable to girls than to boys, but secondary education was more important to girls than to their brothers.

The increase in the number of girls in the higher institutions alarmed Bishop Andrews of the Methodist Church South. In 1853 he estimated that approximately six hundred young men and fifteen hundred young women were being turned out of the "collegiate institutions of Georgia" annually, and in addition that many young ladies were going North, where they learned to "dance gracefully, dress elegantly, and above all to spend freely and handsomely." He feared that the problem of finding suitable husbands for all of them would soon become insurmountable.[48]

The difference between the early secondary schools for girls was not the curriculum, but the method of financing them. The "county academies" were organized under the Academy Act of 1783. They received grants of land, which they might dispose of as they pleased, and gifts of money from the state treasury. As a result, they were usually less expensive than other schools of the same grade. Those schools designed simply as "academies" were private institutions and got no state subsidy. The seminaries, although their patrons frequently thought them more fashionable and found them more costly than the academies, were financed like them. In 1837 the free school system was established and the state withdrew its aid from the county academies. This removed the only general distinction that had existed between the schools, and the terms were applied almost interchangeably after that time.[49]

Some county academies were for boys and some for girls, but many admitted both sexes,[50] although frequently, as at the Academy of Richmond County—the oldest of all such institutions in the state—there were female departments using separate teachers, classrooms, and recreation grounds.[51] Any discrimination that the state might have exercised in grants to the county academies does not seem to have been based on sex. Some children, both boys and girls, were educated in them at state bounty, but county academies were not free schools. They were likely, however, to be more reasonable than private institutions.[52]

In all secondary schools the tuition varied widely according to subjects taken. Monticello Female Academy is perhaps a fair example. There, "boarding, lodging and washing, etc. [were] $110 per annum payable quarterly in advance," and the following terms for tuition were advertised:[53]

Reading and Orthography: $ 3.50 per cr.
the same with writing: $4.50

Do. with English Grammar and Arithmetic: $6.50
The above with Composition, Geography, Astronomy, the use of Globes, History, Rhetoric, Philosophy, etc.: $8.00

In addition to the above:
Needle-work and Plain Sewing: $1.00
Drawing and Painting alone: $8.00
Drawing and Painting, Filligree, Tambour, and Embroidery: $10.00
Music: $10.00
Entrance to the Academy: $3.00

In the academies, boys were taught the classics and mathematics, including the higher branches, whereas girls got English, grammar, writing, and arithmetic as their major subjects, and, in addition, a wide variety of "ornamentals."[54] In the latter part of the period, the courses of study indicate that the classics were offered girls, but Elbert W. G. Booger, who has made an exhaustive study of secondary education in Georgia, states: "actually no specific instance has been found of a girl studying Greek in either academy or private school,"[55] and affirms that "the education of females . . . was decidedly inferior to males."[56]

The courses that Georgia girls were taking in the North seemed to parallel those at home. From a Philadelphia school, Maryanne MacKay, of Savannah, reported that she was "engaged in grammar, geography, writing, and cyphering," and that while Elizabeth Stiles was "very clever" and had won "twelve prizes," still "she is not learning Latin that is quite a mistake," although "she intends learning it when she returns to school after spending next winter in Savannah."[57] And Sarah Semmes, from the same Northern city, informed her friends in Washington, Georgia:

> I am so different from what I used to be not in appearance, I am the same *fat old Sal*, but in disposition my tastes have altered even with regard to the books I read. I care nothing for morals and take pleasure in something more solid and substantial. Every Saturday we have Geography, History, and English Grammar and they are decidedly our most difficult studies. We have nearly finished with Logick and will take in its place Weyland on the human responsibility. Arndt's physics will take several months yet.[58]

A typical curriculum for a "Ladies Academy" was advertised for Mount Salubrity, near Augusta, where they were "enabled to add Filligree, Tambour and Artificial Flower making, to the useful and fashionable needleworks which for six years has met general approbation. Polite literature as heretofore."[59] And a Milledgeville "lady" desired to teach in an academy "all that comprises the most finished English Education with the use of maps and globes, painting on velvet and satin, wax works, rice-work, filigree, needle work and music."[60] If a young lady survived the extras she might be exposed to such lectures as Dr. Hoyt gave, in the Athens Female Academy in 1842, on: "the Palm tree, the ostrich, the goat, the camel, the elephant, the horse, dwellings of the ancients, particularly of the Jews, the ancient nomads or shepherds, and volcanoes."[61]

Music formed an important part of a girl's education, but "to play" was more of a parlor trick than an artistic achievement, as Anna Harden, writing to her grandmother, indicated:

> I improve rapidly both on Piano and guitar, I can play almost any piece on the guitar, I know how gratifying it would be to you to hear me sing and play. If only I had some pretty rings to look at I would be content.[62]

All music was not, however, equally as permissible, for the academy at Sparta was suspended because it taught the violin, which was considered an instrument of the dance.[63] There is small wonder that a teacher would find:

> It is dull giving lessons all day long to such a set of dull scholars as I have now, glad am I that I have but thirteen. In singing I have divided the school into two parts. The Young ladies sing one day and the children the next—and singing in my room too—it is an admirable plan. I regret that I have not tried it before. I intend the young ladies shall read church music better than our present choire. . . . I wish you could hear them sing "Mountain Bugle" in two parts the children singing too sounds much better without the young ladies . . . Sarah . . . is progressing finely. I wish I could say the same of all my scholars.[64]

Washington Female Seminary was a progressive institution and provided an "excellent apparatus" for chemistry, but admitted:

> The preparation of chemical experiments is so laborious, and demands so much time; their success so often depends upon exact proportions and delicate adjustments, and many of them are so dangerous from the highly explosive nature of the preparations used, that they are unsuited to Ladies, and should be confined to the hands of experienced lecturers.[65]

At Washington, "vocal music" was considered so important that it was given "gratuitously to the whole school," and even "calisthenics" were attempted. The young ladies sang as they exercised, and discovered that the "variety of steps and figures together with the accompanying music" gave "interest to the occasion." The exercises were pronounced "eminently useful, in contributing to the ease and grace of movement so desirable in a lady." "Calisthenics" were considered entirely fitting for prospective Georgia belles, since, in New England, where they had been given "most decidedly under religious influence," they had proven "innocent and useful exercises."[66]

Booger found, from a list of forty-five female secondary schools advertising courses of study in Georgia from 1788 to 1856, that the following subjects were being offered:[67]

Spelling: 8	Physiology: 1
Reading: 13	Calesthenics [sic]: 1
Writing: 15	Mental Philosophy: 9
English Grammar: 31	Moral Philosophy: 7
Composition: 13	Natural Philosophy: 14
Rhetoric: 13	Evidences of Christianity: 1
Elocution: 4	Natural Theology: 1
Logic: 6	Ethics: 1
Belles Letters: 12	Political Economy: 3
Arithmetic: 28	Latin: 18
Algebra: 26	Greek: 14
Geometry: 19	Hebrew: 2
Trigonometry: 5	French: 23
Geography: 24	Spanish: 3
Use of the Globes: 3	German: 2
General History: 22	Italian: 1
History, Greece: 1	Swedish: 1
History, Rome: 1	Music: 16
History, England: 2	Drawing: 22
History, Ancient: 4	Painting: 13
History, Modern: 3	Needlework: 11
Astronomy: 21	Sewing: 1
Chemistry: 19	Embroidery: 5
Botany: 5	Tambour: 1
Zoology: 1	Wax Flowers: 2
Geology: 4	Dancing: 0

From the kaleidoscope of life within these Georgia schools come broken bits:

I'm going next to turn my attention to Stephens Hist. of Georgia but I believe his name is spelt Stevens. Mr Stephens [sic] sent me his likeness by Lou Toombs, an excellent one . . .[68]

. . . .

I intend asking papa to let me spend the vacation up home because I can't study next term if I do not have a change the doctor says I ought to have a change. Last summer I was very sick I did not go to school but one day in August I laid on the bed the rest of the month and to make it better I had sore eyes all term so I did not do much last term. There is an old teacher here with a nose three inches and a half long that I am certain of how much longer that I can't certify she is English, a pure specimen, a regular busy body . . .[69]

. . . .

Mrs. Howard lost her youngest baby she is so cross she is all time punishing Sissy and myself. I don't like her as much as I used to. I wish Papa would send me away. Tom Thumb is here we went to see him. He has a beautiful carriage it was one of the greatest wonders I ever saw. . . . Mrs. Howard won't let us go out to walk but once a week which is a great sadness to us girls . . .[70]

. . . .

Something has occurred in school . . . singular and peculiar . . . spread abroad [it] would mar the reputation of one (at least) fair lady of the South . . . [the] Honorary S. Hunter and Miss Pickett . . . were found to spend most of their time in one of the brick recitation rooms where the girls practised. In time the cause of it was suspected. They had seen from the window three or four young men boarding next door entire strangers. They scraped an acquaintance and met and talked every day from the windows. It went so far that notes had been passed between them. . . . Miss Helen found it all out and made them confess it . . .[71]

. . . .

I am very glad to see John but as soon as he leaves me I can't help crying and feeling homesick it feels just as if I were in sweet Savannah . . . he says . . . I speak just like a Yankee . . . I am sorry to hear it . . . love to [the family] and all the servants . . .[72]

The conduct of the young ladies was regulated by the most minute rules[73] and usually enforced by the faculty, although Washington Seminary adopted an honor system that provided that:

Instead of depending . . . upon the powers of espionage possessed by the teachers . . . each pupil in the school [was] required to give testimony concerning herself. . . . Knowing that she must herself report every violation of the rules, and every deficiency in recitation, or be guilty of a deliberate falsehood; each one is stimulated to greater watchfulness and application. . . . From these daily reports, which each one makes herself (subject however to the approval of the teacher) is determined the standing of the pupil in the *Monthly Record Book*, which is always open to the inspection of parents and visitors.[74]

The seminaries provided a superficial education. Change could not be expected, however, so long as a progressive man with the prestige of Dr. Arnold, of Savannah, was "pleased" that his daughter had "commenced drawing," as it would be a "great amusement" to her, and "besides to draw well is an accomplishment which will always add to the reputation of a young lady."[75]

If Dr. Arnold represents conservative public opinion at its best, it is not surprising that the seminaries, at their worst, produced a South where:

> The daughters are often quite uneducated in the current literature of the times, and in all things else evince a simplicity of mind and character altogether refreshing. Sometimes, 'tis true, they are sent to Boarding Schools, (which are becoming more common in the South of late years) are there exposed to a false and shallow system of hot-bed culture for a few sessions; and emerging therefrom in due time make their debut in life, possessed of full as much pride and affectation, as well as conceit and vanity, as of artificial graces of person and manner; and boasting a superficial knowledge of twenty different branches of learning, but in reality having a perfect mastery and comprehension of none. Southern young ladies of this character, however, are usually the daughters of tradesmen, village store-keepers, and the like, who constitute a pretty fair proportion of the Southern Middle Classes.[76]

The mission of the seminaries continued to be to provide a girl with "that kindness and cultivation which would insure her the imposing title of amiable."[77] With the coming of the high school, the male academies began to fall by the wayside, but the female continued in popularity for another twenty years. The new institutions for girls were unable to cope with the varied curriculum of the old; moreover, the high school was primarily to prepare for college. There were few of these open to women and, on the whole, the seminaries still provided an education that was satisfactory to the upper classes from which the colleges might expect to draw their patronage. Southern fathers were not indifferent to the best interests of their daughters as they saw it. Within the narrow bounds set by tradition and social prestige, the seminaries had developed into excellent institutions for their kind, and comparable with any of their day. On their foundation the colleges were later built.[78]

Education offered women both North and South was inferior to that provided for men.[79] However, recent investigators think that southern antebellum education has been very much maligned. They find little evidence that the North made better provisions for its girls than did the South either in its colonial schools[80] or its seminaries,[81] and Georgia chartered the first college in the United States for women. After that time, however, the South yielded its leadership in the movement for equal educational opportunities to the North.[82]

Most of the academies and seminaries were not "boarding schools" in the sense that the students lived there. Some schools had "boarding departments," but the majority of these could accommodate only a limited number of students. Most of the young ladies lived in the neighborhood with "respectable" families,[83] where "board could be obtained for fourteen or fifteen dollars per month, fuel lights, washing, etc., etc., included."[84] However, they remained under the discipline and regulations of the school.[85]

The student body in Georgia institutions was drawn almost entirely from the state. That of Washington Female Seminary, for example, with an enrollment of 104 girls, including six from Charleston, one from Barnwell (both in South Carolina), another from Irwinton, Alabama, and the remainder from Georgia.[86]

Although women taught in the classrooms and served as headmistresses in many institutions, it was more usual to find men as executives and teachers of the "higher branches" in schools for girls.[87] The officials of Washington Female Seminary, where the principal and faculty were women, but the board of trustees men,[88] explained:

> In our Southern county, female schools of the higher order have more frequently had a male head, it has been owing more to the pecuniary responsibilities necessarily incurred in such undertakings, than to any want of ability in the female sex to control them.[89]

There were no restrictions against married women teaching, and it was quite customary to find a husband and his "lady" employed in the same institution.[90]

Antebellum Georgia girls were expected to get married, and the schools were expected to make them attractive to prospective husbands. This objective did not change throughout the period, but masculine fancy did; and when it did, the schools sought to adjust their curriculums accordingly. Then the purpose of the schools became not to provide higher, but different, education

17

for girls, for the seminaries supplied charming sweethearts, but extravagant and boring wives. It was men's consideration for men that led to the establishment of the so-called colleges.[91]

The father of higher education for women in Georgia was Duncan Green Campbell, Georgian by adoption, teacher of girls in Wilkes County, Secretary of the Board of Trustees of the University, and member of the state legislature. In 1825 he introduced a bill providing for state support for a woman's college equal to the University. It passed the house, but was killed in the senate, for Georgia was not ready for equal education.[92]

Where Campbell failed his son-in-law, Daniel Chandler, succeeded. In an address at the University of Georgia in 1835, advocating a "female college," he attracted attention, created interest, and finally produced results.[93] In it he opposed the "common opinion . . . that the culture of the female mind is inconsistent with the domestic duties of a wife." On the contrary, Chandler painted a picture of men deserting "dissipation's paths" for wives, who, with better educational advantages, "would cease to delight in giddy amusements," and for homes where the "conversation would assume a more refined tone."[94] He said so well what everyone else was thinking that the next year the legislature responded with a charter for Georgia Female College, later called Wesleyan, in Macon.[95] This was the first institution in the United States having the right to confer upon women "all such honors, degrees, and licenses, as are usually conferred in colleges or universities."[96]

The colleges for women crept forth timidly. In reality, however, they were only glorified seminaries. There were two powerful enemies to higher education for women—the genuine concern lest Eve desert her predestined sphere and become unsexed; and, as Dr. John S. Wilson put it in 1854, the masculine "hereditary sexual pride which revolts at the idea of being placed on the level with a woman."[97] So the colleges, as the seminaries had done, molded women as men liked them.

Even the Georgia Female College, with its high hopes written into its charter, was no exception. It failed to reach the standards of the male colleges in its early age of admission—twelve years—whereas that of the University of Georgia was fourteen; its low entrance requirements; its sacrifice of academic standards; its failure to require Latin and Greek; and, finally, in its issuing a certificate of graduation, not like those of the male colleges written in Latin and specifying the *Artium Baccalaureata*, but in English and modestly granting the "First Degree" as the seminaries had done.[98]

George F. Pierce, the first president of the Georgia Female College, undoubtedly struggled to establish an institution superior to the old seminaries. The college, however, was faced with problems that he was powerless to solve—a student body that was inadequately trained; a slender purse that demanded the lowering of academic standards to insure tuition fees; and a public opinion that was always critical, seldom sympathetic, usually indifferent, and frequently hostile. Pierce recognized and deplored the shortcomings of the institution, but he was forced to yield to conditions.[99]

When the college opened in 1839, it taught "not only whole courses of English Letters and Science, but also vocal and instrumental Music, Drawing and Painting, together with Latin, Greek, French, Spanish, and Italian Languages; and 'last but not least,' . . . operated . . . a system of Domestic Economy, by which the young ladies under the instruction of experienced teachers [were] enabled and required to prepare, and keep in good order, all their own clothing, thereby avoiding milliner's bills while in school, and at the same time preparing themselves creditably to do this work for themselves in future life."[100]

Other colleges followed, among them the Greensboro Female College, which, likewise, granted a degree. With a faculty of five, including the president, they undertook three divisions: an elementary, with fourteen children under ten years enrolled; an academic, with thirty-two pupils; and a college, with sixty students. The course of study for the collegiate division had eleven departments: language and literature, mathematics, history, natural sciences, chemistry and physiology, astronomy and natural philosophy, modern languages, ancient languages, drawing and painting, and music.[101]

The Georgia Female College, at Scottsboro, "pledged" itself "to impart in one year's time to any young lady who possessed a good mind and can read fluently, a handsome handwriting, a correct knowledge of Arithmetic, Geography and Spelling."[102]

Nothing could be more indicative of the character of these pioneer institutions than the commencement exercises of Madison Female College, where:

> A great variety of talent was exhibited by the class. The religious, and gay, and poetic and argumentative, the satirical and agreeable were united to amuse and gratify the audience. . . . Perhaps more of the poetic element would have better suited the character of the female mind.

. . . they were "dressed very fine"; their compositions decorated with ribbons and bow, they were read loud enough to be heard generally and only lacked a little *suaviter in mode* to make them perfect.

[One young lady gave] "Life on the Ocean" in true spirit of Woman's romance. Her pictures . . . were beautiful if not real. The feeling deepened into the pathetic when Miss B. of Louisville, read "Holy as Heaven is a Mother's Tender Love." Then we were brought to the climax of the sentimental when the apostrophe "Moon, what hast thou Seen" cut us loose from all tangible objects. . . . "The True Gentleman" presented us with some pictures of *soit disant* gentility. The moustaches and cigars fared badly yet justly.

. . . Exercises closed with a rich debate . . . "which is stronger Love or Money?" As you may guess the money argument carried it.

. . . Miss Martha A. Fannin of Morgan County [read her composition] "I would not be a child again" . . . When her name was called she came on the stage and commenced in a full, round tone of voice, but before one sentence was concluded the tide of childhood fears came rushing too strongly for her character and she took her seat bathed in tears. Every heart was touched as we looked upon that half shaded face, now smiling, now blushing, and all the time bathed in tears.[103]

Seven years later this institution was advertising:

Every pupil attends to Arithmetic, Grammar, Geography, Spelling, Penmanship and Composition throughout the whole course. Vocal music will be taught daily, to the whole school. A Uniform has been provided for Sundays and Examinations.[104]

H. V. Johnson of Georgia, in an address at Wesleyan College, gave his ideas of a suitable college curriculum for women, which was fairly representative of what cultured and progressive people in his state wanted:

Ethics are to be studied; they inculcate the doctrine of morality; they teach dependence on God, they promote humility. Biographies of the eminitely learned and pious are of priceless value. They delineate human character in its highest manifestations, and stimulate a laudable ambition by presenting in bold relief, the golden fruits of persevering toil and sublimer triumphs of christian faith. The natural sciences enter legitimately into female education. They are enobling and elevating, in their moral influences, as they are useful, in the practical concerns of life. . . . Geography and history should be studied. . . . These and such branches, are indispensable auxiliaries to that elevation of mind and expansion of heart, which qualify woman for her lofty mission.[105]

The South was not prepared for radical changes in the course of study for women. When Wesleyan College, attempting a constructive experiment, established a department of domestic economy, *DeBow's Review*, which voiced the reactions of conservative people, retaliated:

> We do not believe in female colleges under any circumstances. We believe the fire side to be the best college for young ladies, their fathers the best president, and their mothers the best matron and teacher of domestic economy. It is all nonsense in the extreme to talk of "department of domestic economy" in the Georgia Female College, or in any female or male college. It is like absurdity of the "manual labor department" once attached to Emory and Mercer University.[106]

The discipline of the early colleges was patterned after that of the seminaries, and in keeping with the code of conduct expected from young girls. That at Georgia Female College was considered mild in comparison with other institutions of its day and time.[107] There they even refrained from "regulating the hours of sleep." The President explained that "no rule was made," because "none could be executed, and we esteem it a bad policy to make a law that we know would be violated, and the enforcement of which is utterly impracticable."[108] Such difficulties in discipline as had arisen, he felt, were not "of serious magnitude," but were "the mischievous kind rather than the rebellious—ebullitions of playful feeling—the giddy thoughtlessness of a spirit full of life, rather than the wicked disrespect of authority and rule."[109]

There could have been very little time for "acts of disorder," as:

> At sunrise of each day the young Ladies who board in the college building are summoned by the ringing of the bell to meet in Chapel for family prayer . . . study till breakfast then have recreation in Autumn and Winter till 9, and Spring and Summer till 8 o'clock . . . then . . . assemble for morning prayer. Then recreation till 11, two hours to each class, then study till 12. . . . From 12 to 2 o'clock dinner and recreation . . . study . . . till 4, when all classes recite together at 5 p.m. prayer and dismission, study and recreation til 7, then study till 9, and *afterwards retire to sleep at will*.[110]

At Greensboro Female College "the pupils [were] boarded in the village, subject at all times to the control of the faculty." They were "required to attend church on the Sabbath," but not allowed to go there or to any "other meetings of the kind at night, unless in company with the family in which they board, or the President of the College." But no lessons were assigned for

21

Friday evening "except in cases of delinquency," for "on this evening alone," the young ladies were permitted to "exchange visits or enjoy whatever advantages there may be for social intercourse in the families where they board."[111]

The theory of the mental inferiority of women became the central theme in the debate over the education of girls. Men were divided on the subject into four groups. The first, like George Pierce, believed that "girls can learn and deserve to be taught."[112] The second, like Daniel Chandler, hoped it was possible, but wasn't sure, for as he said, "the intellectual capacities of females have never been fairly developed, or accurately tested." Yet he granted that if women were "not equally gifted with the other sex they are by no means deficient in sprightliness of imagination, originality of thought, and depths of reflection."[113]

The third, like Dr. John Wilson, stoutly affirmed that women couldn't learn, but secretly feared that they could. He, under the sanction of the *Southern Medical and Surgical Journal*, edited and published in Georgia:

> Refused to enter into a discussion of the mental equality of the two sexes, in every branch of science or pursuit in life; we simply declare our conviction that no such equality exists.[114]

Dr. Wilson advocated medical education for women on the grounds that it would relieve men of a disagreeable part of the profession, and because he was "convinced that the *safety and happiness of a large portion of the most refined and lovely women* . . . DEMANDED it"[115] as a protection against their own modesty and the malpractices of midwives and quacks. Yet he proposed to withhold from women enough of the regular medical curriculum to "deprive them of any just or well founded claims to the degree of 'Doctor of Medicine.' "[116]

The fourth group in the debate over higher education for women, like Eugenius A. Nesbit, believed that girls could learn but feared an equal education would unsex them. There was almost general alarm lest the hand that performed a chemical experiment be unfit to rock the cradle, and the belief was nearly unanimous that to look on Homer and Euclid would destroy the pure in heart. In an address before the Cullonden Literary and Scientific Association in 1839, Nesbit said of women:

> That their actual mental organization is the same [as man's] I do not believe; but that they have all the elements of mind in common I do not doubt. . . .

Assign both to the same place in society . . . and . . . no greater difference be found to exist between the sexes than between individuals of the same sex.

But he believed that their spheres were different, and that it was fitting they should remain so, for Nesbit "knew of no queen whose state has not unsexed her but Victoria."[117]

The orators who opposed equal education for women did not shout down the movement in Georgia, but the turn of events in the North strangled those who favored it. In the North, the cause became associated with the humanitarian forces that were threatening southern institutions. As the danger became acute, the South united against radical change of any sort and struggled to preserve the old order, in which "men were sufficiently men without asking aid from the other sex," and preferred their "women as God made them."[118]

At the same time, northern colleges for women were growing both in quality and quantity,[119] yet the southern woman, bound by tradition and sectional expediency, was unable to take advantage of them. She remained at home, to "perform her part in the sphere of action, to which she has been assigned in the order of Providential arrangement." There, her "mission" was "to dispense the amenities and charities of social life and to direct as well as adorn the domestic circle," as "man is expected to be learned—woman cultivated."[120]

It was believed that "the education of the Southern Matron must be a Southern Education," for the "caste of study at the North" had "unsexed women." It had "produced those monstrous assemblies, *Women's Rights Conventions*."[121] The "external forces of Bloomerism and Women's Rights" were frequently considered to have tainted northern colleges with "hetroclitical errors." Moreover, as the war drew nearer, southern men were likely to think that southern "females" should be relieved of the "necessity of making a trip to Yankeedom . . . that 'higher law' land."[122]

Nesbit, the beloved friend of "female education," solemnly warned in an address to the Griffin Synodical Female College:

There are those . . . who invite you to step out of your sphere, and unsexing yourselves enter the list for honors of those pursuits which Christianity and civilization have assigned your sex. . . . they would inaugurate a social reform, which remits you to a position worse than that which paganism and oriental bigotry has provided for you. I believe your sex has not originated it, but that it has its origin in the vile passions and rank infidelity of ours . . . they assail the government of God . . . and they hurl you from your seat of empire—the hearts of men. Their flatteries have enlisted few recruits among you but not here. This our dear Southland is the home of conservatism, especially on the conservatism of female character. In the educated circles of the Southern States woman reaches her highest level. . . . You are here the beloved and honored co-equal companion of man. You can remain so long as you fill . . . the place which God and nature have allotted you.[123]

Education for both sexes, before the Civil War, was for the upper classes, but a greater traditional and economic importance was attached to masculine than to feminine learning. The meager support that Georgia granted did not discriminate against girls. The excess of boys in the schools and the lower illiteracy rate among men, considered in connection with the excess of girls in secondary schools, indicates that elementary education was economically valuable to men, while secondary education was socially valuable to women.

The school increased a girl's social status, but unless it resulted in an advantageous marriage, it seldom altered her economic worth. Fashion rarely goes trailblazing, and blue stockings did not fit into the French-heeled conception of women that was held dear by the upper classes. The seminaries produced a type in keeping with the [prevalent] mores and masculine vanity. The movement for higher education began in Georgia, gave some promise, but suffered retardation in the general conservative reaction that bound the South anew to its own institutions, and kept women in their traditional sphere.

THREE

Courtship and Marriage

In the State of Georgia prior to the Civil War, an unmarried woman stood equal to her brother before the bar, but in her husband she found her legal grave, and by his death her resurrection. The code under which she lived was biting with the acid of an old bachelor—St. Paul—and stinging with the vengeance of a henpecked husband—Lord Coke.[1]

On the statute books, a wife's account was always in the red. Her husband's property was his own to use as he pleased and to deed as he would—minus her dower—and all she possessed was his also to hoard, squander, or settle on another—except her separate estate. He was within his conjugal rights when he beat her, and if another "trespassed" upon this privilege, he was entitled to collect damages, while she retired to lick her wounds.[2] If she drove him out of her home, he might have the law on her; but if he drove her out, he might have the law on whosoever gave her shelter.[3] He was her guardian at all times; she became his only when he was insane.[4] His children might inherit [her] wealth, while hers came away penniless. The legitimate children were his—the illegitimate, hers.[5] He was her "baron," she his "femme covert."[6] If he murdered her, it was as though he had "killed a stranger." If she murdered him, it was as though she had "killed the king,"[7] high treason for which she might be burned alive, as, indeed, was one woman in North Carolina at the time of the Revolution.[8]

Yet, as paradoxical as it may seem, a woman's best chance for happiness was in matrimony, and she seldom failed to take it when offered. For, if the legal hurdles seemed high for the married, those of the social and economic world for the unmarried were higher.

There was no place in the antebellum social system for the unmarried. A single woman of independent means had a measure of security, but there were problems of isolation and protection common to rich and poor alike, and the few occupations that existed for women were all crossed with the bar sinister of either pity or gentility. Marriage became, therefore, not only the goal of the enamored, but the career of the adventuress, the habit of the widow, the ambition of the plain, the pride of the fair, and the refuge of the timid.

Victorians sometimes avowed that marriages were made in heaven, usually arranged them on earth, wisely secured their daughters' property by marriage settlements and prenuptial contracts, customarily provided the most elegant wedding they could afford, and probably sighed with relief, hoped for the best, and frequently got it.

In antebellum Georgia, "it was a *quasi stigma* of reproach to fail to receive an 'offer' after a girl advanced into long dresses,"[9] and many people professed having a "natural antipathy to old maids."[10] Few women had sufficient courage to put themselves willingly in a position where "damsels in the primrose-season of youth" might "mockingly," "happy mothers . . . pittyingly," and "broken hearted wives . . . indignantly," called them "old maids."[11] Any husband at times might be preferable to none. The years of courtship were short and vital. The time between a woman's "entrance into society" and her marriage "was perhaps the most important and most perilous of her career," even though she enjoyed "more fame, and more worldly glory than during any other of her life."[12] For the fear among the upper classes of being a "Leah among the Rachels,"[13] and in the lower of having to dangle in the "hog troft,"[14] was justifiable. For "she that continues unmarried until twenty is reckoned a stale-maid which is a very indifferent character."[15]

Women were not expected to live alone. There was no place for them in the social and economic system except the home. If they did not have their own, they usually became "like the furniture or the servants," an "inevitable" part of the household of a relative.[16] Public opinion was not inclined to sympathize with the few women who were bold enough to revolt against this fate.[17]

The "spinster" occupied an unenviable position. As the word indicates, the unwelcome tasks in the family fell to her. She might expect to be tolerated or ignored, to become the butt of jokes, and to be regarded as a proverbially sensitive, sour, and unattractive person.[18] Her economic status was frequently low, and her social position insecure, although it rose in proportion to the "offers" or rumors of "offers" she had declined. The much courted Mary E. G. Harden of Athens[19] could briefly say, "I never expect to marry,"[20] and remain a romantic figure, but there were few successful imitators. About the limit of toleration an old maid might expect was to have it said of her that "her soul is widowed."[21]

So young girls did their best to attract attention, and their parents to arrange advantageous marriages, although sometimes, "like the unlucky sportsman, who fires right and left to no purpose," they were left "to deplore the lavish expenditures of caps and powder."[22] And, if a game of "Old Maid" at White Sulphur was a "laughing party engaged at cards," until a young lady, "left with the queen," found she had "no patience to stay longer,"[23] who is there to blame her?

The chances of getting a husband were fairly good. From 1790 to 1860 there were more men than women both in Georgia and in the entire United States.[24] Unfortunately, however, at the marriageable age, fifteen to twenty-six, there was reported a "large and growing excess of females," but, as it was pointed out in 1850, the number was "attributable in some slight degree . . . to the anxiety of the sex to retain this interesting age."[25]

The surplus of women was disposed of in various ways. Mrs. Farnham, at the time of the gold rush, was of the "opinion that female society is the great want of California." She "projected the transportation of a number of young ladies from the Atlantic coast to the Pacific," and "located [them] on a ranch, seventy miles south of San Francisco." Mrs. Farnham was joined there by "a lady . . . for the purpose of opening a girl's school," and they reported a "fine community of young girls coming on."[26]

The excess of women was also absorbed, in part, by what might be brutally called the "quick turn-over." Buckingham reported that "many are the instances in which a man marries two sisters in succession . . . and even a third, so rapidly to they give place to each other."[27] Widowers were back in circulation often, but young ladies had potential rivals in widows, for both men and women frequently remarried. In addition to other considerations, the rich found that the plantation needed both a master and a mistress, and the poor, that motherless children must be cared for and fatherless ones supported.

The wedding of very young people was customary. When a girl "left school she began quilt making . . . looking toward matrimony, and it was nothing uncommon to get married early as fourteen or fifteen."[28] There was no happy alternate for young ladies, the youth argued: "if the married state be a state of happiness—if it is intended by providence to improve the lot of man here below—then why not enter into it as soon as possible?"[29] Their elders believed that early marriages reduced "elopements," "seductions," and "domestic infidelity."[30]

In the early part of the period, the attitude toward youthful marriages was explained by the ease of making a living in the South, which obviated the necessity of waiting for established resources.[31] And, even in 1859, the young ladies graduating from LaGrange College were assured it was "cheaper to marry . . . than to remain single."[32] Nevertheless, a young man who professed to love the ladies "from the spangles on their shoes to the ribbons red and blue upon their jaunty bonnets" was forced to "keep [this] distance" simply because of insufficient fortune.[33] Young men were discovering that "Hooped Dresses" were expensive,[34] and "Eudora Unhopped" was costly and selfish,[35] so, when "felicity" was within "reach," they were finding it wise to reverse the practice of the previous generation and refuse "to accept it."[36]

Girls not only hoped, but were expected, to be married. Mrs. Rebecca Felton could recall "nobody" who had actually "said to a daughter, 'You have got to marry,' " but remembered "plenty . . . who did say, 'I am sorry for so and so with a house full of old maids.' "[37] Parents were naturally anxious for the security of their daughters, and marriage offered the best opportunity. Nevertheless, as Governor Gilmer regretted, many did not hesitate "to acquire for them and for themselves distinction by marriage,"[38] and wealth was frequently the only consideration.[39] The young ladies of Wesleyan Female College were told such practices were a "growing evil,"[40] those of LaGrange that "an eligible match, a desirable alliance, these mean nothing more in the estimation of most parents, than such a connection will bring in a proper quota of this world's pelf, and extend the circle of pretentious family relationships."[41]

Medical science was concerned over the frequency of the intermarriage of cousins. It recognized four types of human temperaments: "the sanguine, bilious, lumphatic, and melancholic." These, a Savannah physician warned, if incorrectly combined, would end in most mournful results on the "progeny or no progeny at all."[42]

An Englishman believed that the large number of pecuniary marriages in the slave states were due to the fact that: "The chief, if not the only certain method, of insuring homage or consideration from the mass of the community is by the acquisition of wealth." He thought that in the South a well-planned marriage was one of the modes by which it was "most easily achieved."[43] But a Georgian explained that parents "ambitious" for their daughter's "honorable settlement in life, and confident of their own superior knowledge of the world, or impatient lest the golden period shall have past before the important event is consummated . . . are sometimes induced to take the matter in their own hands and themselves make the selection."[44]

In spite of those who thought to "weight" was a "misfortune," and regretted that "many parents and guardians for the sake of a little worldly consequences sacrificed their children,"[45] impoverished families could be found who were willing to lay their heads together and secure "protection in toto" by the marriage of a daughter even to an unenthusiastic groom.[46]

The businesslike attitude toward marriage was sanctioned by the clergy. Jesse Mercer, a Baptist minister who was able to leave $40,000 to found a university at Macon, informed a young girl at Fishing Creek, Georgia, that:

> Next to religion, the married state . . . is the most important and claims both our desires and our prudence. . . . Mr. H. Pope has had his attentions directed to you as suitable to receive his virtuous matrimonial advances—to you he is a stranger. I have been acquainted with him and his family for more than twenty years. I have never known anything disgraceful in him at any time. . . . I have seen him much concerned and some think him to be a Christian. His family is respectable and his property competent to a comfortable living.[47]

Young daughters no doubt sometimes consciously participated in efforts to contract mercenary marriages for themselves, and occasionally one was unconventional enough to admit "she would willingly get married if she could get a good offer";[48] but, on the whole, the Georgia girl of the upper classes who attracted admirers moved in an ether of exquisite innocence, real or pretended, that separated her from worldly considerations.

An antebellum girl was expected to be the spirit of romanticism and a counterpart of the heroines of Scott and Sims. If she failed to materialize, her contemporaries could not be blamed for lack of diligence. Orators thundered at her the "sovereignty of [her] delicacy,"[49] and the pulpit pled with her for "the modesty of nature and the decorum of her sex."[50] The school taught her to make wax flowers and to play a harpsichord, and eligible young men sought for wine with the "qualifications which adorn the female character." These they defined as being "souls all alive to the feelings of nature, hearts which can melt at the tale of sorrow, and eyes which will drop the tears of sympathy when they alight on the poor child of want and affliction."[51]

By the time of the war, the romantic movement was at its height in literature and music, and in 1842, when Richard Henry Wilde published "My Life is Like a Summer Rose," the school of self-pity, which was to sob itself out later, was well underway. In this morose period, around the theme of love and marriage "crept a tender gloom."[52] "A wind came out of a cloud by night chilling and killing my Annabel Lee."[53] "They fitted a slab of granite so grey" and left Ben Bolt's "sweet Alice under . . . the stone,"[54] while the admirers of "Hally" listened to "the mocking bird still singing on her grave."[55]

To separate cause and effect is difficult. Many of these women were ill,[56] and it is possible that they capitalized on their infirmities. At the same time, George Fitshugh probably did not overstate it when he wrote: "We men of the South infinitely prefer to nurse a sickly woman to being led around by a blue stocking."[57]

The older generation could remember frontier days and women "born before nerves came in fashion," and before "it was fashionable for the sex to faint at the sight of an old ruminating cow, or squeal at the buzz of a beetle."[58]

Occasionally, a rebel among the men wished "for the sake of self interest, of common sense, that we would quit calling women angels, sylphs, fairies, and consider them as warm substantial flesh and blood, capable like us of living on beef-steak and butter milk, as well as nectar and ambrosia."[59] Or a lover might write: "That as much as I love and dote on you, my respect, my esteem and veneration for your mind and character equal my love—are in fact its basis."[60]

On a whole, nevertheless, moronic simplicity, piety, innocence, and smelling salts were the indispensable equipment of a Georgia belle. The "lady" stood on a pedestal. Southern gentlemen seldom shook it, and rarely offered to help her down. Her quarters were uncomfortable and precarious, for, as Mrs. Almira L. Phelps of Baltimore, teacher and writer of scientific textbooks for boarding school girls, discovered:

> If beautiful she will be condemned as vain; if graceful, as affected in manners; if frank and ingenuous, she will likely be called imprudent; and if cautious artful. If, to be agreeable to many, she talk on common-place topics, she may pass for one who has shallow intellect; if she introduce into fashionable circles, literary or religious subjects, she will probably be shunned as pedantic or bigoted. If she should have admirers, she will be called a flirt; if she should have none, she will be pitied for her supposed disappointment and mortification.[61]

Women were known as "the sex," and in alluding to them men used extravagant and fulsome words even when the sentiments were not as elevated as the language implied. Robert Lewis wrote to another young man, giving him the news of the neighborhood girls:

> Emma Neyle is just about the same kind of a gal as she was when you were here. . . . Miss Sally you know whos not of gentile faith she seems quite sumpsious. But I had almost forgot to mention the beautiful, lovely, amiable, and almost to be "beadised" . . . Lavada it is utterly impossible to describe her

more particularly. She is just the very thing itself the cream of perfection—her horse is very harty and she jiist had her gig brushed up. I havn't much time to go among the buties tharfore it is I cent say much about them. They will be worth looking at this winter, becase I persoon the will war frocks as short as there nees, for they have worn them half-way this yare, by which we may not only see the ancle bones, but there neese. I have some sort of notion of trying to marry one of them.[62]

The period of courtship was possibly a glamorous time, but it was also a trying one in a girl's life. During it she was not "to seek but to be sought . . . not to woo, but to be wooed." Frequently a girl was forced to "suppress the most violent feelings . . . and at the same time to wear that face of contentment and ease" that "an inquisitive and scrutinizing world" made advisable.[63] "In solitude," even the pose was kept. She was cautioned to "turn aside from thoughts too alluring" by "playing on a harpsichord, painting a flower, or reading from a work of genius," lest her very thought betray her.[64]

Southern belles were famous coquettes. Courtship was the one period in a woman's life when she enjoyed power, prestige, and glory; so, in spite of the fact that "coquetry" was rated "next to want of chastity in the scale of female vices" by rejected suitors, a girl with talent and spirit seldom neglected to make the most of it.[65] A contemporary wrote: "the theory on this subject is that there are no broken hearts among them; that they do not surrender their tender affections unitl their papas have been duely consulted; but . . . then the gentle feeling darts like lightning into their souls, subduing, controlling and changing the character."[66]

As a matter of fact, both sexes were frequently guilty of flirting,[67] and there was probably a tied score on broken hearts. Men did most of the complaining, for it was subtly romantic for a man to be a victim, but, outside of song and story, humiliating for a girl. Flirtation "was not lovemaking, nor coquetry . . . nor friendship," but, according to a young man of the period, it had a technique all its own. He considered it "worthy of a man's best efforts," for like "every science," it had its "pretenders." He warned others not to "enter into a flirtation with a lazy mind," and assured novices that no man can flirt "with a woman of talent and feeling without being greatly improved thereby both mentally and morally." However, he cautioned, "the least touch of lachrymose and a man is gone."[68]

Among the upper classes, decorum was strictly insisted on during courtship. A six-year-old girl might write to her five-year-old sister: "Hatty has taken William Bower for sweetheart and he sends her honey and sweet potatoes and kisses her";[69] but the propriety of a young lady of fifteen posing in a private theatrical tableau, "The Stolen Kiss," became a matter of much controversy.[70] Nor was it surprising that after John McIntosh Kell participated in the "gazing matches" customary in Uruguay, he "laughed immoderately," for they seemed "so outrageously impudent"[71] when contrasted with the code of etiquette in Georgia, which instructed gentlemen, before bowing to a lady in the street, to "permit her to decide whether you may do so or not, by at least a look of recognition."[72] Public opinion, however, did not wish courtship to be hampered, and the *Columbus Enquirer* even defended the right of young people to "sit up" after the "old folks" had gone to bed.[73]

A marriageable daughter was chaperoned even to the point of pain to the father and embarrassment to the girl. One writes that:

> Whenever young men come here in the evening . . . Father stands it like a martyr-hero—he never flinches (tho' you can see the iron has entered his soul) until the clock strikes *nine*—but that is the death-knell to his fortitude . . . how sour he looks . . . how long he yawns and how "vig'ously" he winds up his watch, and how loud he locks all the doors—and how restlessly he walks from the sitting room to the water pail, and then back into his seat with the most agitated expression and with what determination he resumes his seat, as if to let them know he *would* sit them out, even if they stayed till *ten o'clock*, and he died in the attempt. . . . he intimated yesterday that we had better try to see which of us could get married first, as he didn't intend the other one should at all.[74]

Conversation between the young people was usually trivial and frequently vapid or gossipy.[75] Nevertheless, courtships flourished. The beaux and belles lingered in the moonlight for "three hours in the full tide of enjoyment,"[76] young ladies sent valentines, played "Upon Honor,"[77] treasured tender notes,[78] gave locks of their hair that rendered the lover "mad with love," and made sleep "too sordid, too vulgar an enjoyment for a mind so elevated to think of."[79] They even studied theology when the minister was new and unmarried.[80]

In a drawing room a young lady, to the tune of a harpsichord, invited her admirer to "Call me sweet names, dearest, call me a bird," while in a saloon her errant sister reminded hers that "Frankie and Johnnie were lovers."[81] In a country parlor, a cracker beau might "sot and sot lookin all sorts of love . . . but without ever venturin to open his mouth on the subject."[82] But the "daredevils" of Oglethorpe County "pinched their sweetheart's ears and cheeks until they squealed; slapped them with vigorous love-licks, that made them grunt; hugged with a bear's grip, and kissed them with ravenous appetites."[83]

A southern woman wrote: "With us society is instituted almost exclusively for the benefit of the very young and the unmarried, and its chief object seems to be to afford the opportunity and facilities of courtship. Beardless boys and boarding-school misses almost monopolize the privileges, from which persons of riper years are entirely banished."[84]

Any gathering might provide the proper setting for courtships. Romances flourished on Sundays. "On reaching the interior" of the Methodist, and frequently of the Baptist and Presbyterian churches, "the sexes separated; the ladies all sitting together in the center, and the gentlemen all repairing to the side-pews, where they sat apart."[85] Nevertheless, "more young people than old" attended church. It is quite possible that many did not find the service as attractive as the opportunities for courtship that the walk there and back provided.[86]

In the country everybody who could went to church and the big "meetings were convivial gatherings." For them, "the turkey eggs and fatted calves were kept, to entertain friends coming from a distance."[87] All wore their best to church. "The pretty girls dressed in striped and checked cloth, spun and woven with their own hands, and their sweethearts in sumach and walnut dyed stuff made by their mothers."[88] "Courting was done when riding to meeting on Sunday, and walking to the spring when there."[89] "One of the most dextrous and admired feats of the gallantry was for a young spark to cut out his rival—that is to ride between him and his girl as their horses watered at a creek, or on some other sought for occasion."[90]

Religious gatherings offered opportunities to see and to be seen, and even in the mellowing society of Savannah assembled for worship, an elderly deacon was not above asking who was "wearing the blue bonnet."[91]

Resorts were the best places for the rich to nourish sentimental ideas,[92] and camp meetings served the same purpose for their economic or social inferiors.[93] "Most watering places," observed a Georgia gentleman at Saratoga Springs, "might with equal propriety be called fishing places, being much frequented by female anglers, who are in quest of such prey; the elder for their daughters, the younger for themselves." However, he found "it is equally amusing to see many gentlemen, both old and young, who are trying to *run* in love," for he says, "to run in love is as when one *runs* into debt, [but] to *fall* in love" is as when one "falls down stairs."[94]

Barbecues,[95] balls, dances,[96] and candy pullings all played an important part in courtship,[97] but none of these, at least according to one witness from Elbert County, were more important than singing bees.[98] There the music teacher himself was "more dangerous even than love-powders." He dressed in a manner that impressed the backwoods from his "boots to paper collar, his swinging watch—seals and bright breast pin; his many finger-rings as he beats time with his hands." To make him completely irresistible, there was "his well brushed hair fragrant of cinnamon-oil and odorous bear's grease." Nevertheless, he did not have it all his own way, for there were "many matches made at the piano."[99]

Apparently, the entire masculine population that wished to "undergo marriage" approached the "penance" of the proposal with tied tongues, shaking knees, and bleeding hearts. To say to a young lady simply, "Will you marry me?" was considered to require a "degree of nerve," which only a "bluff soldier like Zac Taylor," or a "brave tar, like Perry" possessed.[100]

The proposal of marriage was such a "general and delicate problem" that the *Southern Literary Messenger* published directions for the aid of its masculine subscribers.[101] "Any body," it considered, could "manage to finish . . . the chief stumbling block" was the beginning. First the victim must break ground by keeping the lady "constantly impressed with the idea" of his superiority. He was advised, "she thinks she is superior to all others, if you convince her that you are superior to herself she must regard you as more worthy of her regard than any other human being."[102] The enamored swain was taught that although "husbands may be humble . . . humility does not become a lover."[103] Next he was cautioned to remember, even if he forgot all else, that it is "time enough to open valves . . . when the days of courting are over."[104] The candidate for matrimony, now ready for the ordeal, was warned that "men make opportunities or never have them . . . day or darkness, alone or in a crowd, in the parlour or along the highway—anywhere and everywhere, opportunities present themselves, where a man is ready for work."[105]

Examples of technique that had been used successfully by others were submitted to guide the timid to the altar:

"Go to Guinea," said a young lady in anger.
"There or any other spot in the world if I may have your good company!" replied the young man romantically.
They compromised on the parsonage.[106]

Another romance was sealed by Machiavellian guile and the bold intercession of the cat:

"Pussy," said the lover, picking it up, "May I have your mistress?"
"Say yes, Pussy," prompted the grateful lady.
It did.[107]

The church hymn book was reported to have been used successfully during the service. A valiant lover showed his sweetheart the words:

'Tis thee I love—for thee alone
I shed my tears and make my moan;
Where'er I am, where'er I move
I meet the object of my love.

She doing ditto:

I yield, I yield, I yield.
I can hold out no more.

Now it was his turn:

—when shall it be,
That I find my heaven in thee
The fullness of the promise prove,
The pledge of thy eternal love?

She, with suspicious promptness:

Soon as they wilt.

He, probably decorating himself for bravery under fire:

O happy day that fixed my choice
On thee.

They lived happily ever afterward.[108]

A widow was recommended for the "extremely bashful."[109] If a man was anxious to become "a candidate for the unexpired term of her late husband," as a politician of Columbia, S.C., was accused of having declared himself,[110] he was advised that "the suitor would need no instructions," to "give himself no concern." If he were "acceptable to her" and he were "backward," she would "supply his speech" or "even do the courting."[111]

A simple and direct method of getting a wife was through advertisements in the newspapers. A prospective groom from Batesville, Arkansas, sought:

> Any gal what got a bed, calico dress, coffee-pot and skillet, knows how to cut our britches, can make a hunting shirt, and knows how to take care of children, can have my services till death parts both of us.[112]

To reduce the number of workmen on the treasury building at Washington, the unmarried men were discharged. They hastened to meet, decided to advertise for wives, appointed a secretary to "receive propositions and report the same," and agreed on a meeting to consider them. "For the information of such Damsels as may wish to apply," and for the benefit of the home market, the Athens *Southern Banner* carried the advertisement:

> Wives Wanted!
>
> The subscriber has been authorized to issue an advertisement for wives of the Stone Cutters at the Treasury Building who still remain unmarried! They are about 28 in number, and between the ages of twenty-three and thirty-five years. A good opportunity is now offered to those ladies who wish to enter the matrimonial state.
>
> Applicants must be between the ages of seventeen and thirty three years, of good moral character and good disposition. Applications sent through the Post Office before Saturday next at 12 M. addressed to the subscriber, will be thankfully received and immediately attended to.[113]

The direct method of "addressing" a young lady was both terrifying and treacherous. Tom Merriweather tried it when he courted Governor Mathew's daughter, but "found the question sticking in his throat."[114] "Heath" also tried it on Sarah Semmes. She admitted to her friends that it was "nothing more" than she "had heard was going to be." When he "expressed his feelings," however, she was forced to "confess it was rather abrupt." She met Heath on the "way to the spring" the next morning and felt it proper to "return his salutation quite cooly."[115] Frequently a young man would decide it was wisest to avoid peril by writing to the young lady for permission to speak to her on the "subject of matrimony" if she were "not already engaged to some more worthy gentleman."[116]

John Howard Payne courted Mary E. G. Harden of Athens. His affections seem to have been returned, for there is ample proof that she would not marry another. There were parental objections to the actor-poet because he did not appear to have any future. After she refused him, he secured an appointment to the consulate in Tunis and died there sixteen years later, unmarried.[117] His letter is a good example of the formal and stilted character of a proposal of marriage.

Madame
I did for a long time indulge in the fallacious hope that fortune would have favored and placed me in a more suitable situation for making this communication to you. I have unfortunately been disappointed and have endeavored to calm my feelings and submit to my fate, yet the more I have strived to do so, the more I have been convinced that it would be useless for me any longer to attempt to struggle with the sentiment I feel toward you.
I am conscious of my unworthyness of the boon I have desired from you and cannot, dare not, ask you to give a decisive answer in my favor now, only permit me to hope that at some future time I may have the happiness of believing my affections returned, but at the same time I conjur you to remember in making up your decision that it is in your power to render me happy or miserable.
Having frequently through the kind permission of your honored Parents the pleasure of being in your society I every day find it more necessary to come to some conclusions to my future conduct for when I was obliged to leave you, it was only to renew the agitated state of my mind and to contemplate the image of one too dear to me to resign forever, without making an effort I was unequal to when I was in your presence.
You will perhaps tell me this is presumption on my part and true it is I have nothing to offer to you but a devoted heart and hand, however, be assured Madame, whatever your decision may be, fervent wishes for your happiness and wellfare shall be the first in my heart.
I have felt it essential to my peace of mind that I should inform you of the state of my feelings satisfied that your amiableness of heart will plead my excuse. I entreat you to reply to this letter (if but a word) indeed I am sure if you knew how anxiously I shall await your answer, compassion alone would induce you to send me an early reply.
Allow me Madame to subscribe myself
Your humble and devoted admirer
J. H. Payne[118]

After a man was engaged, he was in a position to give full play to all the sentimentality of romanticism. A fair specimen was Felix Gilbert, who wrote:

I am this moment landed after a pleasant passage—How beautiful was the last night, how deliciously melancholy were my feelings while I sat on deck, my whole soul full of your image. . . . I saw you in imagination pensively viewing the moon's silver image. . . . I became for once romantic and spoke in soft whispers to the dear vision of my imagination. The delusion was too happy to be lasting—painful images succeeded—and presented your little Barque contending with angry waves . . . yourself sick, weary and desponding—My gloomy forebodings became excessive . . . do not think my dear angel, that I speak the Language of romance, when I tell you that they pursued the dark prospect, till I saw you buried in a watery grave. . . . I feel most poignantly that to perish with you would be infinitely more desirable than to live without you.[119]

Whatever form a proposal took, decorum demanded that the father's consent be asked. His decision was usually abided by.[120] Parents were urged to teach their daughters to "consider any man an enemy, who would presume to speak on the subject of love," without first having gained their permission.[121] The Methodist Church took positive action on the subject. It demanded parental consent and refused its blessing to any girl who was married without it, unless she were "under the necessity of marrying," or "her parents absolutely refused to let her marry any Christian." It taught, however, that even in the latter case, while "she may, nay, ought to marry without their consent. Yet even then a Methodist preacher ought not to be married to her."[122]

Courtship, as an institution, was usually social in its implications and offered as much spontaneity as Victorianism would permit. The giving and accepting of a marriage proposal took the form and intent of a social contract with legal status. A woman was privileged to grant a release or to break an engagement with or without a good reason. But neither the code of a gentleman, the bar of public opinion, nor the laws of the state[123] permitted a man to repudiate his agreement. The difference in the reaction toward male and female offenders indicates that in the first half of the nineteenth century it was an accepted fact that marriage was more important to a woman than to a man. It would seem that contemporary forces recognized the justice of the woman's claim and united to protect it.

With the proposal safely behind her and public opinion her ally, the prospective antebellum Georgia bride might prepare for the wedding. These were the supreme social events of the period.

The usual form of the announcement was:

Married

At Fontenoy, Green Co. on the 17th inst. by Rev. Mr. Lumpkin, Rev. Adiel Sherwood, of Lexington to Mrs. Ann Adams Early, relict of the Hon. Peter Early, former governor of this state.[124]

But occasionally, marriage notices became poetic, as:

Married, on Thursday, the 25th ult. Mr. Epps Brown of Hancock county, to the amiable Miss Eliza Shackelfford of the same county.

Observe the maiden innocently sweet,
She was fair white paper, on an unfilled sheet,
On which the happy Man whom fate ordains,
May write his name, and take her for his pains.[125]

Or in Franklin County, where:

'Twas in this dark and stormy weather
This man and maid were joined together.

To which the editor of the paper added his acknowledgment of "wedding cake received."[126]

Weddings varied in elegance in proportion to class, wealth, thrift, and fancy. The supper for one might cost three hundred dollars,[127] while the less lavish would send "two very thin pieces" of wedding cake to a friend, "about three inches square—no icing," which a young daughter thought "looked too funny but mother would not let me say so."[128]

The bride usually wore white, and when one, "after seven years" courtship, was married in a church with four bridesmaids in a "brown muslin de laine dress," her contemporaries pronounced it an "odd fancy."[129] Robert Toombs' daughter on her wedding day was said to have answered "the romantic descriptions in novels of 'fair and fragil' brides—almost too fair and frail . . . for much of the wear and tear of life."[130] She "looked perfectly lovely" in white silk, with:

Deep Honiton lace around the neck and sleeves, which would not have cost less than fifty dollars, and her veil and wreath and handkerchief were all handsome enough to correspond. She had a beautiful pearl necklace and bracelet and she looked almost as fair as the pearls themselves.[131]

Lou Toombs Alexander died two years later.

Wedding festivities did not end with the ceremony. One "splendid occasion" was on Saturday. Sunday the bride and groom were sponsors at a christening. On Monday there was "a grand dinner" in the barn that was "fitted up and adorned with shrubs and flowers for the occasion, a holiday and feast to all the people," and a ball in the evening. Tuesday was a "day of rest." Wednesday there was a "dinner and ball at Mr. B. Huger's, on Thursday a ride to the sea beach, then to 'Alderly' where they were to have *dejune a la fourchette*," after which the young couple were permitted to retire to their own home.[132]

The poor strove to compete with the rich in wedding festivals. A critical guest reported such an incident:

> We arrived in good time and were ushered into a room lined with unplained boards, no carpet, and a row of ladies stuck bolt upright all round the walls and looking stiff as pokers after a while the spell was broken by the entrance of the bridal party who all looked prodigiously frightened. The bride was shockingly dressed having on a veil with lots of starch in it and which of course hung in every way but the right one. It was confined by a wreath of white tinsel on which I heard many expressions of admiration lavished while "thinks I to myself" how very ugly: There was a good deal of music to which nobody listened except Mr. North who looked daggers at the noisy people which they never even saw and at last we were marched off to supper where there was quite a set out of jellies, cakes and trifles but nothing more substantial these being put on the side table for the benefit of the gentlemen nobody ate anything and the instant we left the room I ordered the carriage and sneaked off all my myself. While the gentlemen were at supper having had quite enough of my frolic which you will imagine was not a very late one when I tell you I was safe back in my room before 11 o'clock—having come to the determination that very poor people should not have company unless they are clever enough to make up for all deficiencies in bright lights handsome furniture, etc.[133]

The weddings in the newly rich and uncultured regions of the state were typical of their background. A belle of Wilkes County described such an event in Lincoln County:

> We went by private conveyance the day before the wedding. On the wedding day we set the table in the morning soon after breakfast, and I counted sixty large iced cakes which they had provided. Cake, meat, biscuit, fruit, and every thing was piled up on one long table all at once, and after the table was loaded down, there were at least eighteen or twenty large and beautifully dressed cakes not touched. I wondered why they had provided so many but afterwards I found every single soul who came expected to take home a good supply of cake.

The wedding was to be at eight o'clock in the evening and the company commenced assembling about three o'clock, many coming with babies and children. They came in and sat in a solemn row all around the room from three till eight, putting the children down in the middle of the floor to play. It was more like a prayer-meeting than a wedding, for no one said anything to anybody. Candles were put in tin sconces all around the wall, and about dusk in the evening the lady and gentleman of the house came in, got up on chairs, and lit the candles. The men did not come into the house at all but collected in the yard, where they had fires built on raised stands. The young men on the porch looked at the girls but did not come in, nor have anything to do with them.

The bride and bridesmaids were dressed about two hours before the ceremony, and about a half hour after the ceremony was over they were all invited to supper. After supper a few of the brave young men ventured in where the young ladies were, and tried to persuade and coax others to join them. Three of them went out and took hold of one very bashful fellow and brought him in, kicking and struggling and introduced him to some of the girls. The minute they let him go, he turned and rushed out as fast as he could possibly go.

Many of the company stayed all night and the bedrooms and floors were covered with pallets where the women and children were packed like sardines in a box.[134]

In the Creek territory, Benj. Hawkins wrote simply:

James Shearly and Minna Brind did this day in my presence agree to take each other as man and wife, and having done so they are to be considered as such and respected as such.[135]

Kellogg, when visiting in Georgia, was interested to learn that at weddings, "the Parson very commonly kisses the bride," and that the "same notion of the prophetic character of dreams with wedding cake under the pillow obtains here, which prevails in New England," with this difference, "to make the prophecy sure the cake . . . must be drawn through the wedding ring, and that by the officiating clergymen. Accordingly . . . a loaf is placed before the priest with a knife and the ring. He cuts proper pieces from the loaf and passes them through the mystic ring. These divining crumbs are then carried off by all who please to take them."[136]

The marriage ceremony itself was of minor legal importance. "Marriage is encouraged by law," states the first section of the marriage code of Georgia,[137] and almost any form, excuse for form, or simply the understood intentions of the parties was sufficient.[138] The Georgia law and the Georgia courts called it a legal marriage if both parties were able to contract, if they actually entered into a contract, and if there was consummation according to law.[139]

Common law marriages have almost continuously been valid in Georgia. They were written into the Code of 1861,[140] and before then were upheld by the Supreme Court in cases of inheritance,[141] prosecutions for bigamy,[142] and provision for alimony.[143] Protestantism made marriage a civil contract, and both the statutes of Georgia and the common law of England, from which they were derived, recognized it as such.[144] In Georgia, regulatory marriage statutes existed[145] that closely followed the English common law,[146] but they were directory only. There was no state supreme court until 1845, but the superior courts held that failure to prescribe to the legal forms was penal but did not annul the marriage, as the statute contained no nullity clause.[147] The Supreme Court, in 1857, confirmed the earlier decisions.[148]

The spirit of both legislative and judicial procedure in Georgia was to protect a woman under a marriage contract, which in general followed a form of her own choosing. The interpretation was in her favor both in contracts made *"per verba* de *presenti"* and *"per verba* the *futuro"*[149] [sic]. The absence of the nullity clause in the statutes and the adolescent age of consent—twelve years for a girl and fourteen for a boy—were intended for a woman's protection.[150]

Common law marriages were frequent in the isolated regions of Georgia. The problem of taking the church to people living there was not solved until the day of the Methodist camp meeting. Before then, the visits of the "preacher" were rare, so the poor and sometimes even the well-to-do, were accustomed to "pairing." It was to this class that Lorenzo Dow made his appeal in his *Reflections on the Important Subject of Matrimony*.[151] He maintained that no forms of ceremonies were necessary, for if they were, "who married Adam and Eve?"[152] However, he advocated that legal procedure be followed as the *"evidence of matrimony"* in order to protect the woman and children from possible desertion and nonsupport, and to establish their rights to the man's estate if he died intestate.[153] Judging from the number of children legitimated in Georgia who bore the name of Lorenzo Dow,[154] his congregations must have followed his advice and blessed him for it.

In the social and economic structure before the '60s, the only groove in which a woman fitted with any degree of comfort was matrimony. It gave her status and stability. In a reasonably successful union she had nothing to fear. The public, the law, and the courts all agreed that marriage was a woman's career, and united in giving her every advantage in making a desirable contract. Once made, the same forces insisted that she keep her bargain.[155]

The legal score between the sexes stood: Courtship—a matter of skill, no support for either side; Betrothal Agreement—women gained considerable yardage; marriage contract—women scored; Marriage—odds went to the man.

FOUR

Political and Civil Status

Except for a short period, Georgia women had the right to vote until 1861.[1] The original charter did not deny it to them,[2] and although the constitution of 1777 restricted the suffrage to males,[3] those of 1789[4] and 1798[5] did not. This does not mean that women voted nor that Georgia intended that they should. Neither were negroes explicitly disqualified until 1861.[6] Rather, the fact that the public law did not specifically withhold citizenship from women is significant of their political insignificance. Only once, before 1861, did the Georgia constitution show that men were conscious of women's political existence. When their status was touched by the vogue for democracy that accompanied the Revolution, it appears that Georgia men fortified their prerogative by the constitution of 1777. By 1789, the flurry, if it ever really existed, was over, and so completely over that women were ignored by the framers of the constitution. If one had attempted to vote in Georgia, however, it is safe to say, a study in masculine blood pressure would have been of permanent interest.

Nevertheless, women were not wholly negative in politics. They rarely entered into political discussions, in part because they were uninformed, or found it socially expedient to pretend so; in part, perhaps, because the same code that demanded that a gentleman never contradict a lady expected that a lady should never embarrass a gentleman with a controversial issue. When there was uniformity of public opinion, however, women who enjoyed politics had their inning. Buckingham noticed that in the struggle between the "nullifiers of South Carolina and the General Government of the United States," women "took a very important part," and, according to him, long afterwards "retained . . . more of the enthusiastic feeling of that period than the men."[7] This was not surprising, for, except for the young and unmarried, life for antebellum Georgia women was drab indeed.

Sometimes a woman held political power. Such a one was Nancy Rumsey. She was able, through the profits of her traveling restaurant,[8] to build a comfortable house, called "Goshen," in the Chinquapin settlement, near Elberton. It was said of her that:

> The first thing a candidate had to do before entering the canvass, was to subsidize this influential lady . . . several aspirants for public office learned that she had taken tribute alike from all. Each got her promise of favor and she got money from each. The candidates soon found this out, but they knew also, that if they did not pay tax to the queen of Goshen, they would get her earnest opposition; so this white female levied black mail on all the office-seekers in Elbert county, for half a century.
>
> For the last twenty years of that period, after the throne had been well established, not only candidates stopped to have a word with Miss Nancy, but the lawyers, who were looking up business took care to say pleasant things to her as they passed, and the Judge, as he went by, paid his respects.[9]

Feminine good will was considered important enough for women to be "flattered and appealed to by political orators, and by the newspapers, whenever the occasion presented itself for so doing with effect."[10] It was common to see the ladies in the gallery of the legislature.[11] Their interest was not always limited to lawmaking, however, for they were sure to come out for a good murder trial.[12] At one, "they filled the gallery and even took possession of the floor of the Senate—so great was the crowd of ladies."[13] They were frequently taken to political celebrations, toasted at political dinners, and danced with at political balls.[14] But that was about the limit of their public activities. What political influence Georgia women had was usually individual, exercised socially, and unacknowledged as such by the men of their state. Both married and single women shared some civil disabilities. Neither did jury service, and the testimony of both, except in criminal cases, was taken out of court,[15] but there the likeness stopped. The law allowed unmarried women to contract; to sue and be sued; to act as administrators of estates and guardians of children; to hold, bequeath, inherit, or purchase property; and to work, keep their earnings, or to spend them as they pleased. All of which they did, as bountiful court evidence proves.

The state of Georgia legally adopted[16] all the British common law not repugnant to the state or federal constitutions, and under that:

> By marriage, the husband and wife are one person in law; the very being or legal existence of the woman is suspended during the marriage, or at least is incorporated and consolidated into that of the husband; under whose wing, or protection, and cover she performs everything; and is therefore called in our law

french a femme-covert . . . under the protection and influence of her husband, her baron, or lord . . . a man cannot grant anything to his wife or enter into a covenant with her; for the grant would suppose her separate existence; and to covenant with her would be to covenant with himself.[17]

And Georgians wrote into their statutes:

In this state the husband is the head of the family and the wife is subject to him: her civil existence is merged into the husbands, except so far as the law recognizes her separately, either for her own protection, or for her benefit, or for the preservation of public order.[18]

When a bride was enfolded in the arms of her husband, one ecclesiastical and the other secular, the right, truly, knew not what the left did. While the bridegroom was promising, "With all my worldly goods I thee endow," simultaneously the courts were turning deaf ears to the church and vesting in him all his bride possessed—even the ring with which he made his vow. For the common law of England gave a husband unconditional title to his wife's personal property,[19] while the Georgia statute of 1789 vested in him her real [property] on the same terms.[20]

Until 1856, husband's and wife's estates were mutually liable for debts[21] existing at the time of marriage;[22] otherwise the man's financial responsibilities were reduced to a legal minimum. He was required to provide his wife with the "necessities suitable for her habits and conditions of life,"[23] although for "anything besides necessaries he is not chargeable."[24] After his death, she was entitled to dower rights in his estate[25] or to her part, under the law, in its distribution if he died intestate;[26] and to a year's support for herself and their children, even though the estate was insolvent.[27] Otherwise, what a wife had was her husband's, free from all rights of survivorship, to sell, dispose of, or bequeath as he wished, regardless of whether his wife's property was derived from parents, relatives, friends,[28] her former husband,[29] the child of a previous marriage,[30] or the profits of her own labor.[31] Even if a husband deserted his wife, prior to 1851 he might appear periodically and collect her earnings, those of the children, or anything else she chanced to have accumulated,[32] and when a man had exhausted the combined family resources, his wife was required by law to share his debtor's prison.[33]

The following wills from Wilkes County are typical of the period: John Bowen left "to wife Rachel all that her father gave her, a slave boy Adam, the dun mare, and her bed and furniture."[34] And Samuel Jack's will reads:

"Whereas at the time of our marriage my wife owned a house and lot at Chambersburg and three hundred acres . . . willed to her by her former husband Alex. Stewart, she shall hold it."[35]

A striking case that came up in the Cobb County Superior Court was that of Penalton and Co. *vs.* Mills and *al.* A mother gave or lent, thereon hangs the case, a negro girl to her daughter. Subsequently, both women were married. The mother's husband sued the daughter's husband for the return of the slave, not as his wife's property, but as his own. Both women were left out of the case altogether. It was a question of whose husband owned the slave.[36]

The story of Fanny Kemble is that of a rebel against the code of her day. When the beautiful and successful English actress married Pierce Mease Butler during a brilliant theatrical season in Philadelphia, there was a clash of two cultures that soon led to unhappiness, separation, and divorce. With a background of Drury Lane and Covent Garden, of Sheridan and Kembles, in the full flood lights and adoration of two continents, the niece of Mrs. Siddons could not be typical of the average woman of any generation, and certainly was not that of her own on a remote Georgia rice plantation. Butler was charming, educated, wealthy. She apparently never inquired the source of his wealth—slave labor on Butler's Island at the mouth of the Altamaha. Theirs was a union of two different worlds, and the daughter of the English strollers was perhaps no more acceptable to his than he was to hers.[37]

Fanny Kemble always disliked slavery, and her disapproval blazed into such a burning hatred the winter she and her husband visited his plantation that it brought the holocaust.[38] The system that she so violently attacked he as jealously defended. Slavery came to serve as a battleground for all the differences that lay between them.[39]

While it is true that Fanny Kemble was English, only spent one unhappy winter in Georgia, and that most of her legal controversies were in Pennsylvania, still she was the wife of one of Georgia's richest planters. The problem of her right to earn, to dispose of her earnings, and to retain the custody of her children, were the product of the English common law, which would have been equally binding in England or in Georgia. The attitude of Pierce Butler is that of a Georgia planter toward a rebel in his world.[40]

One of their early quarrels was over her *Journal of a Residence in America*. Fanny Kemble had contracted for its publication soon after her arrival. In the meantime, she was married. When the proof of her book came, her young husband edited and altered it, over her violent protest. That was his marital right and Pierce Butler knew his rights. The *Journal* appeared with the marks of his censorship still there.[41]

It maddened her that she was not entitled to earn and to enjoy the fruits of her earnings. She had been accustomed to it; besides, it was humiliating to her to live on the production of slave labor. In 1842, when she owed a milliner's bill of £97 and wished to pay it by translating and adapting for the stage Dumas' *Mademoiselle de Belle Isle*, her husband stopped her by reminding her that the income from her writings was not her legal property.[42] To her friend Harriet Martineau she wrote:

> In thinking over the position of women with regard to their own earnings, I confess to something very like wrathful indignation; impotent wrath and vain indignation, to be sure—not the least intense for that, however, for the injustice undoubtedly great. That the man whose wits could not keep him half a week from starving should claim as his the results of mental processes such as composing a noble work of imagination . . . seems too beneficent a provision of the law for the protection of male superiority. It is true that, by our marriage bargain, they feed, clothe, and house us, and are answerable for our debts (not my milliner's bill, though, if I can prevent it) and so, I suppose have a right to pay themselves as best they can of all we are or all we can do . . . I wish women could be dealt with not mercifully, nor compassionately, nor affectionately, but justly; it would be so much better for men.[43]

In Georgia, married women were hampered in their control of their earnings by the law and the courts. A case that was tried three times in the Supreme Court of the state[44] was that of a woman who had made a little money keeping boarders and from renting property belonging exclusively to her. Although her husband was in no way involved in her enterprise, he took her earnings and invested in land that he subsequently lost. She protested against the seizure, but the courts ruled against her on the grounds that the earnings of a married woman were her husband's, "whether derived from a boarding house or any other labor."[45]

In establishing a husband's claim over his wife's property there was one important qualification. He must "reduce it to possession" during coverture.[46] For the wife had the right to her "choses in action," which had its origin in common law.[47] This meant that debts due her—such as rents, legacies, residuary personal estate, money in funds, or shares—which at the time of her marriage were in the possession of a third person, remained here unless her husband took steps to "reduce them to possession"—gain control. To do this he had only to show his intentions together with some overt act to give it force—such as receiving payment on a debt due his wife, having stock belonging to her transferred to him, or bringing action for an offense against her property in his name.

In the case of the woman and the boarding house,[48] the husband had received the money and invested it; he had not recognized the title as being his wife's, but had kept the property in his own name until the lien of a judgment against him had attached it. The court had held that he could not then set up her equity and defeat the title of a *bona fide* purchaser; that whether he took the money with or without her consent, the purchaser must be protected, and that by the man's action his wife's earnings had been "reduced to possession."[49] In Oglesby and wife *vs.* Hall, Oglesby had permitted his wife to sell cakes, she had put her money in the bank in Athens, and borrowed more from her brother, which she paid back from the profits of her baking. With it she had bought a negro woman, Mary, and her four children. Her husband, who at the trial admitted he was ignorant at all times and drunk at that particular one, had secretly deeded the slaves away, retaining for himself and his wife a life interest only. This he said he did for "love and affection." The court held that since he had neither reduced her earnings nor the slaves to possession, that the property was hers and the deed void.[50]

The opinion of the Philadelphia lawyer that "the law presumes a husband to have at all times a complete control of his wife's actions; and that in nine cases out of ten, this presumption resolves itself into fiction!"[51] was not without foundation, both in Georgia and Pennsylvania. Yet there were times when the results of the harshness of the laws were grim. George Paschal found that during the financial crisis of 1837, the outcome of the transfer of the "property of the wife to the profligate husband" produced "moral and social" effects "impossible for the present generation to understand."[52]

The marriage contract or settlement constituted a woman's greatest protection against an unfortunate marriage. It originated in English law[53] and did not appear on the statute books of Georgia until 1847.[54] A woman's separate estate was created in several ways: by conveyance to a trustee before her marriage;[55] by prenuptial agreement between the parties;[56] postnuptial settlement—under which a husband conveyed it to a third party to hold for his wife;[57] and by gift or legacy specifically establishing the woman's sole ownership and legally disavowing her husband's claim.[58]

"Without the aid of statutes," the wife had, under the common law, "substantial control" over her separate estate, while the husband had "no control except as he may be trustee by implication; and even then he is bound to follow her directions and may be removed if he fails to do so."[59] In 1875, Judge Bleckley, of the Supreme Court of Georgia, defined the object of the marriage settlement as being to protect women who were too much exposed to the "kicks and kisses" of their husbands.[60] A wife's separate estate had the full protection of the law. In Georgia, an agreement creating it whether or not in writing could be enforced in the courts of equity. The wife was a free agent under the contract and bound only by it. The courts were inclined to be friendly to the woman's interest and in legal controversies might be expected to construe the agreement liberally so as to carry out the intentions of the parties.[61] Even the Married Woman's Act of 1866 and the constitution of 1868 were held to have no effects on a woman's estate.[62] If husbands abused their authority over the property of their wives, the fault was not in the inadequacy of the law, but in the failure of women to avail themselves of its machinery. Harriet Martineau found:

> On the whole the practice seems to be that the weakest and most ignorant women give up their property to their husbands; and the husbands of such women being precisely the men most disposed to accept it; and that the strongest-minded and most conscientious women keep their property, and use their rights; the husbands of such women being precisely those who would not deprive their wives of their social duties and privileges.[63]

Fanny Kemble believed that the trend toward a woman's control of her possessions was not "without its possible advantages for the magnanimous sex . . . by settling upon their wives large sums of money, or estates which by virtue of a woman's independent legal tenure of property, effectually enables their husbands to baffle the claims of their creditors."[64]

Gradually the laws in regard to women controlling their earnings were liberalized in Georgia. Beginning in 1851, certain wives who applied to the legislature for "reliefs" were allowed to become "free traders" and, in their business ventures, independent of their husbands. During 1851 and 1852, there were four women so recognized; from 1853 to 1854, there were ten; and from 1855 to 1856, the number rose to fifteen.[65] After that, a woman, with the consent of her husband, became a "free trader" if she published a notice of her intentions in the paper for a month before beginning business. She was then liable for her own contracts and entitled to her profits.[66] It was not until the Married Woman's Act of 1866 that a wife had unqualified control of her property.[67]

In general, a woman's share in her husband's estate was for life only. The law required him to support her while he lived, but, even though a man sometimes, like Samuel Bradford, left "all property to my beloved wife, Elizabeth, to dispose of as she think proper. She sole Excx.,"[68] the majority of wills only provided a life interest.[69] The best legal protection a woman had for a share in her husband's estate was her dower, which the courts defined as "the favorite of law and neither the husband nor the courts, nor any other human power can compel the wife to relinquish this right."[70] Although the law was altered from time to time, its intention was to restrict the husband's disposal of his property during his lifetime so as to protect the wife's dower rights.[71] The act of 1826 established a dower claim to "all he died possessed of;"[72] which the supreme court of the state interpreted to mean free of any mortgages that might be on his estate at the time—as though no encumbrances existed.[73] The law was also liberal in permitting a woman to choose what property her dower should consist of.[74] In addition, a widow and her children were entitled to a year's support under both statute law and judicial decision, even though the estate was insolvent.[75]

A woman came off poorly under the laws of inheritance, both as a wife and a mother. The trend was to keep the estate in the male line. If a woman without children died intestate, her husband became her sole heir,[76] but not until 1829 was a widow recognized as the sole heir of her husband under any circumstances.[77] Before then, the property of a husband who died intestate and without children was subject to division. Half of it went to his widow and the remainder to his next of kin.[78]

The status of a wife under the law was, in part, that of a minor whose husband was her guardian. In general, public opinion accepted this theory, although it was not always practiced. Like a minor, her contract was void;[79] her husband was answerable for her words[80] and her misdemeanors;[81] if through commands, threats, coercion, or persuasion, he induced her to commit a crime not punishable by death or life imprisonment, he must pay the penalty in her stead;[82] and, if she disobeyed, he was entitled to administer punishment.

"Under the old law" that Georgia brought from England and legally adopted, a man "might give his wife moderate correction. For as he is to answer for her misbehavior, the law thought it reasonable to intrust him with power of restraining her by domestic chastisement in the same moderation that a man is allowed to correct his apprentice or children." However, he was required to confine it to what "reasonably belongs to the husband for due government and correction of his wife." The civil law for some offenses permitted a man to "beat his wife severely with scourges and sticks . . . in the politer reign of Charles the Second this power of correction began to be doubted," and both husband and wife were given security of peace against the other. "Yet the lower ranks of people who were always fond of the common law, still claim and exert their ancient privilege."[83]

What was true in England was equally so in Georgia. The upper classes likewise felt the effects of the "politer reign of Charles the Second" and laid down the lash, but women were expected to obey. Something of a code of honor among them reinforced a husband's discipline, for both privately and publicly women were coached in their responsibilities. It was probably not new to the young ladies of LaGrange College when they heard, in 1853, that:

> A woman ought not to speak what she pleased, because, if common reputation were true, she sometimes spoke too fast, too much, and too strong, and that whatever she said that did not prove true, her husband had to answer for either by fight or by law—the first threatening his person, and the last invading his purse.[84]

Yet Georgians, like their English ancestors, could say "the lower ranks of people still claim and exert their ancient privileges," for husbands continued to administer corporal punishment to disobedient wives. The law, however, required that the stick be no larger than a man's thumb,[85] and public opinion was increasingly antagonistic. When "a Benedictine was fined $5.00 for whipping his wife" in the factory region of Augusta, the *Evening Dispatch* trusted "that the old maxim that the cheapness of the luxury always increases its use" might not "hold true in this case."[86]

Sometimes the public interfered. In Columbus, it was reported that:

> A person of the name of Powell or Powers, living in the vicinity of Coweta Falls Factory . . . was married . . . to one of the factory girls, whom it is said, he was in the habit of abusing while in a state of intoxication. Having committed this offense of conjugal propriety on Saturday afternoon, a mob of some fifty young men collected after supper, and took him to the river . . . where he was ducked till he was as crest fallen as a drowned rat; he was then taken to his house where, in the presence of his wife and other females, he was bound to a tree with a large rope of "hawser" and soundly beaten with laths, sticks, fist, etc., etc. . . . he was next hoistered on a rail preparatory to the grand ride, without saddle or bridle. The rail, however, broke, and the victim fell, hurting himself considerably, but another was procured . . . several citizens earnestly

remonstrated with the crowd of lynchers, and succeeded with some difficulty in restraining them from further violence—on the promise of Powell to clear out.[87]

In 1857 public opinion became law, and beating or mistreating a wife was made a penal offense, for which the husband could be imprisoned not to exceed six months. The wife was, in this case, permitted to testify against her husband.[88]

A wife was the property of her husband to this extent: he had the right of action against another for abducting, harboring, seducing, or beating her. These were actions at common law for which the husband might collect damages.[89] Such advertisements as John Kilgore's were frequently seen in papers:

> Whereas my wife Elizabeth, hath gone and left me; I do hereby forewarn any [sic] person or persons from dealing with, harboring, or concealing her . . . for if they do, I shall deal with them as the law directs,[90]

which he was entitled to do both under the common law and the Georgia statute.[91]

Not only the law but public opinion expected from women unquestioning obedience, submission, and loyalty to masculine dominance. The *Southern Literary Messenger* thought J. P. Kennedy "particularly successful in the delineation of his female characters" at a time when "almost every attempt of the kind has turned out a failure." They found the heroine of *Horseshoe Robinson* "in her confiding love, in her filial reverence, in her heroic espousal of the revolutionary cause, not because she approved it, but because it was her lover's . . . a truly feminine portrait."[92]

Dr. David Ramsay, physician and author of South Carolina, in writing of his wife, who had been educated both in England and France and was a woman of unusual abilities, perhaps expressed the widespread view of a wife's proper relations to her husband:

> In practice as well as theory, she acknowledged the dependent subordinate condition of her sex; and considered it as part of the curse denounced on Eve as being the first in transgression . . . the most self denying duties of the conjugal relations being thus established on a divine foundation and illustrated by those peculiar doctrines of revelation on which she hung all her hopes, and other duties followed by easy train of reasoning, and were affectionately performed.[93]

Pierce Butler, in defending himself, said "perhaps the fundamental" reason for the failure of his marriage was found in the "peculiar views which were entertained by Mrs. Butler on the subject of marriage . . . she held that marriage should be a companionship on equal terms—partnership, in which if both partners agree, it is well—but that at no time has one partner a right to control the other."[94]

In support of his statement, Mr. Butler published a letter from his wife written to him from London after the birth of her first child:

> You ask me . . . how I like my independence, and whether I remember how vehemently and frequently I objected to your control over my actions. . . . Neither my absence from you, nor my earnest desire to be again with you, can make me admit that the blessed and happy relationship, in which we stand to each other is anything but perfect companionship, perfect friendship, perfect love . . . there is no justice in the theory, that one rational creature is to be subservient to another; nor can there be any high or holy feeling where there is no freedom and independence. . . . But, dear Pierce, upon what grounds should you exercise this control over me? Is it because having full power to withhold the gift, I freely gave myself to you, to add to my fellowship as I could your happiness? Is it because you are better than myself? I am sure you will not say so, whatever I may think. Is it because you are more enlightened, more intellectual? You know that is not so, for our opportunities have been the same.[95]

Fanny Kemble did not know the word "obey," and it was not in the service of the Unitarian Church in which she was married.[96] Pierce Butler offered his wife terms of reconciliation, which she "unequivocally refused" as being "impossible." He probably represented the opinion of his day when he explained that he only demanded:

> the customary and pledged acquiescence of a wife to marital control—nothing more. As it is unnecessary to argue a point generally conceded, and always absurd to attempt to prove an acknowledged truth, nothing is required to show the error of this principle of equal rights in marriage so obstinately contended for. No one who is not morally astray can fail to feel and see the heedlessness of the pretension.[97]

Fanny Kemble was emotional and spoiled. She would not stoop to subterfuge nor was she like the Georgia girl who though married "unsuitably" remained "yet truly faithful and a pious christian."[98] Neither was Pierce Butler like Julia Barnsley's "poor papa," who looked "pulled down already," even though he was still on the safe side of the "consequences" should "mamma" discover "he has had any resources" of which she was unaware.[99]

Nor would Fanny Kemble have stooped to intrigue as did the preacher's wife, Mrs. Norton, who appears to have deceived her husband, but not her feminine neighbors, one of whom wrote of her:

> She appears to be a very clever woman, but she seems perfectly helpless, so dependent that it pains you almost to be about her. She has a splendid sewing machine, nothing to do but put in your work and work the machine with your foot and it works very easily, I could work it right off. But does she work it? No indeed her husband does it all, every bit and does work for others that they help her *baste and cut*. She has a royal time I think; but she's so lifeless in conversation and every thing; she thinks she [is] unable to do anything she's too weak but I must differ from that for when she was here last spring she walked to the Light House one evening after three o'clock 2¼ miles went up to the top which is near two hundred feet and walked back.[100]

The *Columbus Enquirer* cynically remarked that "when a woman accustoms herself to say I will, she deserves to lose her empire." It published a "Dictionary for Ladies," in which it advised:

> Avoid contradicting your husband. . . . Occupy yourself only with household affairs; wait till your husband confides to you those of a high importance; and do not give your advice till he asks it.

> Never take upon yourself to be a censor of your husband's morals, nor read lectures to him. . . . Command his attentions by being always attentive to him; never exact anything, and you will obtain much;—appear always flattered by the little he does for you, which will excite him to perform more.

> All men are vain, never wound this vanity not even in the most trifling instances. A wife may have more sense than her husband but should never seem to know it.

> When a man gives wrong counsel never make him feel that he has done so but lead him on by degrees to what is rational with mildness, and gentleness; when he is convinced; leave him all the merit of having found out what was just and reasonable.

> When a husband is out of temper, behave obligingly to him; if he is abusive never retort! and never prevail over him to humble himself.[101]

With such tricks as these even Pierce Butler might have been beguiled.

A man was the head of his family. His wife and her minor children were his wards. The common law provided that "a mother as such is entitled to no power, but only to reverence and respect," but that "the Empire of the father continues even after his death."[102] Both the law[103] and public opinion gave the father undisputed authority over his minor children. Fanny Kemble once wrote from the fullness of her experience:

> I think the women who have contemplated *any* equality between the sexes have almost all been unmarried, for while the father disposes of the children, whom he maintains, and that endows him with the power of supreme torture. What mother's heart is proof against the tightening of that screw?[104]

Her acceptance of her husband's right to the custody of their children speaks volumes in itself. She was a rebel against many things, and there is no doubt of her affection for them. Even Pierce Butler admitted, "her care and management of our children was admirable; we have never once disagreed about them."[105] Her conduct, apparently, was immaculate, whereas her husband's fidelity was questionable. During their controversy, he was challenged and fought a duel involving an unsavory affair that occurred early in their married life. Fanny Kemble found letters in evidence of it after her estrangement. There were also rumors of Butler's irregularities with the governess, to which he forced his wife to sign a denial. Yet she did not apparently question his just claim to the children, struggled only to be near them, and accepted the most humiliating terms to accomplish it. When the Butlers were divorced in 1849, the custody of the children remained with the father.[106]

Fanny Kemble and her husband both regarded the children as a species of their father's undisputed personal property. The Butlers' difficulties began early in their married life. With their separation in mind, Fanny wrote her husband concerning their second child, who was yet unborn: "There is abundance of time for me to reach England before my confinement; and if you will appoint means for your child being brought over to you, I shall of course observe them."[107] Nor did Pierce Butler consider the possibility of the children being given to their mother. Writing to his wife's friend, Mrs. Sedgwick, about his domestic troubles, Butler said:

> And what would our children lose in being bereft of their mother's guardian care? What could I do with two little motherless children? And would Fanny be

57

happy parted forever from those darling children. . . . She seems resolved to part and asked me if I would allow her either of the children.[108]

Although Butler did not print his reply, it is safe to assume his wife never expected him to agree.

The mother never had unfettered legal control over legitimate children, even if the father died, unless he so provided in his will. Although the law was altered from time to time, a widow was always eligible for appointment to the guardianship of her children, and the tendency of the courts was to give it to her; but if she remarried, she was likely to lose it to their father's next of kin, to their stepfather, or someone else named by the court.[109] Even the liberal act of 1845 only vested the guardianship of the children in the mother until remarriage, and the courts retained the authority to dismiss her.[110]

The same act brought into question the father's complete authority over the children. It provided that in case of the separation of the parents, on writ of *habeas corpus*, the court might assign the custody to either father or mother as appeared most beneficial to the child's interest.[111] And the code of 1861 granted the children of divorced parents to the innocent party.[112] A father still retained his jurisdiction over his children and their earnings until they were twenty-one years old. His rights only abated with his own consent, desertion, or cruel treatment.[113]

A widowed mother's estate was divided among her children, but under the law of 1804 she was entitled to nothing from an intestate legitimate child whom she might survive.[114] If such a child had no descendants, father, brothers, and sisters shared his estate. Whole and half blood on the paternal side inherited equally. If the father was dead and the mother had remained a widow, she was entitled to her husband's part of the estate, but if she had remarried, the father's next of kin inherited his share.[115] But married or widowed, a mother had no claim on the estate of the only child, or the last surviving one. That unconditionally belonged to its father's relatives.[116] In 1841, this provision of the law was repealed,[117] and two years later reenacted in an amended form. Remarriage still barred a mother from participation in the estates of all except her last or only child, but that she might inherit unconditionally.[118]

In 1845, the laws of inheritance were so altered that if a widow with children married again, and came into an inheritance from an intestate estate during the second marriage, it did not become the property of her husband. Half went to the children by the first marriage, who received theirs immediately, and the other half to her and the children by the second marriage. Since her part vested in her husband, everybody was taken care of but the woman who got the legacy. She was still out in the cold.[119]

An interesting decision in equity, delivered in 1848, dealt with the estate of William Harrell, a posthumous child born in 1845. The mother remarried Uriah Holder and by that marriage had a daughter, Mary. Two days after she was born, her half brother, William Harrell, died intestate. The lower courts ruled that his estate should be divided between his mother and her husband, as one party, and his half sister, Mary, as the other. This was contested on the grounds that the mother, together with her husband, was entitled to the entire estate; but the Supreme Court reversed the decision and acknowledged the half sister as the only heir, interpreting "last child" to mean "first surviving child of the mother." Mary got all the estate of her mother's first husband.[120]

The illegitimate children, however, were the mother's, unless the father legally adopted them,[121] for such children had "no blood except that given by the law."[122] Under the laws of inheritance, it was as though the father were dead and his relatives had never existed. The child shared equally in the estate of its mother with legitimates, and, if it died intestate, provided there was no wife or lineal descendants, the estate was divided alike between mother, brothers, and sisters. If none of these were living, the property went to the mother's legitimate children.[123]

The primary concern of the laws regulating the control of illegitimate children was not the interest of the child, the morality of the parents, or even public order, but the pocketbook of the taxpayers. While the law provided that both the man and woman accused of misconduct should be indicted, in the words of the Supreme Court, "the primary object of the Act of 1793 was to protect the county from the charge of bastard children."[124] The mother of an illegitimate child might choose between revealing the name of the father or giving security for its support. If the man was known, he was forced to provide for the expenses of its birth and maintenance, and whosoever the mother accused was held guilty until proven innocent. The father's offense was not his paternity, but his failure to provide for the child. The law held this to be a misdemeanor.[125] The "Bastard Bonds" themselves are not concerned with a man's responsibility as a father, but with a child who was "likely to become chargeable to said county." Most of them seem to cover the care of the child until it was fourteen years of age. Sometimes they were posted before and sometimes after its birth.[126]

The fate of such children was always sad, but the county was determined it should not be their liability. Among the court records, such items as: "Lucy Sheet, illegitimate child of Anna Shorter, four years old bound to Joseph Barker," tell their own story.[127] Yet it is probably significant of the attitude toward common law marriages[128] that fathers frequently named their natural children in their wills.[129] Henry Duke, however, was being more conscientious than most men would have thought necessary when he left his "saddle and bridle to a daughter of Nancy Cup's supposed to be mine."[130]

A father's denial of his paternity of an illegitimate child was regarded as a civil offense, but a mother's as criminal. If she concealed its death, she was held guilty of murder under the common law unless she could prove her innocence.[131] Anyone who helped her during its birth was held on a capital charge if afterwards the mother killed the child.[132] The courts do not appear to have taken a light view of these cases.[133] Later laws made the mother culpable only if proof was offered that the child was born alive; but even though the child lived, if the mother concealed it she was subject to fine or imprisonment.[134]

The civil status of a woman who had contracted an unfortunate marriage was grave under any circumstances, but at least she had the redress of the divorce laws. Many women, for social or economic considerations, hesitated or refused to avail themselves of the courts, but many others accepted their protection. The severity of divorce code originated in the canon law of the Catholic Church, and with the coming of Protestantism passed almost unchanged into the civil law of England. Commentators were "led to wonder that the same authority which enjoined the strictest celibacy to the priesthood, should think themselves proper judge in causes between man and wife."[135] Still, Rome wrote the English divorce code and Georgia adopted it, and that code was "tender in dissolving" the marriage bond, even when:

> It became improper or impossible for the parties to live together: as in the case of intolerable ill temper, or adultery. . . . For the canon law which the common law follows . . . deems so highly of the nuptial tie, that it will not allow it to be loosed for any cause whatsoever, that arises after the union is made. And this is said to be built on divine revealed law; though that expressly assigns incontinence as a cause, and indeed the only cause why a man may put away his wife and marry another . . . but with us in England adultery is only a cause for separation from bed and board.[136]

Action for divorce began in the Superior Courts of Georgia and was perfected by a two-third vote of each house of the legislature[137] until 1833. Then, by constitutional amendment, the power was given to the courts and the verdict of two concurring juries made it final.[138] The Georgia law followed the English and provided that divorces should be classified as complete and partial. The latter were free from "bed and board" only and prohibited remarriage.[139] The constitution provided that divorce should be granted on "legal principles."[140] Since these were not defined by the Supreme Court until 1846, there was a lack of uniformity both in the degree and causes for which divorces were granted.[141]

The Supreme Court of Georgia was organized in 1845. The next year it decreed in the case of Head *vs*. Head that the only grounds for divorce permissible under the state constitution of 1798 were those recognized in the laws that the colony had brought from England.[142] This temporarily put an end to current practices to the contrary, for the English permitted complete divorce only for causes that existed before the marriage, and partial for infidelity and cruel treatment. The first was authorized by the canon, and the second by the common law.[143] Whereas in Georgia, according to Judge Floyd in the Head *vs*. Head decision, "they were had with flagrant facility; some refused that should have been allowed and hundreds granted that should have been refused." He felt that the division of responsibility between courts and legislature was in part responsible, but that the outcome of a divorce suit largely depended on the strength of the council, whether or not the case was defended while in the courts, and "the wealth and standing of the parties, their political and social relations, or perhaps the personal beauty and address of a female libellant."[144]

In 1849 the constitution was amended and the General Assembly was allowed to determine the grounds on which divorces should be granted.[145] The act of 1850 revised the divorce code. Inability of the parties to contract as defined by law, inconstancy, and desertion were assigned as reasons for total divorce; in cases of cruel treatment or habitual drunkenness, the jury was empowered to determine whether the decree should be final or separation from bed and board only; and all other grounds permitted only partial divorce.[146]

The common law of England and, since 1806, the statute law of Georgia, prohibited the guilty party from remarrying, but the legislature by granting a "relief" might remove the disability.[147] The acts of the General Assembly are heavy with such legislation, and Representative Seward, of Thomas, said, on the floor of the house in 1859, that not a single such petition had been refused out of the "hundreds of cases that had come to the legislature since 1806."[148] Finally, the Supreme Court, in 1856, decreed that although it was penal for the guilty party to remarry without legislative sanction, the offense was not bigamy, for as a divorced man had no wife the second marriage could not be void.[149]

Throughout the antebellum period there was the greatest confusion in Georgia over the divorce code. In spite of the fact that, by constitutional amendment, the legislature had not been authorized to grant divorces since 1833, Governor Brown vetoed such a bill on December 5, 1859.[150] In so doing, he wrote that "frequent applications have been made to the legislature" to grant divorces since the constitution had been amended, but that only "in a single case in 1837" had it done so, "and then the verdict of the jury and the judgment of the court had been rendered previous to the alteration of the constitution, and the legislature passed an act perfecting a divorce."[151]

When the Supreme Court ruled, in the case of Head vs. Head, that an absolute divorce could not be obtained for causes arising after marriage,[152] the situation was awkward for those people who had secured them on other grounds, particularly if either party had remarried. In 1849, the General Assembly clarified the situation by providing that all marriages already made or to be made in the future under old decrees were valid.[153]

With Protestantism, both Church and State accepted marriage as a civil contract, yet a fondness for the old sacramental doctrine of the Catholic Church had lingered. This, together with the character of the causes for which divorce was allowed, placed a stigma on it for either sex. For a woman, additionally burdened with the biblical basis accepted as her code of conduct toward her husband, it was to be avoided if possible. Nevertheless, by the time of the Civil War, there was a change in public opinion becoming evident.

In 1859, a bill was introduced into the legislature to repeal the provision in the law of 1806 prohibiting the remarriage of the guilty party. The discussions showed a liberalizing of public opinion. One representative dared say:

> God does not put his eternal sanction on everything that is done by preachers and justices of the peace; and a continued cohabitation under the coercion of law, where there is no affection, is but legalized adultery.[154]

As the years went by, divorces were increasing in Georgia. The constitution assigned as the reason for taking the right to grant them from the legislature and giving it to the courts "the frequent, numerous, and repeated applications" that had become a "great annoyance" to the General Assembly, "as well as on account of expense consequent to said application, as the necessary swelling the laws and journals."[155] The number of divorces rose steadily. From 1798 to the close of the session in 1835, they had totalled 291, "averaging from 1800 to 1810, about 4; from 1810 to 1820, 8; from 1820 to 1830, 18; and since then 28 per annum," according to Prince, in a restrained footnote to his *Digest*, which seems intended to imply a solemn warning.[156] By 1859 Representative Wallace, of Taylor, estimated that the state had spent $200,000 in special divorce legislation.[157]

Man and wife stood equal before the divorce laws, but Judge Floyd, in his Head *vs.* Head decision of 1846, gave a clear indication of what a woman might expect from a jury and society under the accepted double standard of conduct:

> It is the prevalent opinion that the adultery of the husband is less injurious to the order and peace of the family than that of the wife and ought not, therefore, to be held an offense of as great enormity and visited with as serious consequence . . . public opinion in this state does not seem to hold the husband's delinquency so great as the wife's. This judgment as illustrative of the high esteem placed on feminine virtue . . . is without foundation in principle . . . it is owing . . . to the prevalence of the vice among men. The moral character of the act is the same. . . . Its consequences to the wife when perpetrated by her husband are as cruel to her peace as her infidelity can be to his. Yet she is required to meekly endure.[158]

The law granted alimony to a wife.[159] In determining the amount, due regards to the condition of the husband[160] and the woman's separate estate and circumstances were given.[161] But no part of any estate of a wife that her husband had previously lost or squandered was taken into consideration in the alimony. It was in these unhappy marriages that the subordinate civil status of women was so disastrous to their interest.

A lower-class wife who was driven out of her home with nothing but a "little flower and a small piece of meat," and forced to seek "sheltor" from the neighbors, could only be "sory" "he have taken my property and gave it away and now sporeting with my carecttor," and tell her troubles to the "Brothers and Sisters of Mars Hill Church."[162] However, her situation was not unique, as divorce testimony shows,[163] either in her own class or among the aristocracy, where husbands were likely to be more subtle in their methods, as was John Rutledge of Charleston. In his efforts to gain possession of his wife's property following her alleged infidelity, and what seems to have been his fatal encounter with her lover, he wrote to Robert MacKay of Savannah:

> Many thanks and very sincere ones, my dear sir, for your friendly letter by the last Post. All the Persons named in it, as your friends at Newport, are well known to me, and the respectability of their characters has very justly obtained to them great influence in that town. They certainly may be useful in negotiation with Mr. Hornestz to induce his desiring Mr. Kollock to surrender to me the letters from the unfortunate Mrs. R. Which are in his possession. Of the propriety of my having them there is but one sentiment in this community and my hopes are kept alive by being assured, by everybody here that Dr. Kollock, when he reflects upon this business, will not withhold the letters. His caution is commendable, and his feelings for the gentleman who died in his arms do him honor. But when time shall have made his feelings subordinate to his judgments, I have no doubt about his conducting himself with propriety. Shall I urge for divorce the letters of Mrs. R. may be useful to me. Should her brothers, who are minors, die under age, an estate of seventy thousand pounds sterling would by her father's will become hers, and my possessing her letters I might, so impress the Court of Chancery of her unworthiness, as to induce them to settle this fortune upon her children. Should one of her brothers die under age, then half of his estate would devolve to her, which might be secured to my children in the event of my possession of the proofs, her letters contain of her behavior and feeling toward me. Should the relatives of Dr. S. hereafter desire to have me tried, the Governor of this State would be obliged to surrender me, if demanded by the Executive of Georgia, and in case of a trial her letters, no less than his might be useful.[164]

A common advertisement seen in antebellum Georgia papers, along with those for runaway slaves, were those for runaway wives. The husband of the truant wife usually informed the public to the effect she "had left his bed and board without the least shadow of provocation,"[165] and "forewarned all others from trading with or trusting her," as he was no longer responsible for her debts.[166]

It is possible that these husbands were frequently as poor risks as the wives they advertised. At least the *Southern Banner* seems to have entertained suspicions. Beginning in 1842 and continuing for years, it charged for "announcing candidates for office $5.00—payable in advance," and for "husbands advertising their wives . . . $5.00—*invariably* payable in advance," while all other patrons got twelve lines for $1.00—on credit.[167]

In summary, the political status of a woman in Georgia from 1783 to 1860 was of microscopic importance and their civil status fickle. That of the unmarried were secure, but in theory a husband spoke from a burning bush and a married woman had no civil status. In fact, however, the law was flexible. It was unobtrusive, but if solicited it would give substantial protection to married women.

The statutes governing the relations between husband and wife were based on a mixed concept. In regard to property they were feudal—she, the vassal, surrendered all she possessed to her overlord for protection; in regard to a wife's conduct her relations with her husband were those of guardian and ward; and, if a wife was stolen, damaged, or abused, the law regarded a husband's loss as though his wife were his personal property and allowed him to collect damages.

A married woman's greatest legal liability was her lack of property rights. She was not without protection, however, for while a wife surrendered her possessions, if she were cautious enough, her separate estate could be established and maintained during her husband's life. After his death she was entitled to a year's support, and in the case of divorce to alimony. The courts were inclined to be friendly to a woman's financial interest, but expected her to keep her marriage contract and usually held the misconduct of a wife as a more serious offense than that of a husband.

Due to the English heritage and American custom, the tendency was to keep estates in the male line, so women were at a disadvantage under the laws of inheritance. But in the antebellum period, public opinion was slowly crystallizing into laws more beneficial to women. While children were the property of the father, here, too, a slight change in favor of the mother was in progress.

A married woman's position in Georgia before 1860 was always hazardous, frequently humiliating, and often tragic. Her true status, nevertheless, was far more commonly determined by her character, that of the man she married, their personal relations to each other, the use they made of the law, and even by public opinion, than by the statutes themselves.

FIVE

Manners, Morals, and Customs

The writers of southern romance have standardized both mother and daughter of the plantation aristocracy, but most of them have forgotten, or have never known, that the majority of antebellum southern women did not live at the end of magnolia avenues, but on "Tobacco Roads" or in back alleys.

Southern society was distinctly aristocratic and divided into many loosely defined classes. The "planter" of established family, with wide acreage and many slaves, stood at the top of the social scale. There were relatively few in this group, however, in proportion to the population, but they were the articulate and ruling class. Beneath them came the yeomen, or "crackers"—deriving their name, some say, from their custom of cracking corn for hominy;[1] others, from the long whips of the wagoners.[2] This constituted the southern middle class, to which the majority of Georgia people belonged. They possessed land in varying amounts and, usually, a few slaves. On a whole, they were "respectable but not genteel."[3] In the twilight zone between the two was the "cotton snob"[4]—the parvenu of the cotton kingdom who had acquired sufficient slaves (tradition says thirty were demanded), but lacked the lineage necessary for admission to the "planter" class. He was important economically and politically, but seldom arrived socially, although his children usually did.

Underneath was the great mass of "poor whites." "Buckra," the negroes called them in contempt,[5] for the term, in southern vernacular, was not an index to a state of finance but to a state of mind that left these people the "laziest two-legged animals that ever walked erect on the face of the Earth."[6] They counted for little in the economic or political life of the South, and constituted a great social problem.[7] As a class, they were ravaged with hookworm—necator americanus.[8] This, in part, was responsible for their condition, although it should not be forgotten that this continent was a dumping ground for European undesirables. England made a prayer wheel of the new world and twisted it over her profligate immigrants, but there is no proof that the stock experienced any transfiguration.

In contemporary opinion, the "poor whites" were a lazy, shiftless people. Licentiousness usually prevailed among them, and ignorance was profound. Drunkenness was common to men and often to women. Most of them were addicted to clay eating, a frequent accompaniment of hookworm. The women usually dipped snuff, smoked clay pipes, and were old at thirty, while the children looked it at ten. With most of them food was scarce, but children and dogs were plentiful. All preferred starvation to motion, else they were not "poor whites" in southern terminology.[9]

There were marked differences between the women of the various classes. The antebellum southern girl in her hoops and ruffles, with her beaux and parties, so well known in song and story, on stage and screen, belonged only to the plantation aristocracy. Even there her reign was short, for after marriage the ball was over, and the southern belle was expected to be transformed into the southern matron, with her inevitable keys at her side. In blindness and with unstudied cruelty, a southern gentleman expected a frivolous girl, kept ignorant in the name of innocence, trained under the theory of inferiority, and selected as a bride for the very qualifications that she must renounce, to become, on her wedding day, a Roman matriarch with the wisdom of Solomon. And the astonishing thing is that many women accomplished it.

Even Miss Martineau, caustic critic of southern institutions, admitted that among the matrons in the slave-holding states, she had found "some few" of the "strongest-minded and most remarkable women" she had "ever known." For, as she observed:

> Women who have a rule over a barbarous society . . . to make and enforce laws, provide for all the physical wants and regulate the entire habits of a large number of persons who can in no respect take care of themselves, must be strong and strongly disciplined, if they are in any degree to discharge the duty.[10]

Yet with the feudal ideal of womanhood that dominated the plantation aristocracy and that played such an important role in education, courtship, and marriage, it is not remarkable that Miss Martineau also had found, among the matrons, the opposite type who shrank from their duties and became "perhaps the weakest women" she had "ever seen: selfishly timid, humbly dependent, languid in body, and minds of no reach at all."[11] These vapid women were so numerous in the slave-holding states that Buckingham seems to have met no other kind in rural sections. He considered "servants and slaves" essential in a planter's household, for as all the women were brought up alike, except the very poor, "all" of the upper classes were "unqualified to superintend the households." He added that southern matrons being "thus relieved of all necessity for exercising their physical strength and mental capacities, they soon become feeble in health and indifferent toward society."[12]

Hundley describes the middle-class southern matrons as "modest and virtuous, chaste in speech and manners; . . . besides very industrious house-keepers, kind hearted mistresses, and the most devoted wives and mothers although . . . not infrequently quite simple and unsophisticated."[13]

And Emily Burke tells of one of the less affluent, the mother of one of her pupils, whom she found:

> Living in a small log house, very neat, but there was nothing belonging to it, to which the term comfortable could be applied. She had a bed, a table, two or three benches that were used instead of chairs and a very little crockery. The kitchen was a separate little building, of course scantily supplied with cooking utensils. The entertainment she prepared for me, while I sat with her in the little kitchen on a stool, consisted of coffee without sugar, fried bacon and corn bread mixed with water only. She had neither vegetables, nor butter, nor any other condiment we consider essential to any repast. In the course of the afternoon she showed me a roll of cloth she had just taken from the loom, which she told me was the product of her own hard labor, commencing with the cotton seed. On inquiring if she could not purchase cloth much cheaper than she could manufacture it, she replied, "she could if her time was worth anything, but there was no labor she could perform that would bring her any money."[14]

In the backcountry, Bazil Hall discovered "Sir John Falstaff, disguised as the old woman of Brentford," whose whole family "of busy pated rovers, with the old gentleman at their head made a tame picture in comparison to that of the mother," who:

> Near the top of her head she wore a little bit of a man's hat, over a linen cap; and round her capacious corporation was drawn a blue checked cotton gown, tucked up in front, higher than I dared venture to be particular in describing but far enough, at least, to betray a pair of feet and ankles, in perfect keeping with a couple of brawny arms, well-known, I dare swear, to the ears, of her hopeful progeny, to the chops of her negroes, and mayhap, to the sconce of her affectionate help-mate![15]

It could not be expected that these cracker women of the backwoods would be cultured and dependent according to the code for upper classes. "Generations of them," as President Eliot, of Harvard, said of all pioneer women, "cooked, carried water, washed and made clothes, bore children in lonely peril, and tried to bring them up safely without medical or surgical help, lived themselves in terror of the wilderness, and under the burden of a sad and cruel creed, and sank at last into nameless graves, without any vision of the grateful days when millions of their descendants should rise up and call them blessed."[16]

Most of the back country women were poor, but they were not "poor whites." Their poverty was inconvenient but respectable, and their isolation physical. The "sand hillers," however, were "poor whites." Their poverty was considered inalienable but contemptible, and their isolation was social ostracism.[17] Of this class it has been said:

> If anything, after the first freshness of their youth is lost the women are even more intolerable than the men—owning chiefly to their disgusting habit of snuff-dipping, and even sometimes pipe-smoking . . . it is not at all strange that the female Sand-hillers should so soon lose all traces of beauty and at thirty are about the color of yellow parchment, if not thin and pale from constant fever. Besides they are quite prolific, and every house is filled with its half dozen of dirty squalling, white-headed little brats, who are familiarly known as Tow-Heads—on account of the color of their hair, as well as its texture and generally unkempt and matted condition.[18]

"In the South the family is more powerful than in any other portion of the Republic," wrote a contemporary,[19] and Georgia women lived most of their lives within the home, few indeed of which were the pillared mansions of romance. In Savannah and its neighborhood the residences were superior in comfort and in elegance of design, some of which—the "Hermitage" reclaimed by Henry Ford, for example—remain a testimony to the artistry of their builders. Toward the latter years of the cotton kingdom, planters, under the influence of Thomas Jefferson and the Greek revival, built handsome residences in the fashion approved by fiction today. Many, such as the Robert Toombs House, are still standing. But while examples may be seen in Washington, Milledgeville, Athens, and elsewhere in the state, they were relatively few in number. In reminiscences and traditions, however, they have grown like Eneas Africanus' fountains, and patriotic Georgians are left to explain the absence of tangible evidence by Sherman's march to the sea.

As a matter of fact, the typical Georgia country house in the early days was the log cabin. As wealth accumulated, this gave way to a plain, two-storied, clapboard structure with a lean-to in the back and a porch across the front. Farish Carter, perhaps the richest man in Georgia,[20] and Alexander H. Stephens both lived in such houses. The remnants of this style of architecture are to be seen along every highway in the state today, unpainted and dilapidated, with doors swinging and shutters gone—like abandoned Noah's Arks.

Olmsted saw no beauty in southern homes.[21] James Stuart considered:

> The common form . . . of all houses that you meet with on the roadside in this country is two square pens with a space between them, connected by a roof above and a floor between, so as to form a parallelogram of nearly triple the length of its depth. In the open space the family take their meals during fine weather. The kitchen and places for slaves are all separate buildings, as are the stables, cow houses, etc. About ten buildings of this description make up the establishment of an ordinary planter, with half a dozen slaves.[22]

And Garnett Andrews remembered that:

> If a young man wished to marry he went on the other side of the spring—or to another on his father's abundant, cheap rich virgin soil—built his log cabin, cleared a turnip-patch and cowpen, married and went to multiplying and replenishing the earth.[23]

As the need of the family grew, additional cabins were added, "containing sometimes no more than a single room," and when company came, they "filled like bee-hives."[24] Amelia M. Murray was entertained in such log settlements by people owning fifteen slaves,[25] and Bazil Hall saw nothing different among "almost all these forest houses in the interior of the State of Georgia."[26] He found that a settler built one cabin and added the others as his needs demanded. Hall was struck by the lack of windows and his host explained: "We never make the windows in the first instance, but built up the walls with logs, then cut out the windows." He hoped "in the course of a year, to put in a couple of glazed ones," and after that to "go on gradually" until it was "all comfortable."[27]

Fanny Kemble found herself, that tragic winter on Butler's Island, married to one of the largest slaveholders in Georgia, but in a house that she describes as "more devoid of conveniences and adornment than any I have ever taken up my abode in before." It consisted of "three small rooms and three still smaller . . . and a kitchen detached from the dwelling . . . with no floor but the bare earth." The furnishings of the Butler house were of "white pine wood" without "veneer of polish," made by the slaves on the place.

As for the elegance of living, Fanny Kemble's servants were summoned by a "packthread bell rope suspended in the sitting room," but from the bedrooms it was necessary to "raise the windows and our voices, and bring them by power of lungs."[28] And Kellogg, when visiting in Georgia, couldn't sleep because "about half a dozen families of hogs growl and squeal nightly for the best place under the house."[29]

Emily Burke, "in answer to the question, 'Why planters have no better dwellings,' " replied:

> They are under the necessity of changing their place of residence so often on account of the soil, which in a few years becomes barren, owing to the manner in which it is cultivated, if they invest much property in buildings, they would be obliged to make great pecuniary sacrifices; therefore, they have but little property that is not moveable. Their possessions generally consist in slaves, herds of swine, cattle, horses, mules, flocks of goats, numerous fowls of all kinds, fine carriages, furniture, plate, etc., which can be transported when occasion demands a removal from old worn out plantation to another of new and fruitful soil. A Northerner, who is accustomed to judge a farmer's property by his buildings, would suppose, when he first went into the country at the South that many of great wealth were poor men, their buildings are so miserable. The manner of estimating a planter's pecuniary circumstances is by the number of his slaves. . . .
> I have visited plantations where the master residence had not a pane of glass in the windows, nor a door between the apartments, and even the outside doors would have been dispensed with, if it could have been done with personal safety. Neither was there the shadow of a board to intervene between the ground floor and the coarse unhewn shingles as seen on the inside of the roof, yet the table was loaded with an almost endless variety of richest delicacies that could be obtained from the woods, fields and creeks, and when night came, beds of the softest down were ready for our reception. The fields, too, were full of men servants and women servants. The poultry yards were full to overflowing, and the woods teemed with numerous herds of cattle, horses, mules, and goats, while scores of red and yellow swine literally turned up the meadow in search of worms; yet with all these possessions that which we consider so indispensable to comfort, was a mere shell, and could all be taken down and removed in a few hours.[30]

Externally, the dwellings of the poor bore less resemblance to a modern tourist camp than those of the well-to-do in that there were fewer cabins; otherwise the distinction lay in the furnishings. In one log house the framework of the beds was made of "four forked poles driven into the ground passing between the puncheons," and, it was said, the entire contents of the house "if exposed to sale would not bring over ten dollars."[31]

As the "rich alluvial lands of Alabama" were opened up, "thousands of families from the washed-out and impoverished soil of the older Southern states" moved into the new territory. Their numbers were "incredible when viewed in reference" to the population from "whence the emigrants are chiefly derived."[32] Many Georgia women found their homes along the line of march and in the new country. Tyrone Power describes the condition under which they lived as they crossed his route from Augusta to Columbus, during the exodus:

> The caravan usually consists of from two to four tilt waggons, long and low-roofed; each laden, first with the needful provisions and such household gear as may be considered indispensable; next, over this portion of the freight is stowed the family of the emigrant planter, his wife, and commonly a round squad of white-haired children, with their attendant; on the march these vehicles are preceded and surrounded by the field slaves, varying in numbers from half a dozen to fifty or sixty, according to the wealth of the proprietor; a couple of mounted travellers commonly complete the cavalcade, which moves over these roads at the rate of twelve or fifteen miles a day. At night or when the team gives out, or the waggons are fairly stalled or set fast, the party prepares to camp: such rude huts as their time and ingenuity may best contrive; the females prepare the evening meal, and perform such domestic duties as may be needful. On these occasions I have frequently passed amongst or halted by them, and have been surprised at the air of content and good-humor commonly prevailing in their rude camps.
>
> . . . Thus they crawl onward from day to day, for weeks or months, until they reach that portion of the forest or cane break, fixed upon for the plantation.[33]

Most Georgia towns were unattractive. Savannah, however, was a city of culture and refinement; but Augusta consisted of a very wide street, a couple of miles in length and composed of a mixed description, and Lorenzo Dow on his visit there met with such a reception that he was forced to stop with "a black family who," he said, "lived in as good a fashion as two thirds of the people of Augusta."[34] In Columbus, Indians thronged the streets, and the outlaws of "Sodom," in Alabama, rode into the city to "enjoy an evening's frolic . . . all armed to the teeth."[35] Washington, toward the latter part of the period, was a town of wealth and culture, but, in the early days, "there were very few other dwelling houses . . . than the rough log-pens, with puncheon floors, and board roofs, with mud and stick chimneys. The food of the inhabitants almost universally was corn bread, sweet potatoes, 'hog and hominey' and 'long collards' with occasional supplies of beef, venison, tame and wild fouls, fish, 'ba-meat' and opossum."[36] The Reverend Robert Finley, in 1817, described an Athens where "the comforts of life are not attended to, nor any of its elegances, either in buildings, nor furniture, either in dress or table, morals low, correct ideas few, manners coarse, and religious knowledge nearly nothing."[37] The local names given to some of the districts in the up-country bear witness to the rudeness of their character—Washington was in "Hornets Nest," and others were "Guinea Nest, Rabbit Trap, Sanke Rag, Sugar Tit, Shampagny, Wolf, The Lick, Dooley, Nigger Foot, the Devil's Half Acre, Hello, Red Bone, etc."[38]

Regardless, however, of whether a woman lived in low-country or up-country, in cabin or mansion, clothes were an important question, and the code under which an antebellum woman lived found its counterpart in her dress. It was as cruel as the earrings that demanded that she "pierce [her] meat";[39] as confining as the "tight body, buttoned up in front," which left her "cup of misery" full when her "puffs" had "expanded";[40] as inflexible as the corset that deformed her body;[41] as deceptive as the "shoulders bare to the lower edge of decorum";[42] as subtle as the watch spring bustle, "the most perfect contrivance possible for giving a graceful backward fall to the dress";[43] as untenable as the theory that "no young wife with 'six small children' ever wore spectacles," that those who did might "dance quadrills but never waltzes," for "flirts, coquettes, prudes . . . have their failings, but at least are women";[44] yet as time worn as the envy that made "Kate . . . odious among the girls," when she walked out under the first parasol seen in the backwoods of Georgia.[45]

The young girl's wardrobe might be gaily colored, particularly for daytime wear.[46] For evening, however, something more dainty was appropriate. At the reception of the President of the University of Georgia, "white muslin" was in evidence among the young ladies, and their ornaments were only "pearls and white ribbons," or perhaps "a few delicate flowers."[47] The married woman adopted subdued tones that increased in sobriety with her years until, at an early age, she was drab indeed. The widow had her "weeds" that must be worn for a year—although one was probably justified in declaring a moratorium when a prospective second husband appeared, for "a widow's cap is so dreadfully unbecoming."[48]

"Everybody, women and children, wore bonnets. Hats belonged to the masculine."[49]

"Cracker bonnets" were used in the country districts. They were "cotton quilted . . . with deep curtains hanging down behind, covering the ears and shoulders."[50] In the cities and villages, bonnets were of varied textures and trimmed in feathers, ribbons, or artificial flowers according to the age, finance, inclinations, and status of the wearer. The young girl's might be gay, the married woman's never, the widow's was crepe, but each who "was religious or became converted . . . laid aside her flowers along with rings and breastpin,"[51] if they were of the Methodist persuasion.[52] And married women "wore lace caps very early after motherhood. It marked the distinction between the married and the single in promiscuous company."[53]

Dress was, naturally, more elaborate in the urban districts, and materials more costly than the home-spuns and calicos of the country. As the '60s drew nearer, however, women's clothing became so ornate that they went about in costumes that had all the variety and intricacies of the Gothic cathedrals—from which they drew their inspiration—even to the flying buttresses.

During this same period the "bloomer" dress appeared in the North. A barrage opened from press, pulpit, and the man in the street, which was so severe that Elizabeth Cady Stanton, who attempted to wear it, wrote: "I have never wondered since that Chinese women allow their daughter's feet to be encased in iron shoes, or that Hindoor widows walk calmly to the funeral pyre, for great are the penalties of those who dare resist the behest of the tyrant Custom."[54] In days of no fashion columns or news prints, the Augusta *Chronicle* actually departed from tradition and published a picture of the "Bloomer Girl!" It was taken from the *Lilly, a monthly Journal devoted to Emancipation of Women from Intemperance, Injustice, Prejudice and Bigotry*, which had originally advocated the costume, together with a full description of it. There was no local comment. This was not a fashion but an issue.[55] The *Savannah News* office was completely upset by receiving a doll dressed in the much discussed costume. The men, finding, however, the model so attractive, were willing "to look upon a real flesh and blood Bloomer, through our fingers" if the opportunity came.[56]

But DeBow's comments mirrored the status of women. He pronounced the costume attractive, becoming, convenient, modest, and of a design that originated in the Orient. Still:

The Bloomer dress has been adopted as a kind of flag of rebellion against established usage . . . it is no eastern dress but the chosen garb of such ladies who consider themselves as having a full right to consult their own sense of propriety, and to indulge the freedom of their nature in the pursuit of health, happiness, and humbug! It is the rallying standard of woman's rights advocates and as such is unfit for a modest female. Had it been the invention of some Parisian modiste or some country field tripping milk-maid, or of any other womanish thing, imagined womanishly, and womanishly worn, we would not hesitate to recommend it to our daughters. But indifferent things become vicious entirely by their uses; and the uses to which the Bloomer dress has been applied condemn it in *toto*.[57]

So Georgia women scurried to the shelter of their "eight petticoats" starched "as stiff as possible,"[58] for many of them believed, with the Savannah physician, "the girl who dresses not to please, will become a slut or a shrew at twenty-five."[59]

It was fashionable to be frail. At White Sulphur, the arbiter of style, a "young lady affecting the delicate and interesting was quite shocked to find that she weighed a hundred" pounds.[60] This was the romantic era, the mood a melancholy one, and no heroine could be both fat and sorrowful. Beginning with John Penalton Kennedy's *Swallow Barn* in 1832, the South developed a literature steeped in the spirit of romanticism. It reached its artistic heights in Edgar Allen Poe, its romantic in Thomas Nelson Page, and was swelled in volume with the works of William Gilmore Sims. This was a school of broken hearts, and a well brought up and properly mannered heroine usually died early. If there was no better excuse, "the winged seraphs in heaven above" who "coverted her and me" did their duty. Stephen A. Foster represents the best of the music, which was of the "graveyard" variety and featured "miseries."[61] The newspapers dripped with sentimental laments over dead children, and women wore jewelry made from the hair of their "departed ones." Every schoolgirl groveled in woe, kept an album dedicated to it,[62] enjoyed a "secret sorrow" and "broken hearts," and longed to "fly away and be at rest," for the "gathering storms were wild and woeful" like her "soul."[63]

All this emotionalism had its effect, but it is sometimes hard to tell whether upper-class femininity of the nineteenth century cultivated frailty because it was fashionable, or made it fashionable because they were frail. Harriet Martineau found, among the women in the south, "an apathy on the subject of health," and could account for it only by assuming that the "feeling of vigorous health is almost unknown." "Invalids," she said, "are remarkably uncomplaining and unalarmed; and their friends talk of their having a 'weak breast,' and 'delicate lungs,' with little more seriousness than the English use in speaking of a common cold."[64]

The census reports, both for Georgia and the country as a whole, indicate that mortality among boy babies was higher than among girls, but between the ages of five and forty, the female death rate rises; after that, the male death rate ascends, leaving more women to die of old age than men.[65] According to the same authority, the diseases most likely to prove fatal to women were cancer, "consumption," and those peculiar to the sex, with childbirth taking a heavy toll.[66]

It is probable that the languor of antebellum women can be explained in part by either malaria, hookworm, or chlorosis. The latter was a blood disease, almost unknown to men,[67] occurring frequently among wealthy women, but seldom among poor ones.[68] The disease was fairly common in antebellum days, but is a "clinical curiosity" now in both Europe and America,[69] and a doctor of the staff of the Johns Hopkins Hospital considers it too rare to justify a diagnosis except in the case of an adolescent girl.[70]

Girls between the ages of fourteen and twenty-one years were most likely to be affected. The causes of chlorosis are not definitely known, but it is generally accepted to be "faulty hygiene, tight lacing, overwork, mental anxiety, food, constipation, and family predisposition, indoor work and lack of sunlight."[71] The onset was "insidious accompanied by weakness, fatigability, and usually dyspnoea and palpitations, perversion of appetites such as cravings for sweets, for sour food, or chalk, sand and other inedible articles," and headaches were common.[72] Emotional and nervous symptoms were usually present, the subject often becoming "morose and despondent, hysterical or melancholic."[73] A striking characteristic of the disease was the pallor of the skin, which in some cases assumed a transparent, waxy, greenish hue. This led it to be commonly known as "green sickness,"[74] though some found it took the "eye of faith" to see the color.[75] Chlorosis seldom resulted in death, although the condition was likely to become chronic, and the victim might even become quite stout.[76]

Many women had pulmonary tuberculosis. The census reported that in 1860, 196 men and 295 women in Georgia died from "consumption,"[77] and the curve rises sharply for girls at adolescence and continues to ascend.[78] Harriet Alexander, from Boarding School, in Savannah, wrote her sister: "Kate Smith and Lizzie Plant within two weeks of each other have we followed to the grave. Lizzie has been declining for two or three months, so that her death was not so unexpected a blow. It seemed sad to see her the victim of

Consumption. She is the fourth daughter of just that age that her parents have lost."[79]

Hookworm, among the poor, produced many of the same symptoms that chlorosis did among the rich.[80] And malaria, which recognized neither class, age, sex, or prior claims of other diseases, was frequently responsible for the listlessness of southern women. While childbearing, begun too soon[81] and attended by ignorant midwives and practitioners[82]—for anyone might have, like the teacher of Twiggs County, "laid down the birch and picked up the scalpel," if he so desired[83]—destroyed the health or claimed the lives of many mothers.

One of the causes for bad health among women was tight lacing. Many ills were attributed and attributable to it. One critic believed that "consumption" was "produced, or if hereditary brought to a speedy termination" by it.[84] Dr. Charles Caldwell wrote:

> to secure . . . are called fine figure . . . the corset screws are applied while they are young girls . . . their ribs, especially the false ones, are pressed inwardly to such an extent that their front ends nearly touch each other, if they do not actually overlap . . . the whole trunk of the body is altered . . . dyspeptic affections follow . . . the compressed organs themselves weakened, are usually liable to further disease . . . the lungs . . . pulmonary consumption, and dropsy of the chest often ensue. Corset-broken constitutions . . . threaten a degeneracy of the human race. . . . A Scottish gentleman . . . examined about two hundred young females in fashionable boarding schools . . . scarcely one of them was free from some sort of corset injury.[85]

Added to these there was an almost complete lack of exercise among the upper classes, and personal sanitation was rare with all. Dr. Lindsly found "The habit of confining the female sex within doors to the certain and irremediable injury of their health is begun in early childhood."[86] Others believed that the violations of simple rules of fresh air and exercise was "filling our land . . . with idle, sickly, extravagant women, who do not live out half their days, and who are perpetual incumbrances to those who maintain them."[87] But it was almost impossible for women to exercise. Femininity laden with hoops, corsets, chlorosis, tuberculosis, hookworm, and malaria, St. Paul, Blackstone, romanticism, and etiquette sat whenever possible; and first wives continued to yield their place to second, and second to third.

Frequent bathing is a modern custom. Its early enthusiasts met with indifference.[88] Dr. Ewell of Savannah, in 1817, recommended that every family "make a bathing vessel as indispensable an article in the house as a table."[89] The *Georgia Journal*, in 1824, published eight rules for bathing, which it assured the timid, "experience has established and physiology approved," while it warned the bold, "every third or second day is often enough to take a bath," and hoped with all "that our baths will soon become a place of fashionable resort, and the exertions of our benevolent fellow citizens be met by an adequate reward."[90] According, however, to Dr. Lindsly, by 1839, the "subject" had been "frequently discussed and its importance urged upon the attention of the public," but "little progress had been made in its general adoption."[91] The progressives, no doubt, were encouraged to learn; "it is said that J. Q. Adams washes his entire body every morning when he rises, both summer and winter."[92]

Because of the extreme modesty of antebellum women, medical science was hampered if not hindered from giving them the relief it had to offer. Dr. Arnold of Savannah wrote to a physician in Philadelphia who was attending Mrs. Arnold: "As the wife of a medical man, she is aware that false delicacy too often injures females, by their allowing diseases to get beyond the reach of medical art before they speak out. I have told her to answer any questions you might think necessary to ask her."[93]

In 1848, Dr. Joseph A. Eve of Augusta, in a review of Dr. Charles D. Mengis' *Females and their Diseases*, said: "much good sense and truth are embodied in the ensuing sentence: 'So great, indeed, is the embarrassment arising, from fastidiousness either on the part of the female herself, or the practitioner or both, that I am persuaded much of the ill success of treatment may be justly traced thereto.' "[94]

Dr. Wilson, however, while acknowledging "the sad consequence of the morbid sensitiveness of females," who retain modesty "at the expense of health, and even life itself," could still add, "we can but admire while we condemn and deplore." He said "every physician who has a practice of any extent, sees almost daily cases which have become incurable, on account of the reluctance of females to submit" to a proper examination. This, he found, threw women at the mercy of quacks and ignorant midwives, "old grannies" who render mothers "miserable for life" and "gorge" babies "not an hour old with fat bacon." To remedy this situation, Dr. Wilson grudgingly advocated medical education for women.[95]

Even with good health, the majority of Georgia women could not have been very interesting, for their lives were lonely and isolated. They for the most part lived where "nowhere and never met,"[96] and as little girls had been like the one Buckingham met at "Tokoah [sic] Falls." She was at home alone when he arrived. Her mother had gone to pay a visit to a "neighbor" sixteen miles away. The child, who was then ten years old, "had never seen a larger town than one containing about a dozen houses . . . though she had heard about Augusta." She was "filled with astonishment and terror at the description of the sea, and had great difficulty in understanding how a ship could be made as commodious as a house, and yet float upon the water."[97]

Social gatherings were almost entirely a part of courtship, for:

> When ladies marry, they usually give up going into company and confine themselves to nursing and household duties, because, they say, they receive no attention from the gentleman after marriage, and it is not, therefore, worth their while to dress for the purpose of sitting on sofas as ciphers. Married men as well as unmarried attend such parties; but married ladies mostly stay at home. The married men usually herd together in standing groups, talking politics, or discussing the price of stocks and the state of markets; as there are few married ladies present, and their attention to the unmarried might be thought indecorous, or, at least an interference with their more legitimate admirers . . . such parties fall into the nearest gossip and inanity.[98]

Buckingham believed this applied to "nineteen out of twenty" parties in America,[99] yet he pronounced one, given by the residents of Pulaski House in Savannah, among "the most brilliant" he had seen in this country, and that it had as "much of the ease and elegance as could be seen in any party of similar number in London or Paris." Among the three or four hundred people present, he "did not remark a single awkward or ill-bred person," and the supper was in "most exceptional style."[100]

The women of Savannah he found "accomplished ladies," well educated and elegant in manners, who moved in social circles with "grace and dignity, blended with kindness and suavity"; and that those of moderate means were on equality with the wealthy. He saw there "no straining for distinction," and felt that he was in the company of "well bred and recognized gentlemen and ladies."[101] He described a party given by Dr. Church, President of the University of Georgia, for the faculty and senior students, to which about two hundred from the leading families of Athens were invited, as "very elegant and highly intellectual."[102] Augusta, he thought, was not as cultured as Savannah; it was more mercantile and a simpler mode of living prevailed.[103] And Columbus society he considered very crude.[104]

Usually weddings were the chief social events,[105] but dancing, although frowned on by the church,[106] played an important part in the entertainment of all classes. For the gentry there was the ball, which, in Milledgeville, was "perhaps the most attractive feature" of the General Assembly for "our young friends of *both sexes*."[107] One young member reported "the amusements during the session were enough for any reasonable man who was fond of the ladies and pleased with continued dancing." At one ball, he counted "about seventy ladies," for Milledgeville was "always crowded with them during the session. They are pleased with hearing the eloquence of Georgia in the council of our state, or they are very fond of seeing men from different parts."[108]

The fancy dress ball was popular, and at Madison Springs, a Georgia summer resort, the costumes included brides, Indian squaws, Swiss girls, and Morning Stars; there southern gentlemen became Apollos, Grand Pashas, and Spanish Dons.[109]

While in the well-settled communities among the upper classes these dances were a "display of beauty and elegance,"[110] in the backwoods they were more like the one at Washington in the early days, held in the old log courthouse, where they called the figures: "Gentlemen, lead out your partners. Them that's got shoes and stockings will dance the cotillion; them that's got on shoes and no stockings will dance the Virginy reel; them that's got nairy shoes nor stockings will dance the scamper-down."[111]

The theater was of slight importance in early Georgia. Judging by advertisements in the papers, it had some vogue in Savannah, where there were professional performances as well as "readings," personal appearances, and those of the "home talent" variety.[112] "In Augusta," however, the drama was "poorly sustained," as the social leaders "never turn out except at a representation that is really *recherche*; and then there is a large religious class who never visit such places."[113] The character of life in the rural community as well as the attitude of the church would bar any efforts to develop dramatic appreciation—although the "revival" unwittingly came to answer the purpose.

Those who could afford it went to resorts in the summer. White Sulphur,[114] Virginia Springs,[115] Saratoga, and Newport were desirable,[116] but Summerville, just outside of Augusta,[117] Stone Mountain,[118] and Madison Springs were enjoyed.[119] As sectional controversy became more vigorous, local resorts increased in popularity.[120] For the married women, the recreational value of such a summer was doubtful. Mrs. David Roath wrote her husband from Stone Mountain:[121]

We get up about half past five o'clock in the morning, breakfast at a few minutes after six. I go to my room about eight, read my letter and paper from home, try to write a few lines to you, busy myself with sewing until eleven, have a lunch, lay down until twelve, get ready for dinner by one, sit down stairs with what ever ladies may be here until three or four o'clock, I then go to my room until tea after that I feel tired enough for bed.

For the young and unmarried the resorts were gay. At White Sulphur there were balls, cotillions, waltzes, picnics, strolls in the woods in search of wildflowers to be pressed, card games, rides, serenades, singing to guitars, with flirting on the side and occasionally weddings at the close of the season.[122]

The camp meeting amounted to a resort with a religious tone to the middle and lower classes who could not afford the more fashionable centers, although they probably did not realize it and would not have admitted it if they had. There each family returned yearly to its own cabin, which is described as being of logs, with a piazza in front and outhouses in the rear—"kitchen, stables for horses . . . pens for swine, folds for the herds and flocks, and coops for the chickens," all ready for the coming slaughter. In addition, there were "kennels for hounds and watch dogs, which are needed even more at such places than on the plantations."[123] The "extremes of good and bad" came together at the camp meeting, for it attracted not only those who sought "spiritual refreshment," but others who congregated in the outskirts to "drink whiskey, smoke cigars, play cards and steal horses." At one campground, the sinners were accommodated at a "large frame saloon erected just a little beyond the church square."[124]

Between camp meetings, the middle classes of the state amused themselves in fashions described by A. B. Longstreet in his *Georgia Scenes*. These are pictures of half-remembered incidents, against a background of rollicking, boisterous fun, of gander pullings, and horse racings, and country balls; of weddings where the men "buss" the bride, and fox hunts, and pranks, and waxworks. Usually he tells of the middle class, sometimes of the lower, but always his story is warm and human.[125]

The legislature regarded cock fighting and horse racing "as harmless and peaceable athletic exercise" fit to "preserve the martial spirit of the people," and to "improve the breed of horses." Pitching dollars and playing marbles it termed a "childish amusement," even though "one hundred dollars per game have been won and lost" at the latter. At the same time, the state "would rigidly interdict even amidst the family and friendly circle . . . a rational enjoyment of chess, draughts, whist, or backgammon."[126]

Nevertheless, in Wilkes County "ladies of the first class generally played cards (Whist particularly) and visited the courses."[127] And at Bowling Green, seven miles from Lexington, in the semi-annual sweepstakes and match races, "the excitement of men and women who attended was even greater than the children. Money was bet almost without limit, and stakes paid apparently without regret."[128]

The race courses were gathering places for "loose and unprincipled adventurers from every part of the country," and the Grand Jury of Richmond County complained bitterly against the "profligate and abandoned wretches who swarm into our cities . . . called together by the spectacle," yet Augusta developed an excellent turf, and, "once a year, by legislative permission" it was "open for the importation of vice and horses from all parts of the world."[129]

The cities had similar underworlds, which in Augusta, at least, the police did little to suppress. The jailor made of Richmond County jail a "House of Riot, disorder and gambling to the great disturbance of the prisoners as well as the neighborhood."[130] And many justices of the peace fell "into those views which their duty compels them to punish in others,"[131] for "gambling, profane swearing and drunkardness" were common.[132] The "tippling houses," some of which were kept by women,[133] were places of general licentiousness; and the "Indiscreet observance of public worship and the countenance given to public gambling in the Town of Augusta" reached such an extent that it held "peaceful inhabitants in Terror of divine vengeance."[134] Harrisburg, just outside the city, where the gander pulling famed in Longstreet's *Georgia Scenes* occurred, was regarded as a veritable Sodom by the grand jury, and they wished to extend the authority of the city over it.[135] "Sabbath breaking" was common. The cock fighting and gambling that occurred in "Hawk's Gulley . . . in the very face of the traveling public thus desecrating the day and inflicting an indelible stain upon the morals of the city" was a source of great concern to the grand jury.[136] Yet in spite of abuses and the gloomy forewarnings of grand juries, many wholesome people continued to enjoy "horse racing, quoit pitching, and 'pitching into each other,' " along with "ball and card playing, dancing, wrestling, gander-pulling, and cock-fighting."[137]

As upper-class society became more refined and Methodism spread, women usually absented themselves from these gatherings. They did not succeed in preventing them, however, for as Buckingham observed, the women of this country did not "possess nearly so much influence in directing the manners and practices of society" as did the women of France and England. He found "the external marks of deference shown to them by men giving them the best places in steam-boats and stage-coaches, and rising to give them seats in public assemblies are not accompanied by a similar deference for their opinion and authority in literature, taste, or manners."[138] As has been said, in the South the "gallantry to woman was the gallantry of the harem."[139]

Decorum among the upper- and middle-class Georgia women was sternly assumed and harshly enforced. Arthur Calhoun maintained that "even the chastity of southern woman (a monopolized excellence) was scarcely a virtue, but rather a matter of course."[140] Any violation of the accepted code of conduct meant ostracism. Mrs. Roath wrote her husband from Stone Mountain: "Mrs. Clute I find the ladies have very little to do with on account of her intimacy with Mr. Thompson and Mr. Hitchcock they spend days together on the mountain and fishing and riding on horseback."[141] Dolly Madison, then "eighty years of age," was described by Edward Harden as being "despised—she paints and plays the fool everywhere. They say she is a very low bred woman."[142]

Mrs. Nathaniel Greene came in for her share of criticism. Nevertheless, she was not without admirers, and one, coming to her defense, laid bare the feminine code of conduct and much of the foundation on which it rested. He wrote:

When I left New England I was told that General Green had made application for a divorce from his wife, because she had been unfaithful to his bed, in his absence. In Newport where the General resided I made enquiry concerning this report and found 'twas all a lie. They said she had no more gravity than an air Balloon, in her acting and thinking, that she had no more affection or regard for her children than if they were no human creatures and consequently paid no manner of attention to their education, that she cared for nothing but flurting [sic], rattling and riding about.

A lady who is superior to the little foibles of her sex, who disdains affectation, who thinks and acts as she within the limits of virtue and good sense, without consulting the world about it; is generally an object of envy and detraction—Such is Lady Green—she confesses that she has passions and propensities and if she has virtue 'tis in resisting and keeping them within due bonds. To make the world speak well of her, she ought to deny that she possesses them she ought, if a Girl commits an error for which the world calls her virtue into question to say—instead of "God forgive her! pool [sic] soul!" 'tis as likely as not that her philanthropy and unsuspecting goodness of heart have paved the way for her falling into the snare by putting her off her guard,—"Impudent vile hussy, strumpet, Whore! such a creature should be banished from society forever and dwell among brutes like which she has acted." Which would imply that it would be impossible for her to do the same, or in other words that she had not the same passions. She has an infinite fund of vivacity, the world calls it levity,—She professes an unbound benevolence which very few possess. The world calls it impudence; in short, she is honest and unaffected enough to confess that she is a woman and it seems to me the world dislikes her for nothing else. As for the report that she is destitute of natural feelings and paid no attention to her children, I cannot for my life see what foundation there is for it, I am convinced that she has a very great share of maternal affection, and I never met a woman in my life who had an idea, or had formed a system of education so much to my mind as Lady Green.[143]

Women of the upper and middle classes usually conformed to the accepted code, but the popular idea that southern gentlemen were likely to meet in the cold, grey dawn of almost any morning beneath the dueling oaks to avenge real or imaginary insults to women is without foundation in fact. Duels were frequent in Georgia, but they usually came from men's quarrels with men, often over business or politics, and the "honor" of far more gentlemen than ladies led to the field.[144]

Nevertheless, if a woman was involved, the rules of the "Code of Honor" were severe. "Any insult to a lady under a gentleman's care of protection" was considered "by one degree, a greater offense than if given to the gentleman personally." And an offense committed in the "support of a lady's reputation" was regarded as "less unjustifiable than any other of the same class, and admitting of lighter apologies by the aggressor: This to be determined by the circumstances of the case, but always favorable to the lady."[145]

From the very character of the duel, it is difficult to tell how frequently women were involved in "affairs of honor." But if the established code of conduct toward a woman was violated, the southern temper became inflammable and the possibilities fantastic, as the plans of Thomas Spaulding of St. Simons Island exemplify. He wrote his friend to come and bring his "dueling pistols as mine are so rusted with disuse and salt air, that the flint does not draw sparks from the steel." It seems that Spaulding's "rascally cousin" had been forced to acknowledge a secret marriage of eight years standing and, although "the two are now living in the home in Camden County, and are most happily placed I am told," still, on hearing the news:

It immediately occurred to me that this cousin had presumed in 1794, before I had obtained Miss Leak's favor, to offer himself as a suitor for her hand. I have subtracted seven years from 1802, it leaves 1795, which was the year of my own marriage. Therefore, while a married man, he had presumed to offer himself to a lady as a suitor of marriage. Nothing remains but for me to shoot him.[146]

It is comforting to know that the affair was settled, and he never did.[147]

The duel was said to have been introduced into this country by French officers at the time of the Revolution.[148] They were fought with swords and pistols by the gentry, and fist and thumbs by the lowly, and became increasingly popular in the South.[149] Anything might end in a challenge, for "if greatly displeased with the conduct of a fellow citizen toward you your proper course was to offer him an opportunity to kill you."[150]

Although the sending and receiving of a challenge was a solemn occasion, frequently with a grim ending, there was a distinct social significance involved in the duel. Meetings were arranged only with equals. To accept a challenge implied recognition of social equality. If a "note" was received from a stranger, time was allowed for investigation of his social position, "unless he was fully vouched for by his friends" with established status.[151]

An interesting phase of the duel is that it occasionally offered a "cracker" a certification of graduation into the "planter" class. This opportunity was too important to be completely overlooked by the "cotton snob," and one which, according to a contemporary account, admirers of Margaret Long, who afterward married Governor Telfair's son, did not neglect. On finishing school in Pennsylvania, she returned to her home in Washington, Georgia, and took "the most certain means of favorable admittance into fashionable society. Two young gentlemen, whose aspirations were most ardent to head the *beau mode*, sought that distinction by going through the forms of challenge to fight a duel upon the pretense of some exceptional incident in the attention of one or the other to Miss Long."[152]

From the time, in childish hand with many corrections, a girl wrote in her first composition book, "Modesty is an interesting concomitant of beauty and virtue the first of all virtues is innocence, the second modesty,"[153] until it laid her away in an early grave, "modesty" was a favorite theme in the feminine code. Some who remembered ladies' dresses "cut beyond what their interest will bear," and the language they listened to in theater and church, feared that "fashion regulated her modesty, her blushes and her opinion." Her critics were moved to such violence that they ventured to predict, "if the fashion of going bare legged were to arrive tomorrow," women would follow it "within a month, and laugh at those for their prudery who did otherwise."[154]

Early Victorians, however, were more inclined to be prudish than bold; and although there were "preachers" who would "read anything aloud from the pulpit, which they find in the scriptures,"[155] there were others whose "fastidiousness" led to "alterations in the prayers of the Episcopal Service" and to the "mutilations of the Scriptures." In the name of "Delicacy" they condemned the serpent of Eden to crawl on his "stomach," and Peter to thrice deny his lord "before a certain fowl shall crow."[156] Propriety demanded that horses go with unmentioned tails;[157] garters became "hose confiners" and "stocking tighteners"[158]—even though it allowed a small girl to be "exempt from reproof" when she gave the alarm, "the damned Yankees are coming," because of the "exciting nature of the news";[159] and demanded that Mrs. Reid order a "few pair of stockings" through the merchant's wife, because she was "afraid or ashamed" to tell him "about the leg," even though she admitted he "ought to know the size."[160]

Among the habits of the people drinking was common. Buckingham said that wine was in general use and "champagne in abundance of which ladies partake as freely as the gentlemen," yet he saw no intoxication.[161] While George Paschal, of Lexington and Auraria, wrote:

> Brandy was manufactured in every neighborhood and kept in every house. It was drunk at births by suffering mothers, the midwives and the gossips who attended. The lips of the infant were moistened with a weak beverage. It was drunk for joy and sorrow, in adversity and prosperity, at house-raisings, corn-huskings, harvestings, at balls, quilting parties, dinners, and suppers; at funerals and administrator's sales. It was a medicine, in cold weather and in hot; in fever and the ague; for colic, headaches, consumption, dyspepsia, and gout. It was upon every sideboard, visitors were asked to drink on arrival, during the stay, and on their departure. The ladies sipped it with honey; the men drank it in their coffee, and called it "laced coffee"; old grandmothers took it to strengthen them. Preachers and their flocks did not escape the temptation: they took it as one of "God's good creatures."[162]

"The disgusting habit of snuff-dipping, and even pipe-smoking" prevailed among the poor white women and "sometimes among the wives and daughters of the Yeomanry, and even occasionally among other intelligent Southern Middle Classes." The technique of snuff dipping was particularly uninviting. It required that the devotee:

> Procure a straight wooden tooth-brush—one made of the bark of the hickory-nut tree preferred—chew one end of the brush until it becomes soft and pliant, then dab the same while still wet with saliva into the snuff-bottle and immediately stick it back into the mouth again with the fine particles of snuff adhering; then proceed to mop the gums and teeth adroitly, to suck, and chew and spit to your heart's content.[163]

Chastity was rigidly enforced among the upper- and middle-class women, but not among the lowly. "A southern physician expressed the opinion . . . that if an accurate record could have been had of the births of illegitimate children . . . it would be found to be as great among the poor people in the part of the country in which he practices as of those born in wedlock."[164]

The figures are in part available, for, until 1854, children were legitimated by act of legislature,[165] and the children of fathers with some conscience, enough intelligence to proceed, and usually with sufficient property to make it worthwhile, can be counted.

The statute books show a steady increase in the number of children legitimated. In 1823 there was one,[166] thirty-four in 1847,[167] sixty-nine in 1850,[168] and in 1854 there were seventy-three.[169] After that, by the Act of 1854-1855, the constitution was amended, and the legislature surrendered this duty to the county courts.[170]

In addition to the children clearly made the "legal heirs" of their "reputed fathers," there were others who were adopted or whose names were changed. Some of these, probably, were also illegitimate. And "William Sermon, an illegitimate son of Elizabeth Sermon," had his name changed to another, "which name he has assumed."[171]

While most fathers by act of legislature acknowledged the paternity of only one child, some listed five or six,[172] and one father from Rabun County legitimated eleven.[173] Frequently the law indicated that in addition to the natural children there were legitimate ones as well,[174] and that in some cases the daughters had been married before their fathers legally acknowledged them.[175]

Children born prior to the marriage ceremony of their parents constituted a legal problem, which in 1856 the legislature of Georgia settled. It allowed "the recognition of such a child by his father" to be sufficient to "render the child legitimate."[176]

Miscegenation was not unknown among white women, and such affairs were not always restricted to the lower classes. A magistrate of Charleston wrote to the Ordinary of Richmond County concerning Medora A. Duvigon, a mulatto girl who was being sought under the act of 1835 preventing free negroes from entering the state:

> You would be advancing the cause of justice if you know anything that may aid in convicting her so as to send her out of this community. Her mother is the

sister of a very fine lady of our town and the family is very large and highly respectable—This is another reason why the law should be enforced.[177]

In 1770, Georgia incorporated into her statutes the old Roman law that children followed the status of the mother.[178] While, of course, the law could not make them white, it did make them free, and intelligent negroes were likely to avail themselves of it. Consequently, cases of this character were not uncommon in the courts.

Austin Dabney of Madison County, Georgia, was freed on proof that his mother was white. He was a remarkable negro. A wound that he received in the Revolution would probably have proven fatal had it not been for the mercy of a white family who cared for him. They were repaid, for he not only served them throughout his life, but became their principal support and eventually educated their children. Dabney lived to acquire considerable property. Some of it, a grant from the legislature for his war service, was a state political issue. The negro died recognized and respected.[179] And Eliza Crawford and her five children sued and won their freedom in a Virginia court on the "evidence being full and conclusive that the Plaintiff, Eliza, was born of a white woman of Georgia."[180]

Public opinion seems to have been increasingly exercised over these conditions, for in 1859 the legislature decreed that: "Any word falsely uttered connecting a slave, negro, or person of color with a white woman shall be actionable."[181]

While negroes of the first generation with white mothers were seeking to become free negroes, on the same grounds, free negroes of the second and third generation, finding themselves free but only free,[182] were suing to become legally white.[183] Eventually, the Supreme Court decided that a person with one-eighth African blood remained legally black; beyond that, he was entitled to the privileges of the white race.[184]

Georgia women from 1783 to 1860 were divided into social classes with very different standards. The young woman of the gentry was expected to be gay and useless; her mother grave and capable, although many were as callow and as inadequate as their daughters. The middle classes were vigorous and busy, and the lower slovenly and inert.

Women were not the arbiters of antebellum Georgia society, but, on the contrary, in most things they were dictated to by it. Men dominated there as elsewhere, and wrote one code for themselves and another for their wives and daughters. What influence women had over customs, manners, or morals was

89

subtle and exercised privately, for those of the upper and middle classes were too well trained not to "walk to heel," and those of the lower were mired too deep in illiteracy and poverty to be a leaven.

Not all women were the tubercular angels of song and story. Many were wholesome, full-blooded people who spent useful lives within the bounds of the creed that they professed, even while the lower classes lived in sordidness and poverty. There was greater contrast between the shortcomings of the high and the low than is frequently observed in other eras. One made modesty a vice, while the other, looseness a practice; and both probably would have lived more enviable lives if the feminine inhibitions in antebellum Georgia had undergone some long division.

SIX

Work

$\mathbf{W}$omen made a sound economic contribution to antebellum civilization. It was seldom, if ever, recognized and respected as such by their contemporaries, unless the frequency of second marriages may be taken as a tacit admittance that wives were needed. The character of the work of Georgia women before the Civil War did not lend itself to tabulation, statistics, and impressive columns of figures, but the swelling receipts of present-day commercial canneries, chain stores, and ready-to-wear manufacturers offer testimony to the value of what they did in their homes. It occupied no page in household account books, for its assets constituted an unrecognized saving rather than a tangible income. Its financial merit was not appreciated, as it rested on the basis of a primitive division of labor to which no monetary value had ever been assigned. It was accepted with unctuous flattery rather than honest acknowledgment of its worth by contemporary opinion, but it deserved a better fate, for it was vital to society.

In an era without apartment houses, clothing stores, electric buttons, and "sliced bread," homes were factories operated under the direction of and by the highly skilled labor of women. These were usually wives or daughters, old maids or widowed relatives, although, if the supply failed, employed housekeepers might do. Little monetary value was attached to this labor, for here again, the status of women had remained feudal. They rendered service in return for the protection of an overlord.

In antebellum Georgia, as elsewhere, women were not commonly employed outside the home, but the duties there were heavy and a high degree of skill necessary to success. Slaves did not ordinarily simplify the tasks of an efficient mistress, but, on the contrary, complicated them. The husband who deplored "how much harder" he and his "poor wife" worked than their slaves, and longed for the comforts he and his "old woman" might have enjoyed in their old age if they "were not hampered by fifteen negroes," was not alone.[1] All the benefits of emancipation did not belong to the negroes. The exclamation of relief from a Georgia woman on being assured that slaves were freed:

"Thank heavens! I shall have to work for them no more!"[2] was doubtless echoed in the hearts of many.

The work of a plantation mistress was difficult, for she must superintend everything in her household and besides act as spiritual advisor, nurse, doctor,[3] teacher, social worker, and friend to the blacks as well.

Often her hands were stained with dye and bore the marks of scissors, for slaves could not be trusted with their own sewing.[4] Always by her side clanked an enormous bunch of keys—symbols of her complex duties. There was spinning and weaving; dyeing and soap making; preserving and pickling; sewing and mending; quilt making and coverlet weaving; kitchen and pantry; and "spring house" and poultry yard—all of which she must superintend. The negroes' wants must be ministered to; younger children taught; older daughters launched into society; and visitors received and entertained. In the slave quarters she must meet stark reality with efficiency and dignity, and in the drawing room pretend ignorance of it with poise and charm—all in the course of a day.[5]

The plantation mistress, however, had no monopoly on a crowded life. The typical day of a woman in a non-slaveholding family has been described as beginning when:

> She "unkivered" the coals which had been smothered in the ashes the night before to be kept alive till morning and with kindling in one hand and a live coal held in the tines of a fork or between iron tongs in the other she blew and blew and blew until the splinters caught fire. Then the fire was started and water brought from the spring, poured into the "kittle" and while it was heating the chickens were fed, the cows milked, the children dressed, the bread made, the bacon fried, and then coffee was made and the breakfast was ready. That over, and the dishes washed and put away, the spinning wheel, the loom, or the reel were the next to have attention. Meanwhile keeping a sharp lookout for the children and the hawks, keeping the chickens out of the garden, sweeping the floor, making the beds, churning, sewing, darning, washing, ironing, taking up the ashes and making lye, watching for the bees to swarm, keeping the cat out of the milk pans, dosing the sick children, tying up the hurt fingers and toes, kissing the sore places well again, making soap, robbing the beehives, stringing beans for winter use, working the garden, planting and tending a few hardy blossoms in the front yard . . . getting dinner, darning, patching, mending, milking again, reading the Bible, prayers, and so on from morning till night and then all over again the next day. It could never have been said of them that they had fed on roses and lain in the lilies of life.[6]

In the upcountry there was less refinement of life, and in addition to their household drudgery, women could be found working in the fields with their slaves.[7] And among the poor, housewives sometimes made an effort to sell the products they manufactured.[8] Home industry, however, was a slow process, and the market too limited to yield adequate returns for the labor involved. Mrs. McGehee of Wilkes County went down in history when she "spun, wove, cut out, and made a petticoat in one day and wore it the next,"[9] and it was estimated that an expert spinner might expect "about six cents per day."[10]

Miss Burke, while teaching in Georgia, learned that:

In the northern part of the State of Georgia, the people manufacture all their own clothing, excepting their hats, and sometimes their shoes. In the spring they go to work, and plough the soil, plant and raise the cotton, then card, spin and weave the cloth by hand. Next they gather the weeds from which they make their dyes, such as indigo, etc., and when the cloth is collected, it is ready to be made into all kinds of needful apparel. Then when their own garments are completed they are ready to take a journey to the city. Accordingly, they take their mules and fasten them with a parcel of white cords to a little covered cart with one pair of wheels . . . then load them with chickens, ducks, geese, hominy, and perhaps a swine or two, or a wild deer; lastly, they put in their cooking utensils, not only to be used on the way, but also in the city to save the expense of loding at an inn. . . .

When night comes, they stop on the wayside, detach their mules from their burden and turn them into the woods to seek their food, while they make preparations for their supper. First they gather up parcels of dried leaves and old limbs of trees, with which to build a fire, and then proceed to make coffee and boil their hominy . . . creep into their carts for a night's repose. In this manner half a dozen of these women will perform a journey of eighty to a hundred miles. . . .

[Arriving in the city] they go directly to the market place, tie their mules around about upon the market square, kindle up little fires in the street . . . and cook suppers as before described. But here, instead of sleeping in their carts, they camp down upon the cold damp brick in the market. . . . I have often . . . seen a good many of these miserable females lying fast asleep.[11]

For housewives trained on the farms and plantations, agriculture was a natural step. Many were engaged in it, and some ably managed large plantations. Mrs. Farish Carter, wife of the wealthiest planter in Georgia, when her husband was away, cared for his extensive interests.[12] Nathanael Greene's widow ran Mulberry Grove successfully before her marriage to her overseer, Phineas Miller; and Mrs. Robert MacKay, after her husband's death, managed

"Kensington," his plantation near Savannah, as long as she lived, and kept it plastered with as many mortgages as her husband had been able to do.[13]

In the original notes from which the volumes on *Agriculture* for the United States Census of 1850 and 1860 were compiled, under "Owner, Agent, or Manager of Farm," are recorded the names of only a few women. It is probably true that the more prosperous ones employed overseers or returned information in the names of male relatives. From what was listed, however, under the names of women, it appears that as independent farmers they were making a struggle without marked success. On the whole, their acreage was limited, its cash value small, and the production scant.

In Floyd, a poor, mountainous county, 455 names were entered in 1850, but only two of these were women's. There both men and women did subsistence farming of the usual corn, beans, and potato variety. One man ginned forty-nine bales of cotton, but he was more fortunate than any of his neighbors. Mary Tate, the more prosperous of the two women, returned her farm for only $300 cash value. According to the record, she had one horse and one cow; produced thirty bushels of sweet potatoes, thirty pounds of butter, and slaughtered $30 worth of livestock.[14] The next ten years brought new settlers into that section, for 903 men and thirty-seven women made returns to the census taken in 1860. Although the cash value of none of the women's land exceeded $4,000, as producers they compared favorably with the men. Where all were poor, the women were no poorer.[15]

Greene County was relatively well-to-do, and the comparative poverty of the women was more noticeable. Of the 492 farmers listed for the census of 1850, only twenty-one have feminine names. These women commonly plowed with oxen. While all appear to have planted some cotton, no woman produced more than forty-four bales, though one man ginned 350 bales. The women raised corn, slaughtered livestock, indulged in home industries, and produced the usual peas, potatoes, and beans.[16] The number of farms in Greene County decreased in the next ten years. Only 412 were returned to the census taker in 1860. Sarah Early appears to have been the most successful of the twenty-two women whose names were listed. She produced sixty-eight bales of cotton, 2,000 bushels of wheat, 200 pounds of wool, her home manufacturing reached $500, and she butchered animals valued at $700. She was outstripped, however, in her cotton production by the majority of the men in her section. One of them produced 221 bales.[17]

It is singular how few women's names appearing in one census survey reappeared in the next. Whether death, marriage, or modesty removed them is impossible to say. Martha Cartwright, of Greene County, is one who survived. In 1850 she had sixty acres under cultivation, the cash value of her land was $500, she had three horses, three cows, two oxen, and thirty-five hogs. Her crop was 400 bushels of corn, and she slaughtered $60 worth of livestock.[18] After ten years labor, she was cultivating only fifty acres, but her livestock had increased and her crop improved. In 1860 she had four horses, three mules, twelve oxen, and made 300 bushels of corn and two bales of cotton.

Rice was a difficult and expensive crop, as Mrs. Manigualt of Savannah and Charleston discovered.[19] The ditches and dams required skilled labor, flood waters were always hard and sometimes impossible to control, machinery was expensive and often broke, harvesting and threshing were trying times, and slaves were frequently ill—at Gowrie, one of the Manigault plantations near Savannah, cholera broke out twice, once in 1852 and again in 1853.[20]

According to the census records, women did not show up well in the rice country. In 1850 in Glynn County, ninety-one individuals made returns to the census taker. Nine were women, only two of whom were raising rice. Their maximum yield was 1,500 pounds, while a man recorded a 1,113,000 pound crop. Neither of the women were cultivating more than 630 acres, and their principal crop was not rice but corn, and livestock seems to have provided their cash. The only one who was cultivating cotton ginned just ¼ bale.[21]

Glynn, like Greene, showed a shrinkage in the number of farms listed in 1860. Only eighty-four were enumerated for the census. Women seem to have prospered there in those ten years. The names of five appear, one of whom produced twenty-seven bales of cotton. The maximum for the county was 131.[22] Florence O'Sullivan was a spunky soul. In 1850 she had thirty-three acres under cultivation; the estimated cash value of her farm was $600; she had two horses, fourteen cows, two oxen, ten sheep, slaughtered $190 worth of livestock, and raised ¼ bale of cotton.[23] In the next ten years her placed doubled in cash value. She went in for rice and produced 300 pounds. She had 865 acres under cultivation, got 300 bushels of corn, eighty pounds of wool, did home manufacturing valued at $40, and butchered $80 worth of livestock.[24]

At best, the census takers have left a testimony to hard work and slender reward of women operating farms under their own names. Olmsted discovered a woman of this type of whom he wrote that he could:

Not soon forget the figure of a little old woman, wearing a man's hat, smoking a pipe, driving a little black bull with reins; sitting herself bolt upright, upon the axle-tree of a little truck, on which she was returning from the market. I was riding with a gentleman of the town at the time, and, as she bowed to him with an expression of ineffable self-satisfaction, I asked if he knew her. He had known her for twenty years, he said, and until lately, she had always come into town about once a week, on foot, bringing fowls, eggs, potatoes or herbs, for sale in a basket. The bull she had probably picked up astray, when a calf, and reared and broken it in herself; and the cart and harness she had made herself; but he did not think anybody in the land felt richer than she did now, or prouder of her establishment.[25]

Women who needed employment outside the home in Georgia were faced with two serious handicaps—it was humiliating to have to accept it, and there was seldom anything to accept. In the South the traditional attitude toward labor was intensified by the slave system. Among the upper classes, an impoverished woman who produced a wage was set apart from the coveted social order and lived in an arctic gloom of undisguised pity; among the lower, competition with negroes had developed a caste system that banned certain occupations to white women of respectability.

Literature was the only profession open to women, and Georgians made a poor showing there. Only the upper classes could be expected to have any education—at the turn of the nineteenth century, a woman who could write in Wilkes County was so unusual that customers in David Hillhouse's store would ask that he bring his wife in for a demonstration![26] What education women had was not of such a quality as to produce authors; the fear of being labeled a blue stocking would discourage all except the boldest; early marriages and the multiple duties that followed left little free time; and the code of conduct for a lady that demanded that she shun publicity, all united to discourage those who were so inclined.

A few succeeded in getting something published, but the merit of what they produced is doubtful. Mary E. Bryan wrote essays and poems, principally for the *Literary and Temperance*. "The Missing Flower," a poem dedicated to a dead child, was perhaps her best known work.[27] Octavia Walton LaVert was a woman of culture. She told of her European experiences in her *Souvenirs of Travel*, not without grace and charm.[28] Augustus J. Evans, Georgian by birth, although she spent most of her life in Texas and Alabama, contributed *Beulah*, a novel popular in its time, but of no genuine worth.[29] Maria J. McIntosh, who was from Sunbury but produced the greater part of her work in her brother's New York home, wrote novels, juvenile stores, and poems of the usual order.[30] Annie R. Blount edited a paper in Bainbridge for two years, but with no conspicuous degree of success;[31] and, under the name of Jennie Woodbine, was an early columnist.[32] Clara Belle Sinclaire wrote novels and verses. Her wartime poem, "Homespun Dresses," is better than her others and far more creditable than most produced by Georgia women of her day.[33] They were, perhaps, the best known Georgia women in literature before the Civil War. It is a slender roster and one of no real consequence.

Teaching was not a profession. It required no special training and was generally held in low repute. The result was that even the presidency of the University of Georgia did not "seem to be coveted."[34] Many Georgians deplored the "odium attached" to teaching,[35] yet they understood the cause. Teaching had been left to "chance and necessity, some strolling idler, too indolent for bodily labor and unfit for mental . . . abandoned to those who teach because they can do nothing else."[36] Still, few Georgians were ready to follow Sarah J. Hale's advice—prepare women for the job, for which they were apparently so well suited, and leave it to them.[37]

Toward the latter part of the antebellum period, there came an effort to raise the standard of teaching[38] and, from the '30s on, teachers themselves began trying to do something about it. They called many county meetings,[39] and there were even state conventions, but the improvement was negligible. The last state convention was held in Macon in 1854. Only four delegates attended, and they failed to find enough teachers in the city who were interested to make up the quorum of ten.[40] The conventions died a natural death unmourned in the midst of the slavery struggle.

Women teachers were not included in the councils of the conventions, and in general condemnation of their occupation by the press, they were neither praised nor blamed, but ignored. Yet many women taught.

Their preparation was inadequate, but only the poor schools required certificates and those were arbitrarily granted.[41] They suffered from lack of public confidence and preconceived notions of their inferiority, and struggled against the stubborn resistance of male vanity; negro men just released from slavery openly objected to being taught by Lucy Stone at Oberlin College because she was a woman. Yet teaching was genteel, and poor relations and the middle class must live.[42]

Many Georgia women became governesses and taught the elementary subjects, needlework, painting, or drilled the younger generation in its scales and "pieces." Some taught the "higher branches," and a few became headmistresses or operated schools of their own, but most were too poorly trained to be risked with advanced work or in the better seminaries. These places fell principally to northern teachers[43] until the activities of abolitionists began to alarm the South. Then "they raised the state cry about native teachers."[44] And, by 1855, Wesleyan College, which was giving "instruction in the theory and practical duties of the school room," felt prepared to meet the demand and advertised for places for its graduates.[45]

As always, the pay of Georgia teachers was hazardous. Miss Burke thought that those "in languages, music and the other sciences, received good salaries."[46] A music teacher in Washington, Georgia, found it "a very difficult matter to command the small sum of $50" for each pupil.[47] Mary E. G. Harden reported that "Miss Gratan . . . has been teaching for a year. She is paid five hundred dollars a year."[48] And Mrs. Hulburd "remained" in the female department of the Academy of Richmond County on a salary of "$300 per annum," and the tuition of $6 a quarter for each girl, although when an assistant was obtained, she was to resign one-third of the tuition money.[49]

The poor schools did not have a salary schedule prescribed by law. Teachers were compensated in proportion to attendance and pupil load,[50] on a basis of "such sums as are paid for like services by other patrons of such teachers."[51] The law does not specify any difference between the pay of men and women. Teachers drew up their "lists" and they were presented to the ordinary for payment. From the records that have come to light, it is impossible to tell whether or not women were discriminated against, for these teachers received many advances[52] and frequently neglected to present their claims to the ordinaries. This they remedied by applying to the legislature for "reliefs." When Sophia A. Clark made such an appeal, the Assembly provided that she be paid "in the same proportion . . . as is hereby authorized to be paid Jonathan N. Hadden."[53]

In the Richmond County Academy, women received decidedly less than men, who, whether they taught in the male or female departments, appeared to have been on a uniform wage level.[54] Since part of the revenue of these teachers came from fees that they were authorized to collect, it is difficult to determine precisely what each received.

A few women, along with anybody else who wanted to, practiced medicine, and prepared the way for women doctors. But they were untrained at best, and in most cases simply ignorant midwives.[55] Mrs. Agnes Paschal, a remarkable Georgia woman, represented the best of this kind. Born in 1776, she lived to be ninety-four years old. During that time, she bore eleven children, including triplets; kept a hotel at Lexington that was patronized by the sick; began her career as a "doctress" during a siege of "intermittent and bilious fever" there; and eventually followed her unsuccessful husband to Skull Shoals in Greene County, where she continued to practice. After his death, she went with her son to the gold fields of Auraria; built a log church; set bones, performed minor operations, and rode horseback to visit the sick—never charging the poor; saw the Indians driven out; kept a tavern; lived through the financial crash of '37; worked among those left after the gold rush; and remained loyal to the Union during the war. At seventy she rode twenty miles on horseback over mountains and performed a successful operation, and, at ninety-four, she helped deliver her grandson's wife.[56]

Her son said that in her practice of medicine she rejected superstitions, such as:

> Tying the ague to a tree, charms and other mad absurdities. She fought the third day ague with sensible remedies such as active stimulants and diversion before the hour of paroxysm. . . . In my own case the ague resisted Peruvian bark, quinine, opium, and all ordinary remedies. My mother prescribed red pepper upon the soles of my feet . . . draughts of strong red pepper tea; and to give the pepper the best chance to force circulation, I would plow until the ague came, then I would urge my horse into a trot while it lasted. . . . At first I was forced to pause during the fever, which I did under a tree drinking cold water until the fever was gone, when I would renew my work.[57]

Georgia women's business ventures were usually the outgrowth of some occupation they had learned in the home. Spinsters of the upper classes who engaged in trade or business were a rarity, but it was not uncommon for a widow, even of the plantation aristocracy, to wear a husband's mantle without losing caste. In some strange way, the marriage bond was held to dissolve the social stigma, but the grace of deceased male relatives does not appear to have extended to spinsters.

It was quite customary for women to be guardians of children, executors or administrators of their husband's estates, even when a fortune was involved, as legal notices and court records show. Mrs. Emily H. Tubman of Augusta was one of these. Her husband left her with a comfortable income, which, through wise investments and careful handling, she converted into a fortune. Her lawyer, Henry H. Cumming, between January 29 and May 22, 1845, collected from her "defendants" alone, $36,065.25.[58]

Mrs. David Hillhouse of Washington, the wife of the publisher of a newspaper, *The Monitor*, was a highly respected and well-known woman in the state. Her son wrote:

> My father died in 1803, and my mother immediately took the management of the paper and learned and practiced every mechanical service pertaining to the office. There was no paper published for many years afterward above Washington. . . . There were about three hundred subscribers to the "Monitor" when my mother took charge of it. The only newspapers printed in Georgia at that time were in Savannah, Augusta, and Louisville.[59]

Mrs. Hillhouse not only managed the paper successfully, but did the job of printing so well that she got the contract for the state laws. She was the first and only state printer.[60]

Although the Savannah City Directory of 1860 does not show whether the women listed were white or colored, it indicates the varieties of occupations in which they were engaged. In the city there were:[61]

Seamstresses	68	Bakery	1
Milliners	12	Confectioner	1
Boarding-house keepers	21	Matron orphan asylum	1
Washerwomen	1	Oyster saloon and bar-room	
Grocers	6	keeper	1
Merchandise		Tailoress	1
Dry goods	3	Doctor	1
Variety shop	1	Music teacher	1
Proprietess of hotels	3	Principal of school	4
Groceries and liquors	2	Teachers	10
Sup't hotel linen	1	Nurse	1

In 1860, according to the United States census report, 2,411 women were supporting themselves with their needles.[62] They were roughly divided, according to the skill of the workers, into milliners, mantua-makers, dressmakers, and seamstresses. To make a bonnet required an eye for style and a cunning hand, so millinery attracted a higher type of workers than most crafts in which women were engaged.[63] A mantua-maker represented the aristocracy of the trade in outer garments, usually specializing in coats; the dressmaker did not claim to do such finished work; and the seamstress was not highly skilled. No one got rich on any branch of the craft, but establishments of the better kind furnished the materials as well as the work, and frequently combined millinery with dressmaking to increase the profits.

Anna Barnsley's receipts show what a lady might expect her clothes to cost. She paid Miss Washington for making a dress $2.50; and to "C. W. Howard for making one silk dress $5.21 ½ and for another $9.64 ½." Her "mantua-maker" submitted the following bill:[64]

For making 1 dress	$4.00
4 yds. fringe	2.00
Buttons	1.00
Lining	1.50
Silk 25 [¢], hook and eye cords	
10 [¢]	.35
Whalebone	.13
Making waist	2.00
Lining, hook and eyes, and	
whalebone	.50
	$11.48

And to Miss Kendrick:

Bl'k veil	$3.00
Pr. gloves	.75
1½ yd. rib[bon]	.27
2 yds. narrow	.13
16 yds. colored silk	15.00
	$19.15

The need of some gainful occupation for lower-class women was so pressing that charitable people began to give it their attention. In 1841 the "Home Industry Society" was organized in Augusta. It established a sewing agency and clothing store, which they advertised had as its objectives:[65]

Not profit but employment of the destitute. . . . Economy, patriotism, and benevolence alike commend this establishment to the people of Georgia. These clothes are made in their own state manufactories and by their own widows and orphans . . . cheaper than articles from the north and are better made.

Within six months, it was considered necessary to appoint a committee of ladies for each ward of the city, to whom "applicants for work must apply for tickets of recommendation," for it was determined that only the deserving should do the sewing. Women who held tickets presented them at the "Home Industry" store and work was consigned to them. The patrons of the society might either leave orders for sewing or buy the ready-made garments that the store carried for field or boat hands and household servants.[66] At first, only crude sewing was attempted, but the quality of the work must have improved, for the "friends of the society" were urged to buy their own, as well as their children's and servants' clothing, from the "Home Industry" store.[67]

This effort to help the indigent women of Augusta was followed by the "Needle Woman's Relief Society" under the auspices of the ladies of the Presbyterian Church,[68] and it continued to function as late as 1858.[69]

Another source of income for women was boarders, but since most people lived at home, boarders were far more likely to be of the temporary than the permanent kind—summer visitors, members of the legislature and their friends, or young people away at school. The profits were not great. Edward Harden of Athens found that he could board his family with Mrs. Hardee in Savannah for $40.00 a month, and that they would be assigned "a good room."[70] Mrs. David L. Roath paid "seven dollars a week or twenty-four dollars a month" at Gordon Spring.[71] And Richmond County boarded out its orphan children for $48.00 a year each.[72]

Women's training had fitted them for hotel or tavern keeping, and they were frequently proprietors. In 1860, the Florida Hotel, City Hotel, and Screven House, in Savannah, were all run by women.[73]

A Georgia lawyer wrote that "the worst taverns were those in the cotton countries," but that the best of these were kept by women.[74] To lie in a cage of mosquito net, on a feather bed, with only planks or ropes beneath was an experience for the uninitiated traveler.[75] In 1837, Sherwood was still printing in his *Gazetteer* a letter written more than fifty years before, which gives sufficient reason for being grateful that Georgia's tavern days are over. It reads:

Home, July, 1783.

Dear Bess—entering on a new sphere of business, you will need advice. I am an old traveler, and know how to give it. The following remarks regard your treatment of genteel company: others will not expect so much attention:

1. Let your house be kept neat. Have your furniture and rooms brushed and wiped every morning.
2. Keep scrapers at the outside doors, and mats at every door.
3. Let your bed have *clean sheets* for every visitor: this is indispensable.
4. Let your bedsteads be cleansed every March, and you will seldom be troubled with *multipedes*, if you should be, use quicksilver and tallow.

5. Have your cooking done free from coals and ashes: Frequently let your hams and chickens be *broiled* instead of fried.

6. Travellers like strong coffee and well settled: but they cannot endure *smoky or greasy* tea.

7. Let your water bucket stand so high that your children shall not dabble in it.

8. Keep a spit box in each room: this will teach vulgar people that the floors were not made to spit on.

. . .

12. Don't allow your children to examine the baggage of your guests: nor to belch up wind at the table.

Yours loving Father
Joshua Clifford[76]

There was seldom a demand for restaurants, but Nancy Rumsey made use of an unusual opportunity in a unique way, which Garnett Andrews described:

When I first attended Elbert Superior Court . . . I noticed a large woman, "fat, square, and forty" or more drive up her ox-cart, back it up near the path way that led to the main door of the Court House, scotch the wheels, unhitch her two oxen, and with the aid of two friends who came forward, tie and feed them. She then removed the hind gate of her cart and exposed the end of a cedar barrel. Another friend climbed over the wheels and handed out a table, cups, pint and quart pots, a box filled with ginger-bread, and finally a small bag of chestnuts. . . . How often Miss Nancy Rumsey had repeated that scene in years past, I cannot say; but I do know she continued it to a late day as regularly as court set, until a lawyer once moved that the minutes be amended by adding, after the words "present, the Honorable _____ Judge, etc. . . . and Nancy Rumsey and her two red steers" as she and they had been coming long enough to make it a good custom at common law; for the memory of man ran not to the contrary . . . and he doubted whether any lawful court could be held with them.[77]

The kinds of work in which the poor white people of the South engaged were limited, for their badges of superiority over the negro were blood and occupation. Since the first was scarcely impressive even to the slaves, they jealously supported it with the second. However, only certain occupations were banned. Olmsted found that in Virginia, and it applied equally elsewhere, the poor whites were:

Not particular about working with negroes, but that no white man would do certain kinds of work (such as taking care of cattle, or getting water or wood for household use), and if you should ask a white man you had hired to do such things, he would get mad and tell you he wasn't a nigger. Poor white girls never hire out to do servants' work, but they would come and help another white woman about her sewing or quilting and take wages for it. But these girls were not very respectable generally, and it was not agreeable to have them in your house, though there were some very respectable ladies that would go out and sew.[78]

Furthermore, he added that a planter told him "that any white girl who could be hired for wages would certainly be a girl of easy virtue."[79]

It is a mistake, however, to assume that the stigma on labor was such that needy white people refused it altogether. As Hundley pointed out: "respectability is one thing and gentility or fashion is quite another. It is respectable to labor all the world over, but where, we should like to know is it fashionable?"[80] It was rather that there was nothing for uneducated and untrained masses of white people to do.

There were thousands of people in the South who were misfits. Their need was desperate and some southern leaders with vision began to believe that it was not slavery, but "the great upheaving of our masses we have to fear."[81] The hope of cementing the cotton kingdom by finding a place for these people within it was one of the moving factors in DeBow's advocacy of cotton manufacturing—bring the mills to the fields.[82] It led William Gregg to plan and establish his model mill village at Graniteville, South Carolina.[83] It prompted Governor Hammond—who estimated that 50,000 people in South Carolina in 1850 had no way of making a living—a few miles away on the Savannah to employ the white women of his neighborhood to sew for his slaves.[84] And it was partly responsible for the "Home Industry" store, and the "Woman's Needlework Depository" in Augusta.

DeBow, backed by the press, recommended manufacturing as a cure-all for southern ills;[85] his logic brought cheers, but not action.[86] There was little southern capital free for investment, and as long as plantations paid, a southern man of sufficient fortune to launch a factory was more inclined to recommend a mill to his neighbor than to desert the cotton patch itself. It took the pinch of hard times, due to the fall in the price of cotton in 1840, to raise the smokestacks in Georgia.[87]

When the price of cotton fell in 1840, Georgians turned to manufacturing and soon led the slave states in the production of cotton goods.[88]

The development of the industry gave the masses of the poor white women of the South an opportunity for employment such as they had never had before. Gregg had thought especially of them when he planned his experiment, and had predicted that when his mill began to operate: "On the Sabbath, when the females turn out in their gay colored gowns you will imagine yourself surrounded by a group of city belles."[89] This high hope might have been accomplished to his own satisfaction in Graniteville, for he attracted an unusual group of operatives and got such surprising results that, in less than ten years, the community had between $8,000 and $9,000 in the savings bank.[90] "City belles," however, were not a byproduct of many plants, for the wage of factory operatives was not conducive to gracious living. In Georgia it ranged from 10¢ a day to children in the Richmond Factory, at Spirit Creek, near Augusta, to $26.00 a month for men at the Milledgeville Manufacturing Company, at Milledgeville.[91] In 1849, the average wage for mill hands in the state was from $5.00 to $10.00 a month for women, and $15.00 for men. At Columbus in the middle fifties, the operatives were said to be mainly "cracker girls, who earn in good times by piece work $8.00 to $12.00 a month."[92] And, in 1859, the Augusta Factory was paying children from $1.00 to $2.00, and women from $3.00 to $5.00 a week.[93]

Estimates available through the census report give an incomplete picture of the earnings of factory workers. Twenty counties in Georgia made no return in 1860; both the reports of 1850 and 1860 fail to distinguish between adults and children, or to divide blacks from whites; and, although the record for men and women was kept separate in 1850, it was not in 1860. According to the figures given, however, the average wage for women in the cotton mills of Georgia was $7.39 a month, and for men $14.57. At the same time in Massachusetts, it was $13.60 and $22.90 respectively. Singularly enough, Florida recorded the lowest wage for women, $5.00 a month, and the highest for men, $32.15, of all states in the Union manufacturing cotton.[94] The Census of 1860 gives the average pay for all cotton mill operatives in Georgia as $148 a year without regard to age, sex, or color.[95]

From the record of those eligible for the benefits of the poor school fund, in Richmond County children began working in the mills at eight years of age. The youngest girl named, a spinner, was only nine and the average age for that work was from eleven to fourteen years. Girls were listed as sweepers, spinners, and weavers. The average age for boys was lower than that for girls, and they did a greater variety of work.[96]

Not only white men, women, and children worked in the mills, but negroes—many of them slaves—as well, apparently without racial antagonism among the operatives;[97] with the blessing of southern leaders;[98] and with only an occasional criticism from the public.[99]

The slaves themselves were not altogether happy in factories. At least those that Farish Carter took from his plantation to his mill near Columbus were not. They found it harder work than they were accustomed to do, so they escaped—from their master's mill back to his plantation.[100] Neither were the manufacturers near Athens content with slave labor. Their objection, however, was not racial, but economic. White labor was paid $7.00 a month and fed themselves, while masters got the same wage for their slaves and the manufacturers provided the table.[101] When the price of cotton rose in 1850, they were more valuable in the field than in the mills, and the practice of using them almost disappeared.[102]

Factory operatives could not have been poor white trash in the sense usually accepted in southern vernacular—a synonym for laziness, shiftlessness, and degeneracy. It would take a sit-down strike to make mill workers out of that brand of humanity, and no indolent woman ever stood at a loom twelve hours a day for so small a wage. There were no refinements of life in a mill village, the health of the operatives was frequently abused, their standards of conduct were customarily low, but they were hardly lazy. In describing the factories around Athens, Buckingham wrote:

> White families engaged in these factories, live in log huts clustered about the establishment on the river's bank, and the negroes repair to the huts allowed them by their owners when they are near, or stay at the mill when their master's plantation is far off.
>
> The whites looked miserably pale and unhealthy; and they are said to be very short-lived, the first symptoms of fevers and dysenteries in the autumn appearing chiefly among them at the factories, and sweeping numbers of them off by death. Under the most favorable circumstances, I think the factory system detrimental to health, morals, and social happiness; but in its infant state, as it is here, with unavoidable confinement in a heated temperature, and with unwholesome associations, it is worse, and I do not wonder that the most humane members of the community deplore the introduction of factories in the South.[103]

There was an effort made by employers to improve living conditions among the workers. Some furnished them houses, but there were never enough to go around;[104] some provided schools for the children;[105] one boasted of a library and of divine services twice a month;[106] one the advantage of Sunday School instruction;[107] one that the conduct of the operatives was "improved";[108] and another that temperance was being enforced.[109] The very virtues that were considered worth enumerating bespeak the sordid conditions that existed. It is not surprising that laborers brought from the North refused to remain,[110] and that the New England factory girls, attracted to Georgia by the low cost of living, soon left because of the undesirable social conditions and the general degeneration of labor.[111]

The Wayman Factory, Thomaston, was probably typical of those elsewhere in the state. There the 125 operatives used weekly:

Bacon	500 lbs.	Tobacco [used for men,	
Flour	700 lbs.	women and children]	20 lbs.
Corn meal	20 bu.	Molasses	20 gals.
Coffee	50 lbs.		

White reported that at Wayman:

No provision is made for the education of the children the character of the operatives is distinguished by the usual traits that mark the poor uneducated class of this country. Of the whole population of the village, which amounts to 240, there are not twenty who can either read or write. They are much inferior in moral deportment to the operatives of New England, where the laws make provision for their education, yet their condition is much improved. Nearly all the families residing here are those who have been driven by necessity to engage their children to work in the mills, whose toil on some worn-out or barren piece of ground is not sufficient to support their wants.[112]

In proportion to men, the northern mills employed a higher percentage of women than the southern mills. This has sometimes been attributed to the presence of the negro,[113] but in view of the fact that few of them remained in the Georgia factories after 1850, this could not have been true there. In that year, 875 men and 1,399 women were employed in cotton manufacturing in Georgia;[114] while in 1860, there were 1,131 men and 1,682 women reported for the census.[115] It would seem, rather, that white men replaced the negroes taken out of the factories, for men were more valuable for some parts of the heavy work than women.

The census report of 1860 is incomplete for manufacturing, but it presents a fairly accurate account of women in the industries of Georgia. There were 130 counties in the state at the time, and 110 of these reported. Forty-nine counties were employing women in a total of seventeen industries, according to the census report. They were distributed as follows:

Women in Industry in Georgia, U.S. Census 1860

County	Manufacture	No. of Establishments	No. Employed M	F	Wage ($)
Baldwin	Brick	2	17	1	5,412
	Cotton goods	1	45	54	13,284
	Liquors and wines	2	2	4	1,550
	Lumber sawed	2	19	4	10,140
	Woollen goods	1	15	16	4,236
Bibb	Clothing	4	22	3	13,416
	Cotton goods	1	38	75	1,800
Burke	Brick	1	2	1	660
Butts	Cotton goods	1	45	30	14,440
Calhoun	Lumber sawed	1	4	1	864
Camden	Arrowroot	1	6	4	1,008
	Turpentine distilled	2	22	4	4,020
	Lumber sawed	4	66	1	15,480
Campbell	Cotton goods	2	36	57	11,112
	Lumber sawed	3	24	1	5,520
Carlton	Turpentine distilled	5	181	3	42,504
Cass	Boots and shoes	3	5	1	1,476
	Tobacco mfg.	1	20	1	2,544
Catoose	Wool carding	2	2	1	600
Chatham	Rice flour	1	76	20	16,560
Chattooga	Cotton goods	1	20	50	9,000
Cherokee	Tobacco mfg.	2	20	1	2,008
Clark	Clothing	1	5	5	4,620
	Cotton goods	3	102	125	29,820
	Paper printing	1	7	6	2,424
Cobb	Boots and shoes	5	16	1	4,992
	Cotton goods	1	155	231	63,600
	Paper printing	2	20	10	8,880
	Woollen goods	1	13	14	5,100
Columbia	Gold mining	1	35	5	6,660
Coweta	Gold mining	1	37	4	9,600
Decatur	Cotton goods	2	13	28	6,360
	Woollen goods	2	5	7	1,692
DeKalbe	Tin, copper, and sheet iron ware	1	12	1	1,680
Dougherty	Brick	4	34	1	7,920
Effingham	Lumber sawed	4	53	3	10,583
Elbert	Cotton goods	1	12	20	4,080
Floyd	Tobacco mfg.	2	8	12	2,280
Gilmer	Boots and shoes	1	1	1	360
Greene	Cotton goods	2	75	85	20,940

Women in Industry in Georgia, U.S. Census 1860 (*cont.*)

County	Manufacture	No. of Establishments	No. Employed M	F	Wage
Hancock	Cotton goods	1	50	100	24,000
Hart	Carriages	1	3	1	820
	Cotton goods	1	2	4	744
Houston	Cotton goods	1	23	27	6,756
Jones	Cotton gins	1	73	1	11,820
	Lumber sawed	2	16	1	3,096
McIntosh	Lumber sawed	8	111	8	27,672
	Turpentine distilled	2	50	1	8,472
Macon	Brick	1	3	1	576
Madison	Leather	2	4	2	924
Merriweather	Lumber sawed	5	24	2	432
Morgan	Boots and shoes	2	12	1	3,744
Muscogee	Cotton goods	3	157	250	52,860
	Paper printing	1	25	10	9,600
	Woollen goods	3	105	155	43,800
Newton	Boots and shoes	8	11	1	3,252
	Cotton goods	2	25	75	8,508
Pickens	Tobacco mfg.	1	3	5	1,020
Polk	Leather	2	3	1	1,080
Pulaski	Flour and meal	4	9	1	2,880
	Leather	1	2	1	1,200
Putman	Boots and shoes	1	10	4	3,840
	Cotton goods	1	30	30	9,000
Richmond	Boots and shoes	3	16	2	5,100
	Bricks	2	95	1	27,096
	Cotton goods	2	131	222	70,320
	Lumber sawed	16	83	2	16,428
	Printing, newspaper and job	4	64	3	42,960
	Woollen goods	1	15	20	5,520
Scriven	Lumber sawed	3	62	4	18,756
Spaulding	Boots and shoes	2	29	1	7,500
Taylor	Cotton goods	1	10	11	2,640
Troup	Boots and shoes	1	13	5	3,720
	Cotton goods	1	40	60	8,400
	Lumber sawed	2	26	5	6,900
Upson	Cotton goods	3	62	95	19,332
	Leather	3	6	1	1,704
Walton	Cotton goods	1	40	40	11,040
Warren	Cotton goods	1	20	16	5,136
	Woollen goods	1	6	4	1,560
Wilkinson	Lumber sawed	12	57	1	11,988

Antebellum Georgia women were not tin toys with keys in their backs. They worked, and what they produced had genuine financial value. As housewives, their labor was still along primitive lines, which, although altered by trade and commerce, had only been touched by the industrial revolution until the latter part of the period. The result was that, while contemporaries willingly recognized the social importance of the work that women did, they were unconscious of the economic rating it deserved.

Outside the home, there were no professions for women, the business opportunities were insignificant, and until the '40s, industrial openings for women did not exist in Georgia. Lower-class women, particularly, were in desperate need of money, and when manufacturing began, did not hesitate to man the looms.

The boasted chivalry that southern gentlemen offered women did not extend to helping them earn a living. It bolted the doors of employment, unless it was to the advantage of men to do otherwise, and protected women by leaving them outside. Nor did it hesitate in paying them less wage than men, or in throwing white women in association with negroes in the mills.

Tons of memorial oratory have been heaped upon the work of southern women during the Civil War, yet there is nothing astonishing in the ability and courage they displayed, for they had been amply trained for the parts they were to play.

SEVEN

Women and the Church

The antebellum social and ecclesiastical order in Georgia, in accord with tradition, inconsistently expected a woman to find her greatest expression in the Church, and demanded that she refrain from expressing herself while there. It took Sarah Grimké, a fallen angel from Charleston society, to ask, "What about the choir?"[1]

Public opinion, however, in antebellum Georgia, was showing a tendency to compromise with St. Paul. Jesse Mercer, a respected and representative Baptist minister, wrote:

There is a sense in which women are not permitted to speak in the church, and yet a sense in which they may speak. Now in what may they not speak? In teaching and governing . . . 1. The Law requires it. 2. Adam was first formed then Eve. This gives the man the rule of government. 3. The woman being deceived, was in the transgression, indicating her weakness, and affording a reason ever afterwards for her being under obedience with all subjection.

In what may they speak? In praying and prophesying. . . . But this prophesying when used by women must not be teaching, but only edifying. *For it is not permitted to a woman to teach.* Now, then if women are not permitted to teach and exercise authority in the church how can they vote in matters of discipline which is government? We are . . . of the opinion that women are . . . debarred the right of voting in the church in all matters of government, because they cannot use this right without being on a par with men, and in many instances taking the ascendancy, which is at palpable variance with the obedience and subjection which is required of them.

We suspect it is the general practice in the churches of our order to allow women this use. But whenever a case of this kind has come under our observation, we have noticed an obvious reluctance in adopting it. And within the sphere of our administration they have *modestly* declined it. We have never had any difficulty on this subject with us, and we hope for the sake of the female Christian character women in no churches will ever make a difficulty of it, and if men should attempt it, in view of honoring them, they will have grace enough to rise up with one consent, and pour the waters of pious, modest and humble contempt upon it and quench it at once.[2]

The Methodist Church ruled that "A woman is in no case licensed . . . to exhort or preach";[3] although "sometimes with the tacit consent of all church authorities women exhort, preach, and labor as evangelists with great acceptability and success."[4] It was not until 1880 that the Methodist Conference "ordered that he, his, and him, when used in the Discipline, with reference to stewards, class leaders, and Sunday School Superintendents shall not be so construed as to exclude women."[5] According to Methodist notions, shouting women, but not praying ones, were acceptable to St. Paul. At revivals the feminine shouters were even estimated to outnumber the masculine. And the difference between "a praying and a shouting woman" was clear to the minds of the brethren.[6] Mrs. Rebecca Felton, the first woman in the United States Senate, remembered vividly the first time she "heard a woman pray in meeting." The good sister had been "talking to a bench of 'mourners' and broke loose, in the fervor of her pleadings." The incident was the "talk of the town," and public opinion was sharply divided. "Some said it would not do at all—others said she was so good that she must be forgiven, but the majority said she should have kept silent."[7]

The Rev. Hugh Smith of the aristocratic St. Paul's Episcopal Church, in Augusta, at the convention of the diocese of Georgia, warned against "officious intermeddling with spiritual concerns" on the part of women. He cautioned against any activities, or excessive religious zeal, that might make them "dictatorial judges—noisy controversialist—restless proselyters—self-authorized, but scripture-forbidden laborers in the work of others, to which they have no call." He condemned such practices as "injurious to the peace of the Church at large and particularly at variance with the sober and well-ordered arrangements of our own Church."[8]

The Presbyterians joined with the Baptists, Methodists, and Episcopalians in holding to the doctrines of St. Paul as interpreted by the church fathers, at least insofar as women's participation in church government was concerned.[9] But when it came to "women's work," they were all equally as sure that was another matter. The cautious Rev. Hugh Smith, for example, was convinced that: "In the department of Religion, as well as in social life, there is a sphere which belongs exclusively to woman," and that "the fear of doing too much" should not induce her to resolve that "she will do nothing." He warned against "that false delicacy and too shrinking timidity which would keep them back from the work of their God"; and sounded a clarion call for women to "become spirited and unwearied auxiliaries, in the good work of extending

Religion to the destitute in our own borders, according to the pure and primitive provisions" of the Episcopal Church.[10]

Just what was classified as "women's work" in the church seems vague, and it was no doubt dictated by expediency, but there was one point on which there was growing unity among the denominations—whatever it was, it should be done. Sam Jones, born in 1847, who was a popular Methodist evangelist in Georgia for half a century, summed up contemporary opinion by saying: "Some people say they don't believe in woman's work. There is an old preacher down in Georgia who preached against woman's work, and that preacher has not had a conversion since the war."[11]

The Sunday schools afforded an excellent opportunity for women to participate in religious activities,[12] and they appear to have supplied the majority of teachers.[13] But that was not enough. Women organized all sorts of benevolent societies for which they commonly assumed administrative and financial responsibility. However, they seem to have carefully avoided the title of "president," and most of them were governed by "directresses," with a first or second directress in possession of the chair.[14] Women of all denominations sponsored both domestic and foreign missions[15] and held fairs to support them.[16] The Methodist ladies of Augusta organized a "mite society" to help pay the bachelor preacher, and Miss Amelia M. Love, its treasurer, afterwards married him.[17] Mt. Zion had its "Educational Society";[18] Augusta one for the benefit of the sick poor;[19] while the Savannah ladies sponsored relief for indigent widows,[20] an industrial school,[21] a "female asylum," free school, clothing and fuel association, announced themselves as the "Seaman's Friend," and sponsored the Sailors Home.[22]

One Augusta organization that seems to have done a particularly fine piece of work was the "Needle Woman's Relief Society." The Board met for years in the Presbyterian lecture room.[23] They opened up a "Woman's Needle Work Depository" with headquarters at Broad and Kollock, and solicited orders for "destitute females." Work was only given out to those whom the board of directors had investigated and certified with a card.[24]

Buckingham was impressed with the sewing societies of Savannah, in which he found the women "religious without being fanatical, and pious without being puritanical."[25] The ladies gathered "once a week at each other's houses" and occupied "four or five hours in needlework," the proceeds of which were sold to support benevolences.[26] He described a meeting, at one of the most "splendid private residences" in the city, of the "Society for Promoting

Education and Christianity in the East." There the ladies gathered in the morning to hear from a returned missionary, and sewed while he talked.[27]

Stephen Elliott, for twenty-five years Episcopal Bishop of the Diocese of Georgia, in his sermon, "The Busy Woman's Religious Difficulties," outlined the attitude his church expected of husbands toward wives:

> Now mark, the man is the head of the woman as God is head of the Church: that is she is subordinate to him, nothing more; he is expected to deal with her as God dealt with Christ, to exact of her lawful duty and no more; not to make a servant of her whom God gave him for wife; not to forget that she has duties, feelings, and above all a soul; not to require that she shall sacrifice her conscience to his pleasure, or even comfort; not to rearrange everything by his disorderly habits, and then require of *her* all his own deficiencies; not to leave servants, children, house-hold economy, altogether to her weakness [since a man knows] how weak her body is and how inferior her authority . . . if he does not give her his support he should be satisfied with imperfection.[28]

Women were not expected to regulate the church, but the church expected to regulate them. Firmly it confined them to the home, and sought to standardize their dress, manners, morals, and amusements.

The Methodist church was firm on the subject of women's dress. It recalled that when the "daughters of Zion" became "haughty" and walked "with stretched forth necks and wanton eyes," they had been visited with a stern judgment.[29] The founders of the church conspired to save the sisters of Methodism from a like fate. The divines agreed: "our one aim . . . is to raise a *holy people* . . . we cannot allow of anything which has an immediate tendency . . . to strengthen and puff up the carnal mind. Few things, perhaps, have a greater tendency to this than gay dress."[30]

Deacons were instructed "to read the thoughts on dress at least once a year in every large society"; to be "mild, but strict"; to "allow no except cases, not even of married women"; and to "give no tickets to any that wear high heads, enormous bonnets, ruffles or rings."[31] Even as late as 1865, the Methodist *Doctrines and Discipline* decreed that "all people conform to the spirit of apostolic precept not to adorn themselves with gold, and pearls and costly array."[32] And Lorenzo Dow, an eccentric Methodist evangelist, in his *School of Babylon*, awarded dress the fifth place among thirteen vices. "For," he said, "dress was ordained in consequence of sin, and may be considered a badge of fallen nature."[33] Before 1823, "one good sister wore some feathers and was dropped for superfluity of apparel" by the church in Augusta.[34] There, by

1845, some of the younger people were "venturing to wear ribbon and artificials on their bonnets, and managed to escape the censor of the young preacher, but the sturdy mothers of the olden days still wore their old-time bonnets and their simple gowns."[35] The other churches were not as strict as the Methodist in matters of dress and adornment. Probably having, on the whole, more of the world's goods, they were not constrained to make a virtue of its absence.

The Episcopalians were usually more tolerant in their attitude toward dancing than the other denominations, and were inclined to leave it to the conscience of the individual member.[36] But Lorenzo Dow put dancing, "the important art of hopping and jumping about," second in his *School of Babylon*.[37] And Sam Jones, even at a later day, was roaring:

> Sow profanity and reap it. Sow cards reap gamblers. Sow balls and reap Germans. The German is the legitimate product of the ball room. I tell you, humanity when you start it down hill ain't going to stop. The square dance, 'Twas said "let's go on with it a while," and then on with it a little while further, and on, and on, and on, and on, and then—the round dance. I could say something that would make your blood boil—."[38]

Whatever differences of opinion the various denominations and individual congregations may have entertained as to the limits of "woman's work" in the church, most pulpits would have joined with Henry Kollock, minister of the Independent Presbyterian Church at Savannah, in acknowledging piety as a cardinal virtue of women.[39] As such it fitted well into the mores, for it allowed full ecclesiastical credit for Bible records of devout women,[40] but in no way interfered with the interpretations of their status included in church dogmas, and gave the sentimental years a golden opportunity.

It is significant of the public mind that not only the church but teachers who knew children and were accustomed to them were favorably impressed with incidents of piety in little girls that, to the modern mind, seem morose, unwholesome, and unnatural. Emily Burke, Northern teacher in Savannah, told of a child in the orphanage there whom she said:

> I soon found she had a source of happiness not derived from this world. Although young in years, she had learned to love her Savior. She had given her affections to God, and it was her delight to be alone, where she might without interruption enjoy his presence. She was often found on her knees in prayer in some secret corner, and many times she was overheard imploring mercy for herself, her teachers, and companions. It was evident to all who knew her, that

115

she was speedily finishing her work in this world. She grew in grace every day and made rapid advances in divine life.[41]

The Presbyterians, in Caroline Smelt, produced an outstanding example of devoutness. Adiel Sherwood, Baptist, unmindful of denominations, pointed with pride to the Augusta Cemetery where rested "the remains of Caroline Smelt—an eminent instance of early piety."[42] And Moses Waddel—teacher, President of the University of Georgia, minister, and Secretary of Education of the Presbyterian Church in the United States—in 1818 wrote the *Memoirs of the Life of Miss Caroline Smelt*. It was considered "so well calculated to illustrate Christian character"[43] by the Presbyterian Committee of Publications, Richmond, and the Board of Publications, New York, that they were having it republished as late as 1875.

Caroline Smelt, according to Dr. Waddel's account, when only two years old had memorized and could repeat "instructive lessons . . . with such pathos, propriety of emphasis, and expression of countenance, as to gratify all who heard her."[44] Between five and six years of age she was taken to dancing school, but "felt such alarm" that she could not stay.[45]

By eight, her "plan of salvation through a Redeemer" was so "clear" that she "understood it as well and believed in it as firmly" as on her deathbed.[46] At ten, dolls were only "painted pieces of wood" to her, but she loved "living babies" dearly, because "our blessed Savior had taken such in his arms and blessed them."[47] At sixteen, she was popular and sought after, but took no part in "what she then considered to be criminal amusements." She only attended one ball and a theater, and, although she frequently went to smaller parties, she went unwillingly.[48]

Caroline Smelt lived to be only seventeen. Dr. Waddel represents her on her deathbed as saying:

> Mother, I wish you to deliver a message from me to my beloved sister-cousin, Cornelia Walker . . . tell her of all the Lord has done for me. Tell her that I desire her never again to participate in sinful amusements. Tell her I requested on my deathbed, that she never enter a theater, a ball room, or attend another fashionable tea-party . . . if one of them is sinful, they are all so . . . I am also of the opinion that the last mentioned are more so, if possible, than either of the others. Tea-parties . . . lead to more extravagance and party spirit, more vanity, more ambition than the others.
>
> . . . I wish you [mother] and her [Cornelia Walker] to keep up rational intercourse with all our dear friends, but let it be done with gospel simplicity.

. . . It is sweet to die. Death is a pleasant friend; the gate to heaven. I long to meet death but still I am willing to wait until I shall have finished the work appointed for me to do.[49]

Not only the church preached piety, to the full accompaniment of public approval, but fashionable ladies cultivated it. Their albums drip with wretched poetry dedicated to the subject. Julia Blanche Monroe, who married John McIntosh Kell, has left the following specimen:

Women's Rights

The right to wake when others sleep
The right to watch, the right to weep;
The right to comfort in distress
The right to sooth, the right to bless
The right the widow's heart to cheer
The right to dry the orphan's tear.
The right to clothe and feed the poor
The right to teach them to endure.
The right when other friends have flown;
And left the sufferer all alone
To kneel that dying couch beside
And meekly point to Him who died!
The right a happy home to make
In any clime for Jesus sake,
Rights such as these are all we crave;
Until our last—a quick grave.[50]

Vineville, 1853

No matter what the attitude of the church toward women, women were convinced that it was both good and just, if membership is any guide. That of the Independent Presbyterian Church in Savannah is perhaps a fair example. Their rolls show in September 1842, 140 white women and seventy-four men, sixteen of whom were elders. Their colored membership followed the same order—twenty-five women and nine men.[51] It is probable that Dr. Arnold, writing to his daughter, Ellen, touched on a pertinent reason for women's loyalty to the church when he wrote:

You were right to avoid any discussion of religion with Mrs. Bryan. People in the country live a monotonous life and even religious excitement is often hailed a pleasure more akin to worldly amusement than the good people are themselves aware of.[52]

The status of women in the church was too well written into the cultural pattern for antebellum Georgia women to feel any resentment toward it. In addition to gratifying what appears to be a basic religious urge, it offered both compensation and emotional outlet for lives that were for the most part isolated and drab.

EIGHT

Slavery and the Status of Women

From the depths of his homesick heart, an American colonist advised: "Whosoever is well off in Europe better remain there. Here is misery and distress same as everywhere. . . . we have the same old world as in Europe."[1] Women who crossed the ocean hoping to improve their status would have done well to have listened. The new world added the cares of pioneer life, but otherwise the condition of women throughout the seaboard colonies remained substantially what it had been in Europe. The concept of woman as a fragile ornament of civilization had no place in frontier or lower-class society. When wealth accumulated in America, women became the index of masculine opulence—a Mandarin's nails.

Yet with the same background, northern women began to throw off their yoke earlier than those in the slave states. The South produced no Lucretia Mott, Elizabeth Cady Stanton, Emily H. Willard, or Lucy Larcum. Her early roster bears only the name of the Grimké sisters, of a wealthy and aristocratic Charleston family, who entered the feminist movement more by accident than design and lived in northern exile.[2] The explanation appears to lie in the almost inseparable interweaving of economic, social, and political life and thought in the South with the institution of negro slavery.

True to their cultural traditions, both the New England and Southern colonist originally settled in towns. But the New Englanders found no temptation to change. They did not discover a money crop. The soil and climate were grim. Instead, they developed industries—notably fishing and shipbuilding. These served to promote town life, and negro slavery gained no foothold.[3]

In the middle colonies, although there was a larger foreign element than in the other two sections, the English urban traditions prevailed. For New York found her way to her richest agricultural lands blocked by the unfriendly and highly organized Iroquois, and the Pennsylvania Dutch farmers quickly usurped the Susquehanna Valley. Hedged in, but with the advantage of ports and position, the middle group became the business center of colonial America.

While the North was developing an urban civilization, the South was evolving a rural one.

In America the southern colonists soon discovered money crops—tobacco and rice. They found a friendly soil and an agreeable climate. The only thorn was the lack of labor. Free men, with the open resources that the frontier offered, were not available. Indian slavery proved a failure. Indentured servants were unsatisfactory. A plantation system with negro slave labor slowly developed.[4]

There were no traditions of slavery in the cultural background of the colonies. The institution was not legally recognized in Virginia until the code of 1705. It grew gradually and without apparent intention, from economic necessity, through lengthening penal sentences, and extending the terms of indentured servants, until laws fixing the status of the children as that of the mother closed the avenues of escape. Massachusetts enacted such statutes in 1698, and one by one the other states fell in line.[5]

Slavery was tolerated rather than approved during the early days of the republic and was regretted by the Jeffersonian school.[6] Then came the cotton gin. The South had found another and a more profitable crop that demanded labor, so it remained rural, and slavery was assured.

In the meantime, the northern cities were flourishing, and the old adage "city air breeds freedom" was to be redemonstrated in the movement for the emancipation of women that commenced there. An analysis of the leadership in the equal rights crusade shows that nearly all the women were city born, that they were educated, and had sufficient income to provide leisure. Their work originated in the urban centers, for an idea to thrive must be heard, and from there gradually spread to the rural districts.[7]

The women's rights movement began as the illegitimate child of the antislavery crusade. That alone would have been sufficient to have doomed it in the South in its early stages, and to have left a deep-seated prejudice against equality for women in slaveholding states. The traditional attitude toward women knew no sectional lines, and any loosening of the bonds was destined to meet stubborn opposition. In the North, even though the crusade was associated with a popular cause, the reaction against it was violent.

Fannie Wright, who probably initiated the movement for the emancipation of women in the United States, began her career in this country with an experiment in abolition. She bought land near Memphis and, in 1826, settled slaves on it, expecting, as they worked out their freedom, to teach them to use it when it came. She became ill, however, and returned temporarily to London. The project was poorly managed and failed. Miss Wright in the end took the negroes to Haiti, where they were freed.

In the late '20s she toured the northern cities, lecturing on slavery, religion, and woman's rights—the first woman to speak in this country on lay subjects. She was mercilessly attacked by the press; proclaimed as the triumvirate of "Tom Paine, Fanny Wright, and the Devil" by the clergy; and as the "Priestess of Beelzebub" by the political enemies of the Working Men's Party, which she likewise sponsored. Nevertheless, by the time Miss Wright left America, the woman's crusade was begun.[8]

When the American Anti-Slavery Society was founded in Philadelphia in 1833, women were allowed to take part in the meetings, but were not accepted for membership. Dissatisfied with this, they organized the Philadelphia Female Anti-Slavery Society, which, a few years later, held its first convention in America.

No one was disappointed in the violence of the storm the meeting provoked. The Massachusetts Association of Congregational Ministers, in 1837, begged not to have these "perplexed and agitating subjects" forced on the church. They declared that "if the vine . . . thinks to assume the independent and overshadowing nature of the elm, it will not only cease to bear fruit, but fall in shame and dishonor in the dust."[9]

When the Female Anti-Slavery Society held its second convention in Philadelphia in 1838, the building was surrounded by an enraged mob that, after the meeting had adjourned, invaded and burned the hall. And when women asked for equality in the American Anti-Slavery Society, it split into two parts, [one including women and the other excluding them]. William Lloyd Garrison joined the organization that accepted women.[10]

In 1840 occurred the event that was to separate the woman's rights movement from abolition. The world's antislavery convention, which met in London, refused to seat the women delegates who had been duly selected. Among those who were banished was Lucretia Mott, a demurely appearing Quakeress of Philadelphia. However, in spite of her apparent defeat, she had dominated the convention; powerful friends, including William Lloyd Garrison, had joined her in the gallery; and she had won Elizabeth Cady

Stanton to her cause. Mrs. Stanton had not been previously interested in emancipation of any kind, and her husband had opposed equality for women in the Anti-Slavery Society. They had been married just in time for her to cross the ocean with him.[11]

In London the two women realized that the real issue was not abolition, but equality for women, and determined on a convention in America with that as its objective. It was held eight years later at Seneca Falls, New York. There they drew up the "Declaration of the Rights of Women," in which they "let facts be submitted to a candid world," and launched their cause on its own merits.[12]

Public sentiment in the North continued to militate against women. Antoinette Brown, pastor of the Congregational Church at South Butler, New York, was an elected and certified delegate to the world's temperance convention held in New York in 1853. When she rose to speak, she was invited to the platform so that she could be heard. A Philadelphia gentleman stamped his feet until the dust arose around him in clouds and shouted, "Shame on the Woman!" The cry rose from the mob, "She is bringing in women's rights!" Antoinette Brown was forced to retire from a scene of mob violence without having spoken a word. Horace Greeley in describing the convention for the *Tribune* wrote:

First day—crowding a woman off the platform.
Second day—gagging her.
Third day—voting she stay gagged.

Having thus disposed of the main question, we presume the incidentals will finish this morning.[13]

The forties and fifties were an age of reform. Everyone minded his neighbor's business. Public opinion in the North was ready to sponsor the emancipation of slaves—which they did not have; but stubbornly resisted emancipating women—which they did have. There was no tradition of slavery, but subjection of women was a Christian practice. Although the barrage continued against equality for women, from the abolitionists came such friends as: William Lloyd Garrison, Wendell Phillips, Ralph Waldo Emerson, John Greenleaf Whittier, and Horace Greeley, all powerful allies.

These very allies, however, only served to unite the southern front. Women of the plantation aristocracy, who alone were prepared for leadership, drew aside the hems of their garments, while southern men fortified the Mason-Dixon line against abolition and women's rights.

As the abolitionist societies grew and their assault on slavery became more and more bitter, a spirited people defended the system with equal fervor. From the original conception of slavery as a necessary evil they came to regard it as the "corner stone of free government," and a positive good,[14] and Jefferson's equalitarian idealism gave way to Calhoun's economic realism.[15]

In the '30s, the South became a conscious minority. In seeking to preserve its civilization it rationalized the slave system by reverting to the theory of Aristotle. It conceived of itself as a Greek democracy, with its superiors freed from drudgery by negro slaves. Southern philosophy imagined a stratified society in which each part accepted its allotted task and cheerfully worked to maintain a South with the harmony of Greek proportions. The slave states developed a doctrine of inequality, with nature itself setting the seal on social rank, and interpreted southern social, economic, and political institutions in terms of it.[16]

Chancellor Thomas R. Dew of Virginia, hailed as a "Daniel come to Judgment," was the father of this school of thought;[17] Chancellor William Harper of South Carolina developed the idea in an extreme form;[18] Alexander H. Stephens[19] and Governor Hammond of South Carolina accepted and advanced it;[20] in John C. Calhoun it found its finite expression;[21] and in George Fitzhugh its enthusiastic publicist.[22]

In this new democracy, women retained their traditional rank. Southern leaders accepted the framework of society as they found it and set about to prove it was good. The subordinate position of women was an established fact. As such, it was fitted into the concept of a stratified society and became an inalienable part of the defense of slavery. The philosophers of this ideal state continued to romanticize women of the upper classes and to forget those of the lower.

It was contended that a slave society was mutually beneficial. Dew claimed that it delivered women from bondage, for in it a woman "ceases to be a mere 'beast of burden'—becomes the cheering animating center of the family circle." He said that as a result of slavery: "we find [woman] at once elevated, clothed with all her charms, mingling with and directing the society in which she belongs, no longer the slave, but the equal and idol of man."[23]

George Fitzhugh wrote: "The duty of protecting the weak involves the necessity of enslaving them—hence, in all countries, woman and children, wards and apprentices, have been essentially slaves, controlled, not by the law but by the will of superiors."[24]

The new southern philosophy avoided discussing the mental abilities of women. It defended the inferior position assigned them on the unalterable fact that they were women, and as such had a definite field of activity; but they were barred from participation in all others. Chancellor Dew maintained that women's place was "not an accidental one, but resulted from the law of nature," and that the relative positions of the sexes were the "results of the forces of circumstances . . . even upon the supposition of perfect intellectual equality at birth." He believed that "occupations produced a mighty influence on character." Women, therefore, must "rely upon the strength of others," and "man must be engaged in her cause." This she might accomplish "by the exhibition of those qualities which delight and fascinate [for] grace, modestly, and loveliness are the charms which constitute her power."[25]

In 1838, Chancellor Harper, in his *Memoir on Slavery*, described the inescapable position of women in a southern society of inequality, which he believed to be altogether ideal. He said:

> Females are human and rational beings. They may be found of better faculties, and better qualified to exercise political privileges, and to attain the distinctions of society, than many men; yet who complains of the order of society by which they are excluded from them? For, I do not speak of the few who would desecrate them; do violence to the nature which their Creator has impressed upon them; drag them from the position which they necessarily occupy for the existence of civilized society, and in which they constitute its blessing and ornament—the only position which they have ever occupied in any human society—to place them in a situation in which they would be alike miserable and degraded. Low as we descend in combatting the theories of presumptuous dogmatists, it cannot be necessary to stoop to this.[26]

George Fitzhugh wrapped his brutality in less sentimental words but held to the same principles. He warned that:

> If American women wish to participate in the hard labor of men, they are right to curtail the petticoat. Queens wear the longest trains, because they have least occasion to labor. The broom girls of Bavaria have to work hard for a living, and find it necessary to amputate the nether impediments. In France, woman draws the plough and canal boat. She will be condemned to like labors in America, so soon as her dress, her education and coarse sentiments fit her for such labors. Let her exhibit strength and hardihood, and man her master, will make her a beast of burden. So long as she is nervous, fickle, capricious, delicate,

diffident and dependent, man will worship and adore her. Her weakness is her strength, and her true art is to cultivate and improve that weakness. . . . In truth, woman, like children, has but one right, and that is the right to protection. The right to protection involves the obligation to obey. A husband, a lord and master, whom she should love, honor and obey, nature designed for every woman—for the number of males and females is the same. If she be obedient, she is in little danger of mal-treatment; if she stands upon her rights, is coarse and masculine, woman loathes and despises her, and ends by abusing her. Law however well intended, can do little in her behalf. True womanly art will give her an empire and sway far greater than she deserves. The best women have been distasteful to men, and unpopular with their own sex, simply for betraying, or seeming to betraying, something masculine in their characters. Catherine Parr, Miss Edgwood, Mrs. Fry, Miss Martineau, and Madam De Stael, are not lovable characters. On the other hand men have adored the worst women, merely for their feminine charms and arts. Rhodope and Aspasia, Delilah, Cleopatra, Mary Stuart, Nonon d'Enclos, Maria Antoinette, Herodias and Lola Montez, ruled men as they pleased, by the exercise of all the charms, and more than the wiles and weakness of their sex. . . . Yet Mrs. Stowe would have women preach. If she sets them to preaching today, we men will put them to the plough tomorrow. Women would do well to disguise strength if they possess it, if they would retain their empire. The men of the South take care of the women of the South, the men of slaveholding Asia guard and protect their women too. The generous sentiments of slaveholders are sufficient to guarantee of the rights of woman, all over the world over. But there is something wrong in her condition in free society, and that condition is daily becoming worse.[27]

Southern men convinced themselves that what they did was for the best interest of women. They developed a chivalry of which they were proud, and conceived an etiquette that accepted mental inaptitude for women and was intended to guard their physical weakness. In the name of chivalry, however, flattery was substituted for justice, masculine brutality was veiled with sentiment, and feminine honor and virtue made synonymous with chastity only. The gallantry of southern men shielded women from unwelcome attentions, but it fed the upper classes on saccharine, and left the lower with a bare plate. Only a code in which the poor were forgotten could have accepted such theories as George Fitzhugh's when he wrote:

Look at the situation of woman when she is thrown into the war of competition and has to support herself by daily wages. For the same or equally valuable service she gets not half the pay that man does, simply because of the modesty of her sex prevents her from resorting to all the arts and means of competition which men employ. . . . We do not set women and children free because they are not capable of taking care of themselves, not equal to the constant struggle of society. To set them free would be to give the lamb to the wolf to take care of.[28]

Chancellor Harper argued that "the tendency" of slavery was:

To elevate the female character, as well as that of the other sex and for similar reasons. In other states of society there is no well defined limit to separate virtue from vice. . . . Here there is a certain marked line, above which there is not toleration or allowance for any approach to license of manners or conduct, and she who falls below it will fall far below even the slave. How many will incur this penalty?[29]

As a result, he maintained that prostitution was practically eliminated from the South, as white women were seldom available, except by "importation from the cities of our confederate states where slavery does not exist"—and negroes were unalluring.[30] "Never but in a single instance," he wrote, "have I heard of an imputation on the general purity and manners among the free females of the slave holding states." With almost comical blindness he continued: "Such imputations . . . we never heard *here*, where divorce was never known; where no court was ever polluted" by action against an unfaithful wife.

Hammond was willing to "broadly assert" from the "records of the courts, . . . the public press, and . . . the knowledge of all who have ever lived here," that licentiousness among the white people of the South was less than "among any other five millions of the people on the civilized earth." He believed that the slave states had produced "a people whose men are proverbially brave, intellectual and hospitable, and whose women are unaffectedly chaste, devoted to domestic life, and happy in it."[31]

Olmsted was puzzled by Harper's defense of slavery, which maintained that it protected white women by supplying negro prostitutes. He had read the *Memoir on Slavery* and had reached the only logical conclusion—Harper had lost sight of the poor whites altogether, as most southern writers had done.[32] For he knew that many negroes owed their freedom to white mothers, and remembered an explanation of a "Southerner" that: "There must always be women among the lower class of whites, so poor that their favors can be purchased by slaves."[33]

At a time when the ancient mores in regard to women were crumbling elsewhere in America, they were being strengthened in the South. "Woman" remained an abstract symbol to the men of the plantation aristocracy, whose imagination stopped with those of their own class. They allotted them virtues—purity, love, piety, gentleness, frailty, and obedience—all of which were best exercised in the home, and assigned them a role in southern institutions. Since it was in harmony with the one sanctioned by Christian tradition, it gave new life to the decaying order in the South, and deprived the opposition of leadership, for which the lower classes were unfitted. As a result, the movement for civil and political equality was retarded in the South. At the same time that the guns for equal rights for women opened fire in the North, in the slaves states southern ladies were teaching their daughters what gentlemen of the old regime had taught them, that: "A woman's name should appear in print but twice—when she marries and when she dies."[34] This was their contribution to a way of life that the South found good.

Notes

EDITOR'S INTRODUCTION

1. Edward T. James, Janet Wilson James, and Paul S. Boyer. eds. *Notable American Women, 1607-1950: A Biographical Dictionary*, 3 vols. (Cambridge: Harvard University Press, 1971); Barbara Sicherman and Carol Hurd Green, eds., *Notable American Women, the Modern Period: A Biographical Dictionary* (Cambridge: Harvard University Press, 1980).
2. New York: R.R. Bowker, 1979.

PREFACE

1. In 1946—two decades after Boatwright was hired—there were forty-four women faculty members, including at least eight who had master's degrees. Nearly all had the A.B. degree, from such places as Vanderbilt, Smith, Syracuse, and the University of Chicago as well as from a variety of southern colleges.
2. Flisch deserves, and may soon get, a biography of her own. Born in Augusta in 1861, she graduated from Lucy Cobb Institute in Athens, Georgia, in 1877 and applied for admission to the University of Georgia, which would not admit women for another forty-two years. Rejected, she wrote a dramatic letter to the *Augusta Chronicle* deploring discrimination against women in Georgia. After teaching at the Georgia State College for Women for many years and writing novels, as well as many articles for newspapers and magazines, in 1906 she went to the University of Wisconsin for an M.A. By that time she was an active member of the American Historical Association. She appeared on its program in 1905 and again in 1908. Her carefully researched paper on "The Common People of the Old South" and an equally careful "Bibliography of the Public Records of Richmond County, Georgia," were published by the Association (see the *Annual Report of the American Historical Association* for 1906, vol. 2 [Washington, D.C.: GPO, 1908]). Both of these are cited in Boatwright's bibliography. Later Flisch returned to Augusta to care for an aging mother and taught at Tubman High School, where Eleanor Boatwright came under her influence. It is generally agreed among the survivors of the Tubman faculty that it was Flisch who set Boatwright on the road to being an

historian, and it is quite plausible to suggest that Boatwright's choice of thesis topic also bore the marks of Flisch's interests and her approach to historical research. Boatwright used many of the documents first collected in Flisch's "Bibliography"; Ann Braddy, Boatwright's closest friend, says flatly, "Miss Flisch chose Eleanor to be her Sword Bearer." When Augusta Junior College was organized in 1926 Flisch became dean of women. She lived until 1939 and until recently had dropped entirely out of historical memory. Robin Harris of Georgia College in Milledgeville, Georgia, is writing her biography. Her novels contain useful social history.

3. I asked Ann Braddy, "Why did Boatwright not go on to get the Ph.D.?" Braddy's response was quick: "Money, and anyhow with Julia Flisch for a teacher who needed a Ph.D.?"

4. Robin Harris, the assiduous biographer of Flisch, can find no record in the Augusta newspapers of either of these strikes. The anecdotal evidence comes from women who were teachers at the time; apparently the newspapers were loath to encourage such goings-on by writing about them.

5. Eleanor Boatwright to J. Harold Saxon, Nov. 12, 1947, to J. L. Yaden, Nov. 16, 1947, in files of Teachers Retirement System of Georgia. I am much indebted to Dorothy Hughes, Administrative Assistant, for providing this and other data about Eleanor Boatwright's encounters with the Retirement System.

6. Florence Fleming Corley to Anne Firor Scott, March 8, 1992. Professor Corley, a distant cousin of Boatwright, graduated from Tubman in 1950.

7. Page 1 of the present volume.

8. Page 25.

9. The essay is reprinted in *Unheard Voices: The First Historians of Southern Women*, edited by Anne Firor Scott, University of Virginia Press, 1993. It was originally published under the title "The Political and Civil Status of Women in Georgia, 1783-1860," in the *Georgia Historical Quarterly*, Volume 25, 1941, pages 301-24. This quote appears on page 176 of *Unheard Voices*.

10. Of course black historians were far more sensitive to this issue, but their concern was overwhelmingly for the black women, usually a slave woman, who was forced into sexual relationships with a white man. In the 1960 edition of John Hope Franklin, *From Slavery to Freedom: A History of Negro Americans* (New York: Alfred Knopf) we find this paragraph: "The extensive miscegenation which went on during the slave period was largely the result of people living and working together at common tasks and the subjection of Negro women to the whims and desires of white men. There was some race mixture that resulted from the association of Negro men and white women, but this was a small percentage of the total" (204-5). In 1970 James Hugo Johnson, *Race Relations in Virginia and Miscegenation in the South* (Amherst: University of Massachusetts Press), which had been a dissertation at the University of Chicago in the 1930s, finally found a publisher. Johnson is an African American. In 1980 Joel Williamson published *The New People* (New York: Free Press), the first definitive work on the subject of miscegenation. Williamson, consulted for this note, confirmed my view that southern

historians were not dealing with the subject at all in the years when Johnson and Boatwright were writing. He tells me that the anthropologists, psychologists, and sociologists were beginning to think about it in the 1920s, but not the historians. And as far as I can determine only the women among white scholars dealt with the white women-black man aspect of the phenomenon. Thus Johnson and Boatwright in this as in so much else were ahead of their time.

11. I continue to be puzzled as to how the idea ever got started that southern women did not organize their own associations. Thomas Woody, *Women's Education in the United States*, vol. 2 (New York: Science Press, 1929), was well aware of the kinds of evidence that would be used by Johnson, and Boatwright on this question. "In the South, female societies were *no less common* [than in the North]. Perhaps they were more so." He went on to list several and added, "All the foregoing are but a handful of the vast number incorporated in the states named and elsewhere during this period." He cited the laws of Virginia and indicated that he had found similar evidence of incorporation of voluntary associations in other states.

12. Just as well. From the record it seems that her salary of $1,800 a year did not change between 1938 and 1943. It did improve after that, though money remained a problem for the rest of her life.

13. Marie A. Hurlburt of Augusta, Ga., interview, Sept. 5, 1991.

14. Eleanor Miot Boatwright to Dr. William Kenneth Boyd, May 9, 1937, Charles Sydnor Papers, Department of Special Collections, Perkins Library, Duke University, Durham, N.C.

15. E. M. Boatwright to Charles Snyder [*sic*], May 22, 1937, ibid.

16. E.M.B. to C.S.S., May 5, 1938, ibid.

17. E.M.B. to C.S.S., March or April 1939, ibid.

18. Boatwright wrote Sydnor on Jan. 14; he replied Jan. 23, and her second letter is dated Jan. 27, 1940.

19. His reply is dated Feb. 24, 1940.

20. The letters to Coulter are in the Coulter Historical Collection, Hargrett Rare Book and Manuscript Library, University of Georgia. I am indebted to Professor John Inscoe of that university for searching these out for me.

CHAPTER ONE

1. George R. Gilmer, *Sketches of the First Settlers of Upper Georgia of the Cherokees, and the Author* (New York, 1855), p. 112. (Hereafter referred to as *Sketches*.)

2. Benjamin Martyn, "An Impartial Inquiry into the State and Utility of the Province of Georgia" (London, 1741), in *Georgia Historical Society Collection* (Savannah, 1840), I:160.

3. Georgia, *Colonial Records*, Allen D. Chandler, ed. (Atlanta, 1904), III:375. (Hereafter referred to as Georgia, *Colonial Records*.)
4. Ibid., I:11.
5. Ibid., III:373-75, 382-88.
6. Ibid., III:287-88, 379, 422-26; V:168, 170, 195-96, 288, 199-400, 404, 602, 603.
7. Ibid., II:500.
8. William Blackstone, *Commentaries on the Laws of England*, with Analysis of Contents by Thomas M. Cooley, ed. by James Dewitt Andrews (Chicago, 1899), 4th ed., I:435-36. (Hereafter referred to as Blackstone, *Commentaries*.)
9. Ibid., p. 434.
10. Oliver H. Prince, *A Digest of the Laws of the State of Georgia* (Athens, 1873), Act of 1789, p. 255. (Hereafter referred to as Prince, *Digest*.)
11. Hugh Smith, "A Plea for the Church of Georgia," in *Protestant Episcopal Church Journal of the Conventions in the Diocese of Georgia, 1823-1853, Convention of 1829*, I:9. (Hereafter referred to as "Plea for the Church," in P.E.C., *Jour. of Conv.*, 1829.)
12. Eugene A. Hecker, *A Short History of Woman's Rights* (New York, 1911), pp. 1-49.
13. Ibid., p. 65.
14. I Peter 3:6.
15. I Timothy 2:13-14.
16. I Corinthians 7.
17. Ephesians 5:22-24.
18. I Corinthians 7:10.
19. Ibid., 11, 39; Romans 7:2-4.
20. I Timothy 5:9-17.
21. I Timothy 2:9.
22. Ephesians 6:28-33.
23. I Corinthians 14:34-35.
24. I Timothy 2:11-15.
25. John Langdon-Davis, *A Short History of Women* (New York, 1927), pp. 222-28.
26. Ibid., p. 226.
27. Ibid., p. 203.
28. Ibid., p. 226.
29. Ibid., p. 225.
30. Hecker, *A Short History of Woman's Rights*, p. 58, citing *Patrologia Latina: edite* J.P. Minge, vol. 171, pp. 1698-99.
31. Ephesians 5:23.
32. Ibid., p. 106, citing Gratian, *Distincto*, 30, c. 2—Friedberg, i, p. 107.
33. Ibid., p. 109, citing Gratian, *Causa*, 30, Quest. 5, c. 7—Friedberg, i, p. 1106.
34. Blackstone, *Commentaries*, passim; Chapters Three and Four of this book.

35. H. C. Peeples, "Women under the Law," in *Report of the 31st Session of the Georgia Bar Association*, 1914 (Macon, 1914), p. 167. (Hereafter referred to as G.B.A., *Report*.)
36. Blackstone, *Commentaries*, I: 445.
37. Peeples, "Women under the Law," in G.B.A., *Report*, 1914, p. 168.
38. State *vs.* Macajah Stevens, Richmond County, Superior Court: Minutes, 1805-1811, p. 407.

CHAPTER TWO

1. Elbert W. G. Booger, *Secondary Education in Georgia, 1732-1858* (Philadelphia, 1933), p. 240. (Hereafter referred to as *Secondary Education*.)
2. Ibid., citing C. W. Howard, "Education of a Southern Matron."
3. "The Literary Wife," in *Southern Literary Messenger* XXIII, p. 408. (Hereafter referred to as *So. Lit. Mes.*)
4. Eugenius A. Nesbit, "Views of Female Education and Character," in *Southern Ladies' Book*, vol. I, no. 6 (June 1840), p. 327.
5. "To the Gentlemen of Georgia," in *Southern Ladies' Book*, vol. I, no. 2 (August 1840), p. 112.
6. "Letters of Richard D. Arnold, M.D., 1808-1876," Richard H. Shyrock, ed., in Trinity College *Historical Papers*, series 18-19, p. 34. (Hereafter referred to as "Arnold Letters" in T.C., *Historical Papers*.)
7. "The Literary Wife," in *So. Lit. Mes.*, XXIII, p. 408.
8. "Advice to Young Ladies," in *So. Lit. Mes.*, XV, p. 250.
9. United States, *Compendium of the Seventh Census* (1850); *Report of the Eighth Census Population* (1860).
10. Adiel Sherwood, *A Gazetteer of Georgia*, 4th ed. (Atlanta, 1860), p. 149. (Hereafter referred to as *Gazetteer, 1860*.)
11. "A Letter to Teachers," in *Southern Ladies' Book*, vol. II, no. 5 (November 1840), pp. 266-69.
12. Orville A. Park, "The Puritan in Georgia," in *Georgia Historical Quarterly*, XIII, pp. 370-71. (Hereafter referred to as *G.H.Q.*)
13. Gilmer, *Sketches*, pp. 233-34.
14. Booger, *Secondary Education*, p. 133.
15. Athens, *Southern Banner*, December 19, 1844.
16. James R. Coombs, *Recollections of a Twiggs County Planter*, pp. 30-34.
17. Savannah Sabbath School Teacher's Society, "Circular," in the Mt. Zion *Missionary*, July 29, 1822.
18. Ebenezer Kellogg, *Notes and Reflections during a Journey from Williamstown to the Southern States in 1817-18* [18], p. 111. (Hereafter referred to as *Notes and Reflections*.)
19. Augusta *Georgia Constitutionalist*, November 9, 1841, citing "A Sketch of the History of Education in Georgia," in Savannah *Georgian*, n.d.

20. Coombs, *Recollections of a Twiggs County Planter*, pp. 30-31.
21. Ibid., p. 33.
22. Ibid., pp. 33-34.
23. *Athens Gazette*, April 4, 1815.
24. Emily P. Burke, *Reminiscences of Georgia* (n.p., 1850), p. 197.
25. Ibid., pp. 201-2.
26. Ibid., p. 197.
27. Kellogg, *Notes and Reflections*, pp. 111-12.
28. Ibid., p. 113.
29. Mt. Zion *Missionary*, July 29, 1822.
30. Savannah Sabbath School Teacher's Society, "Circular," in ibid.
31. Burke, *Reminiscences of Georgia*, p. 197.
32. Prince, *Digest*, Act of 1823, p. 21.
33. E. M. Coulter, *A Short History of Georgia* (Chapel Hill, 1933), p. 268. (Hereafter referred to as *History of Georgia*); Jackson County "Regulations," in Milledgeville *Georgia Journal*, August 31, 1824.
34. Jos. Pothill to William Longstreet, July 13 and August 4, 1829, in Richmond County, Inferior Court Records: Poor School Letters and Papers.
35. Ibid., Poor School List, 1830.
36. Booger, *Secondary Education*, p. 110.
37. Richmond County, Superior Court: Minutes, 1830-1835; Presentments of the Grand Jury, January Term, 1832, p. 198.
38. Fannie Anderson to David L. Roath, n.d., n.p., Richmond County, Inferior Court Records: Poor School Letters and Papers.
39. Ibid., October 8, 1861.
40. Athens *Southern Banner*, January 6, 1846.
41. Augusta *Daily Chronicle and Sentinel*, July 3, 1858.
42. Thomas Woody, *A History of Women's Education in the United States* (New York, 1929), I, pp. 238ff., 418, 563-66. (Hereafter referred to as *Women's Education*); Booger, *Secondary Education*, pp. 242-48.
43. Richard H. Shryock, *Georgia and the Union in 1850* (Philadelphia, 1926), pp. 85-86.
44. Augusta *Daily Chronicle and Sentinel*, October 12, 1858.
45. Booger, *Secondary Education*, p. 218.
46. Ibid., pp. 85-89, 216.
47. Ibid., p. 95.
48. Augusta *Daily Constitutionalist and Republic*, August 18, 1853.
49. Booger, *Secondary Education*, pp. 79-81, 179, 117-216.
50. Ibid., pp. 80, 110.
51. Richmond County Academy, *Minutes*, March 16, 1811; January 14, 1815; January 21, 1817.
52. Booger, *Secondary Education*, pp. 79-81, 117, 120, 179.
53. Milledgeville *Georgia Journal*, January 4, 1825.
54. Ibid., p. 180.

55. Ibid., p. 188.
56. Ibid., p. 181.
57. Maryanne MacKay to her mother, Philadelphia, July 15, 1819, Robert MacKay-W. H. Stiles Letters and Papers, 1762-1899. (Hereafter referred to as MacKay-Stiles Letters.)
58. Sarah Semmes, Philadelphia, November 2, 1840, to Louisa Alexander, Adam Leopold Alexander Letters and Papers, 1785-1909. (Hereafter referred to as Alexander Letters and Papers.)
59. Augusta *Chronicle and Gazette of the State*, April 25, 1810.
60. Milledgeville *Georgia Journal*, March 22, 1825.
61. Athens *Southern Banner*, February 8, 1843.
62. Anna Harden to her grandmother, Dalton, Georgia, March 18, 1859, Edward Harden Letters and Papers, 1732-1930. (Hereafter referred to as Harden Letters.)
63. E. Merton Coulter, "Ante-Bellum Academy Movement in Georgia," in *G.H.Q.*, vol. V, no. 4, p. 33.
64. Julia [?], February n.d., 1842, to Louisa Alexander, Alexander Letters and Papers.
65. Washington Female Seminary, *Second Annual Catalogue*, 1840 (Washington, 1840), p. 12. (Hereafter referred to as *Catalogue*, 1840.)
66. Ibid., p. 14.
67. Booger, *Secondary Education*, pp. 241-47.
68. Clifford Alexander to her mother, Washington, March 13, 1851, in *Alexander Letters, 1787-1900*, ed. Marion A. Boggs (Savannah, 1910), p. 149. (Hereafter referred to as *Alexander Letters*.)
69. Julia Barnsley to Harold Barnsley, Montpelier [Macon], February 14, 1851, Godfrey Barnsley Letters and Papers, 1828-1873. (Hereafter referred to as Barnsley Letters.)
70. Adelaid Barnsley to Harold Barnsley, Charleston, November 7, 1847, Barnsley Letters.
71. Sarah Semmes to Louisa Alexander, Philadelphia, November 2, 1840, Alexander Letters and Papers.
72. Elizabeth A. MacKay to her mother, New York, 1825, MacKay-Stiles Letters.
73. Woody, *Women's Education*, I, pp. 434-41; Booger, *Secondary Education*, pp. 125-32.
74. Washington Female Seminary, *Catalogue*, 1840, pp. 9-10.
75. "Arnold Letters," in T.C., *Historical Papers*, series 18-19, p. 34.
76. D. R. Hundley, *Social Relations in our Southern States* (New York, 1860), p. 100. (Hereafter referred to as *Social Relations*.)
77. Warrenton Female Academy Advertisement, in Mt. Zion *Missionary*, December 29, 1823.
78. Booger, *Secondary Education*, pp. 218, 221.
79. Woody, *Women's Education*, II, pp. 188-89.
80. Ibid., pp. 238ff.

81. Ibid., pp. 418, 563-66; Booger, *Secondary Education*, pp. 242-48.
82. Woody, *Women's Education*, II, pp. 184-92.
83. Booger, *Secondary Education*, p. 100.
84. Washington Female Seminary, *Catalogue*, 1840, p. 13; Sherwood, *Gazetteer*, 1860, p. 148.
85. Greensboro Female College, *Catalogue and Circular*, 1853, pp. 5-9.
86. Washington Female Seminary, *Catalogue*, 1840, pp. 5-8.
87. Booger, *Secondary Education*, pp. 182-83.
88. Washington Female Seminary, *Catalogue*, 1840, p. 3.
89. Ibid., p. 10.
90. Athens *Southern Banner*, January 20, 1843.
91. L. Pierce, "On Female Education," in *Southern Ladies' Book*, vol. I, no. 3 (March 1840), pp. 129-37.
92. Woody, *Women's Education*, II, p. 139.
93. George F. Pierce, "The Georgia Female College, Its Origin and Prospects," in *Southern Ladies' Book*, vol. I, no. 2 (February 1840), p. 66. (Hereafter referred to as "Georgia Female College.")
94. Daniel Chandler, *Address on Female Education*, delivered at the University of Georgia, 1835 (Washington, 1835), pp. 11-15.
95. Pierce, "Georgia Female College," in *Southern Ladies' Book*, vol. I, no. 2, p. 66.
96. Woody, *Women's Education*, II, p. 161, citing "Charter" approved December 23, 1836.
97. John S. Wilson, "Female Medical Education," in *Southern Medical and Surgical Journal* (New Series), X, p. 15. (Hereafter referred to as *So. Med. and Sur. Journal.*)
98. Woody, *Women's Education*, pp. 161-67.
99. Pierce, "Georgia Female College," in *Southern Ladies' Book*, vol. I, no. 2, pp. 65-74.
100. Columbus *Sentinel and Herald*, September 27, 1838.
101. Greensboro Female College, *Catalogue and Circular*, 1853, pp. 4-20.
102. Milledgeville *Georgia Journal*, January 2, 1838.
103. Augusta *Daily Chronicle and Sentinel*, August 10, 1852.
104. Augusta *Evening Dispatch*, January 4, 1859.
105. H. V. Johnson, *Address at the Commencement Exercises of the Wesleyan Female College, July 14, 1853* (n.p., 1853), p. 23. (Hereafter referred to as *Address*.)
106. J. D. B. DeBow, ed., *The Commercial Review of the South and West* (New Orleans, 1846-1880), X, p. 375. (Hereafter referred to as *DeBow's Review*.)
107. Woody, *History of Women's Education*, II, p. 198.
108. Pierce, "Georgia Female College," in *Southern Ladies' Book*, vol. I, no. 2 (February 1840), pp. 65-74.
109. Ibid.
110. Ibid., p. 66.
111. Greensboro Female College, *Catalogue and Circular*, 1853, pp. 5-9.

112. Pierce, "Georgia Female College," in *Southern Ladies' Book*, vol. I, no. 2, p. 66.
113. Chandler, *Address on Female Education*, p. 5.
114. Wilson, "Female Medical Education," in *So. Med. and Sur. Journal*, X, p. 6.
115. Ibid., p. 8.
116. Ibid., p. 14.
117. Eugenius A. Nesbit, "Views of Female Education," in *Southern Ladies' Book*, vol. I, no. 6 (May 1840), pp. 321-25.
118. Booger, *Secondary Education*, p. 240, citing Howard, "Education of a Southern Matron."
119. Woody, *Women's Education*, II, pp. 184-92.
120. Johnson, *Address*, pp. 11-13.
121. Booger, *Secondary Education*, p. 240, citing Howard, "Education of the Southern Matron."
122. Wilson, "Female Medical Education," in *So. Med. and Sur. Journal*, X, pp. 13-16.
123. Eugenius A. Nesbit, *Thoughts on the Beautiful*, an address delivered at the commencement of the Griffin Synodical Female College, June 1857 ("Empire State" Job Office, n.p., 1857), p. 9.

CHAPTER THREE

1. Chapter One of this book.
2. Chapter Four of this book.
3. Blackstone, *Commentaries*, III, 139; Georgia, *Code of 1861* (Atlanta, 1861), comp. by R. H. Clark, T. R. R. Cobb, and D. Irwin, sec. 2949.
4. Cobb, *Digest*, Act of 1819, p. 342.
5. Chapter Four of this book.
6. Blackstone, *Commentaries*, I, 433.
7. Ibid., pp. 445-46, note.
8. Peeples, "Women under the Law," in G. B. A., *Reports*, 1914, p. 168.
9. Rebecca L. Felton, *Country Life in Georgia in the Days of My Youth* (Atlanta, 1919), p. 63. (Hereafter referred to as *Country Life*.)
10. Felix Gilbert to Sarah Hillhouse, July 14, 1804, *Alexander Letters*, p. 28.
11. Anna C. M. Ritchie, "An Old Maid," in Mary Forrest, *Women of the South Distinguished in Literature* (New York, 1865), pp. 96-97. (Hereafter referred to as *Women of the South*.)
12. Thomas Dew, "Dissertation on the Characteristic Differences between the Sexes," in *So. Lit. Mes.*, I, p. 498. (Hereafter referred to as "Differences between the Sexes.")
13. Harriet Alexander to Clifford Alexander, September 4, 1844, *Alexander Letters*, p. 87.

14. M. S. Scarborough to Eugenie J. West, August 30, 1856, George W. West Letters, 1806-1876. (Hereafter referred to as West Letters.)
15. Arthur C. Calhoun, *A Social History of the American Family* (Cleveland, 1919), I, p. 245, citing Dr. Brickett who practiced at Edenton, N.C., about 1731. (Hereafter referred to as *History of the American Family.*)
16. William E. Dodd, *The Cotton Kingdom* (New Haven, 1919), p. 72.
17. Roseline Gauvine Hardin to Eveline R. T. Jackson [1844], Harden Letters; John McIntosh Kell to Margaret S. Baillie Kell, August 26, 1857, John McIntosh Kell Letters, 1841-1865.
18. Hundley, *Social Relations*, pp. 123-24.
19. John Howard Payne to Mary E. G. Harden, February 17, 1854; James Rogers to same, December 10, 1842; William Mitchell to same, February 17, 1854; Harden Letters.
20. Mary E. G. Harden to William Mitchell, February 20, 1854, Harden Letters.
21. Columbus *Sentinel and Herald*, October 18, 1838, citing *Southern Literary Journal*.
22. "Advice to Young Ladies," in *So. Lit. Mes.*, XV, p. 249.
23. Mark (pseudo. for Mary) Pencil, *The White Sulphur Papers, or Life at the Springs of Western Virginia* (New York, 1839), p. 87. (Hereafter referred to as *White Sulphur Papers.*)
24. United States, *Compendium of the Seventh Census* (1850); *Report of the Eighth Census* (1860), *Population*.
25. United States, *Compendium of the Seventh Census* (1850).
26. Augusta *Daily Constitutionalist*, February 22, 1851.
27. J. S. Buckingham, *The Slave States of America* (London, 1842), II, 12-14. (Hereafter referred to as *Slave States.*)
28. Felton, *Country Life*, p. 62.
29. I. S. Bradwell to Adam Alexander, July 26, 1820, Alexander Letters and Papers.
30. Buckingham, *Slave States*, I, 127.
31. Ibid., I, 13-14.
32. W. J. Sasnett, *Marriage*, an address delivered at the Commencement of LaGrange Female College, LaGrange, Ga., July 6, 1859, p. 35. (Hereafter referred to as *Marriage.*)
33. "A Woman Worshipper in Trouble," in *So. Lit. Mes.*, XXIII, pp. 101-9.
34. "Hooped Dresses," in *So. Lit. Mes.*, XXII, pp. 31-39.
35. "Eudora Unhooped," in *So. Lit. Mes.*, XXII, pp. 214-21.
36. I. S. Bradwell to Adam Alexander, July 26, 1820, Alexander Letters and Papers.
37. Felton, *Country Life*, p. 63.
38. Gilmer, *Sketches*, p. 68.
39. Ibid., pp. 62-69, 145, 220-21.
40. Johnson, *Address*, p. 26.
41. Sasnett, *Marriage*, p. 17.

42. Powell W. Bird, "Physiological Incompatibility between the Sexes in Relation to Progeny," in *Savannah Journal of Medicine*, I (March, 1859), pp. 374-76.
43. Buckingham, *Slave States*, II, 13-14.
44. Sasnett, *Marriage*, p. 17.
45. George Barnsley to Godfrey Barnsley, May 12, 1830, Barnsley Letters.
46. [?] to Godfrey Barnsley, August 10, 1828, Barnsley Letters.
47. Jesse Mercer to Nancy Anthony, March 5, 1805, Jesse Mercer Letters.
48. Edward Harden to Mary Harden, December 3, 1843, Harden Letters.
49. Nesbit, *Thoughts on the Beautiful*, p. 5.
50. Smith, "Plea for the Church," in P.E.C., *Jour. of Conv.*, 1829, I, 7.
51. I. S. Bradwell to Adam Alexander, July 26, 1820, Alexander Letters and Papers.
52. Paul Hamilton Hayne, "Marguerite," in *Poems* [of Paul Hamilton Hayne] (Boston, 1882), p. 143.
53. Edgar Allen Poe, *Annabel Lee.*
54. Thomas Dunn, "Ben Bolt," in Kate E. Staton, comp., *Old Southern Songs of the Period of the Confederacy*: Dixie Trophy Collection (New York, 1926), p. 15. (Hereafter referred to as *Southern Songs.*)
55. Alice Hawthorne, "Listen to the Mocking Bird," in Staton, *Southern Songs*, p. 56.
56. Chapter Five of this book.
57. George Fitzhugh, *Sociology for the South* (Richmond, 1854), p. 217.
58. Garnett Andrews, *Reminiscences of an Old Georgia Lawyer* (Atlanta, 1870), p. 54. (Hereafter referred to as *Reminiscences.*)
59. "Female Education," in *So. Lit. Mes.*, VI, pp. 451-57.
60. Felix Gilbert to Sarah Hillhouse, July 11, 1804, *Alexander Letters*, p. 27.
61. Almira L. Phelps, "Belles," in Forrest, *Women of the South*, p. 193.
62. Robert Lewis to Edward R. Harden, October 18, 1831, Harden Letters.
63. Dew, "Differences between the Sexes," in *So. Lit. Mes.*, I, p. 498.
64. *Columbian Museum and Savannah Advertiser*, August 27, 1803.
65. Mt. Zion *Missionary*, May 27, 1822.
66. "Flirtation," in *So. Lit. Mes.*, XV, p. 345.
67. Sasnett, *Marriage*, pp. 23-25.
68. "Flirtation," in *So. Lit. Mes.*, XV, p. 345-49.
69. Sarah Alexander to Louisa Alexander, August 11, 1832, *Alexander Letters*, p. 63.
70. J. H. Reid to Godfrey Barnsley, February, 1847; same to same, April 5, 1847.
71. John McIntosh Kell to Julia Kell, March 31, 1858, Kell Letters.
72. Augusta *Daily Chronicle and Sentinel*, May 7, 1852.
73. Augusta *Chronicle and Sentinel*, January 6, 1845, citing Columbus *Enquirer*.
74. Clifford Alexander to her mother, March 13, 1851, *Alexander Letters*, pp. 147-48.
75. E. M. Coulter, *College Life in the Old South* (New York, 1928), p. 276. (Hereafter referred to as *College Life.*)

76. Ibid., p. 275, citing "Frederick Diary, in the 'Georgia Cracker, November 1921,'" p. 12.
77. Anna Harden to her grandmother, March 18, 1859, Harden Letters.
78. E. N. W. to Louisa Alexander, 1840, Alexander Letters and Papers.
79. Felix Gilbert to Sarah Hillhouse, May 12, 1802, *Alexander Letters*, p. 18.
80. Julia [?] to Louisa Alexander, September 24, 1843, Alexander Letters and Papers.
81. Sigman Spaeth, *Read 'em and Weep* (Garden City, 1927), pp. 34-40.
82. W. T. Thompson, "Supposing a Case" in *Major Jones Courtship . . . [and] . . . Thirteen Humorous Sketches* (New York, 1872), p. 193.
83. Andrews, *Reminiscences*, p. 39.
84. "The Women of France," in *So. Lit. Mes.*, V, p. 302.
85. Buckingham, *Slave States*, II, 135.
86. Ibid.
87. Andrews, *Reminiscences*, p. 12.
88. Gilmer, *Sketches*, p. 179.
89. Ibid., p. 180.
90. Andrews, *Reminiscences*, p. 12.
91. John H. Reid to Godfrey Barnsley, April 5, 1847.
92. Pencil, *White Sulphur Papers*, pp. 76, 134.
93. M. S. Scarborough to Eugenia J. West, August 30, 1856, West Letters.
94. Adam Alexander to Louisa Alexander, August 31, 1841, *Alexander Letters*, p. 73.
95. M. S. Scarborough to Eugenia J. West, August 30, 1856, West Letters.
96. Chapter Five of this book.
97. Andrews, *Reminiscences*, p. 78.
98. Ibid.
99. Ibid., pp. 77-78.
100. "Courtship Made Easy," in *So. Lit. Mes.*, XXV, pp. 13-16.
101. Ibid., pp. 13-20.
102. Ibid., p. 14.
103. Ibid., p. 15.
104. Ibid., p. 16.
105. Ibid., pp. 14-15.
106. Ibid., p. 18.
107. Ibid.
108. Ibid., pp. 18-19.
109. Ibid., p. 20.
110. Augusta *Evening Dispatch*, January 17, 1859, citing "Memphis Appeal."
111. "Courtship Made Easy," in *So. Lit. Mes.*, XXV, pp. 19-20.
112. Augusta *Georgia Constitutionalist*, February 25, 1841, citing Batesville [Ark.] *News*.
113. Athens *Southern Banner*, March 27, 1840, citing *National Intelligence*.
114. Gilmer, *Sketches*, p. 97.

115. Sarah [Semmes] to Louisa Alexander [1840], Alexander Letters and Papers.
116. James Rogers to Mary Harden, December 10, 1842, Harden Letters.
117. *Atlanta Journal*, March 17, 1929.
118. John Howard Payne to Mary E. G. Harden, July 14, 1840, Harden Letters.
119. Felix Gilbert to Sarah Hillhouse, July 11, 1804, *Alexander Letters*, p. 27.
120. John Conolly to Godfrey Barnsley, May 8, 1847; same to same, May 27, 1847; Anna G. Barnsley to Godfrey Barnsley, February 25, 1847, Barnsley Letters.
121. Samuel K. Jennings, *The Married Ladies' Companion or the Poor Man's Friend* (Richmond, 1804), p. 16.
122. Methodist *Form of Discipline*, 1792 (Philadelphia, 1792), sec. 6, pp. 54-55; ibid., 1856 (New York, 1856), chapter IX, sec. 2, pp. 87-88.
123. Harris *vs.* Tison, 63 Georgia 630.
124. Mt. Zion *Missionary*, May 30, 1821.
125. Augusta *Chronicle and Gazetteer* of the State, March 6, 1802.
126. Athens *Southern Banner*, December 18, 1840.
127. H. J. Wayne to Mary Harden, April 20, 1844, Harden Letters.
128. Sarah Mackay to Kate Mackay, September 1847, Mackay-Stiles Letters.
129. H. J. Wayne to Mary Harden, January 11, 1843, Harden Letters.
130. Louisa Gilmer to George R. Gilmer, April 30, 1853, *Alexander Letters*, p. 185.
131. Ibid.
132. Mary E. Huger to Mrs. Sumpter, April 20, 1812, Mackay-Stiles Letters.
133. M. C. Elliott to Kate Mackay, January 1845, Mackay-Stiles Letters.
134. Mary Clifford Hull, "The Family Chestnut Tree," in *Alexander Letters*, pp. 125-26.
135. "Benjamin Hawkins Letters, 1796-1806," in *Collection of the Georgia Historical Society* (Savannah, 1916), IX, p. 302.
136. Kellogg, *Notes and Reflections*, p. 102.
137. Georgia, *Code of 1861*, sec. 1652.
138. Askew *vs.* Dupree, 30 Georgia 173.
139. Ibid., Georgia, *Code of 1861*, sec. 1653-1658.
140. Ibid., sec. 2950.
141. Askew *vs.* Dupree, 30 Georgia 173.
142. Murphy *vs.* the State of Georgia, 50 Georgia 150.
143. Dillon *vs.* Dillon, 60 Georgia 203.
144. Blackstone, *Commentaries*, I, 433-34.
145. T. R. R. Cobb, *Digest of the Statute Laws of Georgia* (Athens, 1851), Act of 1799, p. 282; 1849, p. 287. (Hereafter referred to as *Digest*.); Georgia, *Code of 1861*, sec. 1653-1664.
146. Blackstone, *Commentaries*, I, 433-37.
147. Fitsgerald *vs.* Garvin, *et al.*, Chatham County Superior Court Records, Minute Book "G," February 1810, p. 257.
148. Askew *vs.* Dupree, 30 Georgia 173.
149. Ibid.

150. Ibid.
151. Lorenzo Dow, "Reflections on the Important Subject of Matrimony," *History of Cosmopolite, or the Writings of Rev. Lorenzo Dow* (Philadelphia, 1855), pp. 399-418. (Hereafter referred to as *History of Cosmopolite.*)
152. Ibid., p. 402.
153. Ibid., pp. 399-418.
154. Georgia, *Acts of the General Assembly*, Act of 1832, p. 154; 1844, p. 229.
155. Chapter Four of this book.

CHAPTER FOUR

1. Georgia Constitution of 1861, Art. V, Sec. I, in Walter McElreath, ed., *A Treatise on the Constitution of Georgia* (Atlanta, 1912), p. 232. (Hereafter referred to as *Constitution of Georgia.*)
2. Georgia Charter of the Province, in ibid., pp. 212-37.
3. Georgia Constitution of 1777, Art. IX, in ibid., p. 232.
4. Georgia Constitution of 1789, Art. IV, Sec. I, in ibid., p. 247.
5. Georgia Constitution of 1798, Art. IV, Sec. I, in ibid., p. 264.
6. Georgia Constitution of 1861, Art. V, Sec. I, in ibid., p. 296.
7. Buckingham, *Slave States*, II, 182-83.
8. Chapter Six of this book.
9. Andrews, *Reminiscences*, p. 37.
10. Buckingham, *Slave States*, II, 182-83.
11. I. S. Bradwell to Adam Alexander, May 31, 1820, Alexander Letters and Papers.
12. Ibid.
13. Milledgeville *Daily Federal Union*, November 17, 1859.
14. Buckingham, *Slave States*, II, 182-83.
15. Georgia, *Acts of the General Assembly*, Act of 1829, p. 94; Foster Blodgett, Jr. to David L. Roath, January 18, 1860, Roath Letters.
16. Prince, *Digest*, Act of 1784, p. 570.
17. Blackstone, *Commentaries*, I, 442.
18. Georgia, *Code of 1861*, sec. 1700.
19. Blackstone, *Commentaries*, III, 434-36; Georgia, *Code of 1861*, sec. 1722; Bell *et al vs.* Bell, I Georgia 637.
20. Prince, *Digest*, Act of 1789, p. 225.
21. A woman's debts sometimes served as a serious drawback to romance:

A Methodist at Savannah, brought by Mr. Whitfield from Pennsylvania [wrote the Earl of Egmont in his *Journal*, of Tom Slack] courts the Widow Harris of the same town, a remarkable industrious and thriving woman, and nothing wanting but the minister to marry them; but finding her last husband left some debts, and that she had not administered, so that if he marry'd her he should be lyable to those debts, flys off and declares his conscience would not let him marry one that was no Christian, as he found by her frequenting the Church of England.

Earl of Egmont's "Journal," in Georgia, *Colonial Records*, V, 460-61.

22. Georgia, *Acts of the General Assembly*, Act of 1856, p. 229.
23. Georgia, *Code of 1861*, sec. 1705.
24. Blackstone, *Commentaries*, I, 443.
25. Cobb, *Digest*, pp. 16, 163-65, 171, 178, 228-31.
26. Prince, *Digest*, pp. 233, 237, 251, 253.
27. Cobb, *Digest*, Act of 1838, pp. 296-98; John Silcox, and others, *vs.* John Nelson and others, Richmond County Superior Court, 1842 Term., in *Decisions of the Superior Courts of the State of Georgia*, Part I (Augusta, 1843), pp. 24-25. (Hereafter referred to as Georgia, *Superior Court Decisions*.)
·28. Penalton and Co. *vs.* Mills and *al*, Cobb Superior Court, 1843 Term, in Georgia, *Superior Court Decisions*, Part II (Augusta, 1844), pp. 116-17; Royston *vs.* Royston, 21 Georgia 161.
29. A. Edwards and wife *vs.* B. Leigh and W. Leigh, Richmond County, Superior Court Records: Minute Book, 1805-1811, April Term, 1818, p. 246.
30. Prince, *Digest*, Act of 1804, p. 233; Cobb, *Digest*, Act of 1845, p. 294; Uriah B. Holden and wife *vs.* David Harrell, 6 Georgia 126.
31. Gorman *et al vs.* Wood, 68 Georgia 524, 73 Georgia 370; Wilson *vs.* Wilson Sewing Machine Company, 76 Georgia 104.
32. Georgia, *Acts of the General Assembly*, 1851-1852, Act of 1851, p. 237.
33. Cobb, *Digest*, Acts of 1810; p. 379; 1822, p. 385; 1834, p. 388; 1841, p. 389; 1843, p. 390; 1847, p. 392; Smith *vs.* Taylor and Wife, Louise Lynch *vs.* same, 11 Georgia 22.
34. Wilkes County, *Records*, *Early Records of Georgia*, comp. by Grace G. Davidson (Macon, 1932), I, 47. (Hereafter referred to as Wilkes County, *Records*.)
35. Ibid., p. 85.
36. Penalton and Co. *vs.* Mills and *al*, in *Decisions of the Superior Courts of the State of Georgia*, Part II (Augusta, 1844), pp. 116-67. (Hereafter referred to as Georgia, *Superior Court Decisions*.)
37. Leota S. Driver, *Fanny Kemble* (Chapel Hill, 1933).
38. Frances Anne Kemble, *Journal of a Residence on a Georgia Plantation* (New York, 1863), passim. (Hereafter referred to as *Journal*.)
39. Driver, *Fanny Kemble*, pp. 92-114.
40. Pierce Mease Butler, *Mr. Butler's Statement, Originally prepared with the aid of his Professional Council* [Philadelphia, 1850]. (Hereafter referred to as *Statement*.)
41. Ibid., pp. 22-24.
42. Ibid., p. 125.

43. Ibid., p. 170, citing letter to Harriet.
44. Gorman *et al vs.* Wood, 68 Georgia 524; 73 Georgia 370; Wilson *vs.* the Wilson Sewing Machine Company, 76 Georgia 104.
45. Ibid.
46. Sayre and Sayre *vs.* Flournoy, adm'r and others, 3 Georgia 541.
47. Blackstone, *Commentaries*, II, 397, 398.
48. Gorman *et al vs.* Wood, 68 Georgia 524, 73 Georgia 370; Wilson *vs.* the Wilson Sewing Machine Co., 76 Georgia 104.
49. Gorman *et al vs.* Wood, 68 Georgia 524.
50. Oglesby and wife *vs.* Hall, 30 Georgia 386.
51. Augusta *Georgia Constitutionalist*, June 8, 1846.
52. George Paschal, *Ninety-Four Years, or Agnes Paschal* (n.p., 1871), p. 97. (Hereafter referred to as *Ninety-Four Years*.)
53. Blackstone, *Commentaries*, II, 293 (note).
54. Cobb, *Digest*, Act of 1847, p. 180.
55. Chatham County, Superior Court Records: Minute Book "2 F," Folio 107, Lydia C. Pepper and Alexander Fawnes.
56. Ibid., Book "Z," Folio 507, Joseph Welcher and Ann Miller.
57. Georgia, *Code of 1861*, sec. 1725.
58. Chatham County, Inferior Court Records: Will of William Lowden, no. 50.
59. Blackstone, *Commentaries*, I, 444 (note).
60. Humphrey *vs.* Copeland, 54 Georgia 543.
61. Georgia, *Code of 1861*, sec. 1702, 1725-1735; McBride *vs.* Greenwood and others, 11 Georgia 393; Kempton *et al vs.* Holland and Co., 24 Georgia 52; Hicks *vs.* Johnson, 24 Georgia 194.
62. Georgia, *Acts of the General Assembly*, Act of 1866, p. 146.
63. Harriett Martineau, *Society in America* (New York, 1837), II, 238.
64. Frances Anne Kemble, *Records of Later Life* (London, 1882), I, 28.
65. Georgia, *Acts of the General Assembly*, 1851-1852; 1853-1854; 1855-1856.
66. Georgia, *Code of 1861*, sec. 1708.
67. Georgia, *Acts of the General Assembly*, Act of 1866, p. 146.
68. Wilkes County, *Records*, II, 125.
69. Ibid., I, 58, 60, 67, 78, 92; II, 127, 134.
70. Royston *vs.* Royston, 21 Georgia 161; Blackstone, *Commentaries*, II, 129; Georgia, *Code of 1861*, sec. 1741.
71. Cobb, *Digest*, Acts of: 1760, p. 161; 1768, p. 163; 1785, pp. 164-65; 1842, p. 178.
72. Ibid., Act of 1826, p. 171.
73. Dennis and others *vs.* Ray, 10 Georgia 435.
74. Cobb, *Digest*, Acts of: 1830, p. 230; 1850, p. 231; Georgia, *Acts of the General Assembly*, 1845, p. 71.
75. Cobb, *Digest*, Acts of: 1838, p. 296; 1850, pp. 297-99; Dennis and others *vs.* Ray, 9 Georgia 261.
76. Prince, *Digest*, Acts of: 1789, p. 225; 1827, p. 251.

77. Ibid., Act of 1829, p. 253; Georgia, *Code of 1861*, sec. 2452.
78. Ibid., Act of 1804, p. 233.
79. Blackstone, *Commentaries*, I, 443-45.
80. Smith *vs.* Taylor and wife, Louise Lynch *vs.* same, 11 Georgia 22.
81. Blackstone, *Commentaries*, I, 445.
82. Cobb, *Digest*, Penal Code of 1833, p. 778.
83. Blackstone, *Commentaries*, I, 445.
84. Robert M. Charlton, *Address*, delivered at the commencement of LaGrange Female College, July 1853 (Savannah, 1853).
85. Orville A. Park, comp., *History of Georgia in the Eighteenth Century as Recorded in the Reports of the Georgia Bar Association*. Reprint from G.B.A., *Report*, June 1921, p. 90. [Macon, 1921]
86. Augusta *Evening Dispatch*, February 1, 1859.
87. Augusta *Daily Constitutionalist*, July 4, 1847, citing Muscogee *Democrat*, 1st inst.
88. Georgia, *Acts of the General Assembly*, 1857, p. 126.
89. Blackstone, *Commentaries*, III, 139-40; Georgia, *Code of 1861*, sec. 2949.
90. Augusta *Chronicle and Gazette of the State*, October 14, 1797.
91. Blackstone, *Commentaries*, II, 140; Georgia, *Code of 1861*, sec. 2949.
92. *So. Lit. Mes.*, I, pp. 523-24.
93. Mary S. Benson, *Women in Eighteenth-Century America* (New York, 1935), pp. 184-85, citing David Ramsay, "Memoirs of the Life of Martha Laurens Ramsay," pp. 41-42.
94. Butler, *Statement*, p. 9.
95. Ibid., pp. 9-10.
96. Ibid., p. 11.
97. Dorothie Bobbé, *Fanny Kemble* (New York, 1831), p. 247, citing Butler, *Statement*.
98. "Grandfather" to [?], 1790, MacKay-Stiles Papers.
99. Julia Barnsley to Godfrey Barnsley, August 7, 1834.
100. Emily I. Thomas to Mitta [Thomas], n.d., Alice E. [Andrews] Niles, Niles Letters, 1859-1864.
101. *Columbus Enquirer*, October 18, 1834.
102. Blackstone, *Commentaries*, I, 454.
103. Ibid., pp. 447-52; Georgia, *Code of 1861*, sec. 1783.
104. Fanny Kemble to Harriet Martineau, September 22, 1846, in Kemble, *Records of Later Life*, III, 137.
105. Pierce Butler to Mrs. Sedgwick, May 31, 1839, in Butler, *Statement*, p. 33.
106. Driver, *Fanny Kemble*, pp. 114-56; Butler, *Statement*, passim.
107. Fanny Kemble to Pierce Butler, 1838, in Butler, *Statement*, p. 27.
108. Pierce Butler to Mrs. Sedgwick, May 31, 1839, in ibid., p. 38.
109. Cobb, *Digest*, Acts of: 1792, p. 309; 1799, p. 281; 1805, p. 283; 1828, p. 327.
110. Ibid., Act of 1845, p. 335.

111. Ibid.
112. Georgia, *Code of 1861*, sec. 1685.
113. Georgia, *Code of 1868*, sec. 1783-84.
114. Prince, *Digest*, Act of 1804, p. 233.
115. Ibid.
116. Ibid.
117. Cobb, *Digest*, Act of 1841, p. 286.
118. Ibid., Act of 1843, p. 197; Georgia, *Code of 1861*, sec. 2452.
119. Cobb, *Digest*, Act of 1845, p. 297.
120. Uriah B. Holden and wife *vs.* David Harrell, 6 Georgia 126.
121. Georgia, *Code of 1861*, sec. 1750.
122. Ibid., sec. 1751.
123. Ibid., sec. 1751-52; Cobb, *Digest*, Acts of: 1816, p. 293; 1850, p. 299.
124. Locke *vs.* State, 3 Georgia 534.
125. Cobb, *Digest*, Act of 1793, pp. 148-49; ibid., Penal Code of 1833, sec. 237, p. 818; Georgia, *Code of 1861*, sec. 4640-43.
126. Richmond County, Inferior Court Records: Bastard Bonds.
127. Wilkes County, *Records*, I, 145.
128. Chapter Three of this book.
129. Liberty County, *Records, Annals of Georgia*, comp. by Carolina Price (New York, 1928), I, 84. (Hereafter referred to as Liberty County, *Records*.)
130. Wilkes County, *Records*, I, 42.
131. Blackstone, *Commentaries*, IV, 358.
132. Richmond County, Superior Court Records: Minutes 1816-1819. Charge to Grand Jury, June Term 1817, pp. 168-69.
133. Chatham County, Superior Court Records: Minutes 1841, pp. 108, 131.
134. Prince, *Digest*, Penal Code of 1833, sec. 20-22, p. 624.
135. Blackstone, *Commentaries*, III, 93.
136. Ibid., I, 440-41.
137. Georgia Constitution of 1798, Art. III, Sec. IX, in McElreath, *Constitution of Georgia*, p. 263; Prince, *Digest*, Act of 1803, pp. 187-88.
138. Georgia Constitution of 1798, amendment to Art. III, Sec. IX, in ibid., p. 274.
139. Prince, *Digest*, Act of 1806, p. 187.
140. Georgia Constitution of 1798, Art. III, Sec. IX, in McElreath, *Constitution of Georgia*, p. 263.
141. Chatham County, Superior Court Records: Minutes; Judgments.
142. Head *vs.* Head, 2 Georgia 191.
143. Blackstone, *Commentaries*, I, 440.
144. Head *vs.* Head, 2 Georgia 191.
145. Georgia Constitution of 1798, amendment, Art. III, Sec. IX, in McElreath, *Constitution of Georgia*, p. 278.
146. Georgia, *Acts of the General Assembly*, Act of 1850, pp. 151-52.
147. Prince, *Digest*, Act of 1806, p. 188.
148. Augusta *Daily Constitutionalist*, December 11, 1859.

149. Park *vs.* Barron, 20 Georgia 702.
150. Milledgeville *Daily Federal Union*, December 15, 1859.
151. Ibid.
152. Head *vs.* Head, 2 Georgia 191.
153. Cobb, *Digest*, Act of 1849, p. 227.
154. Augusta *Daily Constitutionalist*, December 11, 1859.
155. Cobb, *Digest*, Preamble to the amendment of 1833, p. 1123.
156. Prince, *Digest*, p. 187.
157. Augusta *Daily Constitutionalist*, December 11, 1859.
158. Head *vs.* Head, 2 Georgia 191.
159. Cobb, *Digest*, Act of 1806, p. 225; Georgia, *Code of 1861*, sec. 1684, 1689-96.
160. Ibid., sec. 1676.
161. Ibid., sec. 1690-94.
162. Elizabeth Harper to the Brothers and Sisters of Mars Hill Church, November 12, 1818, Harden Papers.
163. Chatham County, Superior Court Records: Judgment no. 2899.
164. John Rutledge to Robert MacKay, February 11, 1804, MacKay-Stiles Papers.
165. *Athens Gazette*, June 16, 1814.
166. Milledgeville *Georgia Patriot*, July 11, 1826.
167. Athens *Southern Banner*, June 13, 1842.

CHAPTER FIVE

1. L. C. Gray, *History of Agriculture in the Southern States to 1860* (Washington, 1833), I, 484. (Hereafter referred to as *Agriculture in the United States.*)
2. Charles Lyell, *A Second Visit to the United States of North America* (New York, 1849), I, 244. (Hereafter referred to as *Second Visit to U.S.*)
3. Coulter, *History of Georgia*, pp. 253-54.
4. Hundley, *Social Relations*, pp. 162-90.
5. Kemble, *Journal*, p. 65.
6. Hundley, *Social Relations*, p. 262.
7. Julia A. Flisch, "The Common People of the Old South," in *American Historical Reports*, I (1908), pp. 133-42.
8. W. M. Brewer, "Some Effects of the Plantation System upon the Ante-Bellum South," in *G.H.Q.*, XI, 226.
9. Gray, *Agriculture in the Southern States*, I, 484.
10. Martineau, *Society in America*, I, 104-5.
11. Ibid., p. 105.
12. Buckingham, *Slave States*, I, 489-90.
13. Hundley, *Social Relations*, p. 98.
14. Burke, *Reminiscences of Georgia*, pp. 208-9.

15. Bazil Hall, *Travels in North America in the Years 1827-1828* (Edinburgh, Scotland, 1829), II, 258-59. (Hereafter referred to as *Travels in North America.*)
16. Arthur M. Schlesinger, *New Viewpoints in American History* (New York, 1928), p. 127, citing President Eliot. (Hereafter referred to as *New Viewpoints.*)
17. Gray, *Agriculture in the Southern States*, I, 487.
18. Hundley, *Social Relations*, p. 264.
19. Ibid., p. 74.
20. Ralph B. Flanders, "Farish Carter, A Forgotten Man of the Old South," in *G.H.Q.*, XV, 142-72.
21. Frederick Law Olmsted, *Journey in the Seaboard Slave States* (New York, 1855), pp. 17, 384. (Hereafter referred to as *Journey in Slave States.*)
22. James Stuart, *Three Years in North America* (Edinburgh, Scotland, 1833), II, 106.
23. Andrews, *Reminiscences*, p. 15.
24. Ibid., p. 34.
25. Amelia M. Murray, *Letters from the United States, Cuba, and Canada* (New York, 1856), II, 37-38.
26. Hall, *Travels in America*, II, 271.
27. Ibid., pp. 272-73.
28. Kemble, *Journal*, pp. 25-27.
29. Kellogg, *Notes and Reflections*, pp. 131-32.
30. Burke, *Reminiscences of Georgia*, pp. 118-20.
31. E. Steadman, *The Southern Manufacturer* (Gallatin, Tennessee, 1858), pp. 68-69.
32. Tyrone Power, *Impressions of America, During the Years 1833, 1834, and 1835* (London, 1836), II, 123. (Hereafter referred to as *Impressions of America.*)
33. Ibid., pp. 124-25.
34. Dow, "History of Cosmopolite, or Lorenzo's Journal," in *History of Cosmopolite*, p. 127.
35. Powers, *Impressions of America*, II, 132-33.
36. B. P. Hillhouse to George R. Gilmer, February 4, 1815, Alexander Letters and Papers.
37. Isaac V. Brown, *Memoir of the Rev. Robert Finley* (New Brunswick, 1819), p. 127.
38. Andrews, *Reminiscences*, p. 38.
39. Sarah Gilbert to Felix Gilbert, May 17, 1806, *Alexander Letters*, p. 34.
40. Harriet Alexander to Clifford Alexander, December 1849, *Alexander Letters*, pp. 133-34.
41. Charles Caldwell, "Evils of Tight Lacing," in *So. Lit. Mes.*, VII, pp. 731-32.
42. Augusta *Daily Constitutionalist and Republican*, July 24, 1853.
43. Augusta *Evening Dispatch*, February 15, 1859.
44. Augusta *Georgia Constitutionalist*, August 7, 1841.
45. Andrews, *Reminiscences*, p. 14.

46. Harriet Alexander to Clifford Alexander, 1849, *Alexander Letters*, pp. 134-35.
47. Buckingham, *Slave States*, II, 92.
48. Augusta *Daily Chronicle and Sentinel*, February 12, 1846.
49. Felton, *Country Life*, p. 64.
50. Buckingham, *Slave States*, II, 155.
51. Felton, *Country Life*, p. 64.
52. Methodist *Form of Discipline*, 1848, chapter VII, sec. I, 81.
53. Felton, *Country Life*, p. 63.
54. T. Stanton and H. S. Blatch, *Elizabeth Cady Stanton* (New York, 1922), pp. 171-74.
55. Augusta *Daily Chronicle and Sentinel*, February 17, 1852.
56. Augusta *Daily Constitutionalist*, June 14, 1851, citing Savannah *News*, 12th inst.
57. *DeBow's Review*, XIII, pp. 279-80.
58. Felton, *Country Life*, p. 64.
59. James Ewell, *The Medical Companion* (Philadelphia, 1817), p. 243.
60. Pencil, *White Sulphur Springs*, p. 84.
61. John T. Howard, *Our American Music* (New York, 1930), pp. 134-261; Sigman Spaeth, *Read 'em and Weep* (Garden City, 1927), passim.
62. Julia Blanche Monroe, Album, Darian, Georgia, 1853-1856. (Hereafter referred to as Monroe, Album.)
63. Hull, "The Family Chestnut Tree," in *Alexander Letters*, p. 128.
64. Martineau, *Society in America*, II, 363.
65. United States, *Report of the Eighth Census* (1860), *Population*.
66. Ibid.
67. Surgeon General's *Catalogue* notes a few cases among men.
68. Irby C. Bates, "Chlorosis," in *Transactions of the Medical Association of the State of Alabama* (Montgomery, 1917), p. 307. (Hereafter referred to as *Tr. Med. Ass.*)
69. Paul W. Clough, *Diseases of the Blood* (New York, 1929), p. 114.
70. Ibid., p. 116.
71. Bates, "Chlorosis," in *Tr. Med. Ass.*, p. 305.
72. Clough, *Diseases of the Blood*, p. 115.
73. Bates, "Chlorosis," in *Tr. Med. Ass.*, p. 306.
74. G. Fütterer, "Scrofulosis, Chlorosis, and Tuberculosis and their Treatment," in *Journal of the American Medical Association*, XXV, p. 948.
75. Clough, *Diseases of the Blood*, p. 115.
76. Bates, "Chlorosis," in *Tr. Med. Ass.*, pp. 305-6.
77. United States, *Report of the Eighth Census* (1860), *Statistics*.
78. Ibid.
79. Harriet Alexander to Clifford Alexander, September 1844, *Alexander Letters*, pp. 86-87.
80. Paul H. Buck, "The Poor Whites of the Ante-Bellum South," in *American Historical Review*, XXI, p. 45.

81. Harvey Lindsly, "Observations on the Ill Health of American Women," in *So. Lit. Mes.*, V, p. 92.
82. R. H. Shryock, "Medical Practices in the Old South," in *South Atlantic Quarterly*, XXIX; Wilson, "Female Education," in *So. Med. and Sur. Journal*, X, pp. 8-9.
83. Coombs, *Recollections of a Twiggs County Planter*, p. 78.
84. Augusta *Georgia Constitutionalist*, August 5, 1841, citing Philadelphia *American Sentinel*.
85. Charles Caldwell, "Evils of Tight Lacing," in *So. Lit. Mes.*, VII, pp. 731-32.
86. Lindsly, "Observations on the Ill Health of American Women," in *So. Lit. Mes.*, V, p. 92.
87. Augusta *Evening Dispatch*, April 22, 1859.
88. Richard H. Shryock, "Sylvester Graham and the Popular Health Movement," in *Mississippi Valley Historical Review*, XVIII.
89. Ewell, *The Medical Companion*, p. 245.
90. Milledgeville *Georgia Journal*, May 25, 1824.
91. Lindsly, "Observations on the Ill Health of American Women," in *So. Lit. Mes.*, V, p. 90.
92. Augusta *Daily Chronicle and Sentinel*, July 12, 1842.
93. "Arnold Letters," in T.C., *Historical Papers*, series 18-19, p. 18.
94. Joseph A. Eve, "Review of *Females and their Diseases*, by Charles D. Mengis," in *So. Med. and Sur. Journal*, IV, p. 287.
95. Wilson, "Female Medical Education," in *So. Med. and Sur. Journal*, X, pp. 8-10.
96. Jane C. West to Mrs. Matilda P. West, October 24, 1833, George W. West Letters, 1806-1876. (Hereafter referred to as West Letters.)
97. Buckingham, *Slave States*, II, 161-62.
98. Ibid., pp. 124-25.
99. Ibid., p. 126.
100. Ibid., I, 123-24.
101. Ibid., pp. 122-23.
102. Ibid., II, 92.
103. Ibid., I, 166.
104. Ibid., pp. 511-12.
105. Chapter Three of this book.
106. Chapter Seven of this book.
107. Milledgeville *Daily Federal Union*, November 5, 1859.
108. I. S. Bradwell to Adam L. Alexander, May 31, 1820, Alexander Letters and Papers.
109. Augusta *Chronicle and Sentinel*, August 22, 1849, citing Charleston *Mercury*.
110. Ibid.
111. Hull, "Family Chestnut Tree," in *Alexander Letters*, p. 121.
112. Savannah *Gazette of the State of Georgia*, August 21, 1788.
113. Augusta *Daily Chronicle and Sentinel*, November 4, 1858.

114. R. B. Pollard to Richard Tubman, August 13, 1835, Richard Tubman Letters and Papers.
115. C. M. Manigault to his brother, 1855, Manigault Letters.
116. Buckingham, *Slave States*, I, 166.
117. Ibid.
118. Louisa M. Roath to David L. Roath, May 29, 1856, David L. Roath Letters and Papers. (Hereafter referred to as Roath Letters.)
119. Augusta *Daily Chronicle and Sentinel*, August 22, 1849, citing Charleston *Mercury*.
120. Ibid.
121. Louisa M. Roath to David L. Roath, May 29, 1856, Roath Letters.
122. Pencil, *White Sulphur Papers*, pp. 76-134.
123. Burke, *Reminiscences of Georgia*, pp. 238-39.
124. Ibid., p. 239.
125. A. B. Longstreet, *Georgia Scenes* (New York, 1897).
126. Richmond County, Superior Court: Minutes, 1816-1819, Presentments of the Grand Jury, June Term, 1818, pp. 323-24.
127. George R. Gilmer to D. P. Hillhouse, February 4, 1851, Alexander Letters and Papers.
128. Paschal, *Ninety-Four Years*, pp. 101-2.
129. Richmond County, Superior Court: Minutes, 1816-1819, Presentments of the Grand Jury, June Term, 1818, p. 323.
130. Ibid., 1805-1811, Presentments of the Grand Jury, October Term, 1808, p. 280.
131. Ibid., 1787-1789, Presentments of Grand Jury, 1787, p. 30.
132. Ibid.
133. Richmond County, Inferior Court Records: Retail Bonds, 1847.
134. Richmond County, Superior Court: Minutes, 1787-1789, Presentments of Grand Jury, 1788, p. 75.
135. Richmond County, Superior Court: Minutes, 1816-1819, Presentments of the Grand Jury, June Term, 1818, p. 324.
136. Ibid., 1859-1860, Presentments of Grand Jury, April Term, 1859, p. 344.
137. D. P. Hillhouse to George R. Gilmer, February 4, 1851, Alexander Letters and Papers.
138. Buckingham, *Slave States*, II, 124.
139. Calhoun, *History of the American Family*, II, 323.
140. Ibid., p. 302.
141. Louisa M. Roath to David L. Roath, May 29, 1856, Roath Letters.
142. Edward Harden to Mary Harden, January 1, 1843, Harden Letters and Papers.
143. I. Briggs to Joseph Thomas, November 23, 1785, Isaac Briggs Letters.
144. Thomas Gamble, *Savannah Duels and Duelists* (Savannah, 1923), passim.
145. John L. Wilson, *The Code of Honor* or *Rules for the Government of Principals and Second in Duelling* (Charleston, 1858), p. 40. (Hereafter referred to as *Code of Honor*.)

146. Caroline C. Lovell, *The Golden Isles of Georgia* (Boston, 1932), pp. 107-8.
147. Ibid.
148. Dixon R. Fox, *Ideas in Motion* (New York, 1935), pp. 58-59.
149. Edward Ingle, *Southern Sidelights* (New York, 1896), p. 45.
150. Fox, *Ideas in Motion*, p. 59, citing Dr. Jameson.
151. Wilson, *Code of Honor*, pp. 15, 16, 19.
152. Gilmer, *Sketches*, p. 230.
153. Mary Harden, composition on "Modesty," n.d., Harden Letters.
154. Savannah *Daily Georgian*, August 11, 1831.
155. Ibid.
156. Buckingham, *Slave States*, II, 133-34.
157. Ibid.
158. Athens *Southern Banner*, October 30, 1840, citing New Orleans *Picayune*.
159. Caroline E. Merrick, *Old Times in Dixie Land* (New York, 1901), p. 83.
160. Julia Barnsley to Godfrey Barnsley, July 31, 1834, Barnsley Letters.
161. Buckingham, *Slave States*, I, 125.
162. Paschal, *Ninety-Four Years*, pp. 206-7.
163. Hundley, *Social Relations*, p. 264.
164. Olmsted, *Journey in the Seaboard Slave States*, p. 507.
165. Georgia, *Acts of the General Assembly*, Act of 1856, p. 260.
166. Ibid., Act of 1823, p. 142.
167. Ibid., Act of 1847, pp. 227-32.
168. Ibid., Act of 1850, pp. 321-30.
169. Ibid., Act of 1854, pp. 486-99.
170. Georgia Constitution of 1798, amendment to Art. I, Sec. 26, in McElreath, *Constitution of Georgia*, p. 280.
171. Georgia, *Acts of the General Assembly*, Act of 1854, p. 492.
172. Ibid., Act of 1850, pp. 321-30.
173. Ibid., Act of 1854, p. 493.
174. Ibid., Acts of 1834-1835, p. 157.
175. Ibid., Act of 1854, pp. 189, 497.
176. Georgia, *Acts of the General Assembly*, Act of 1856, p. 260.
177. Charles E. Kanapaux to Foster Blodget, Jr., August 17, 1860, Roath Letters.
178. Prince, *Digest*, Act of 1770, p. 777.
179. George White, *Statistics of the State of Georgia* (Savannah, 1849), pp. 406-9. (Hereafter referred to as *Statistics*.)
180. Augusta *Weekly Chronicle and Sentinel*, June 27, 1855, citing Richmond *Enquirer*, 12th inst.
181. Georgia, *Acts of the General Assembly*, 1859, p. 54.
182. Prince, *Digest*, Acts of 1792, p. 802; 1818, pp. 794-99; 1818, p. 799.
183. Bryan *vs.* Walton, 14 Georgia 185; ibid., 20 Georgia 512; Yancy *vs.* Harris, 9 Georgia 535.
184. Bryan *vs.* Walton, 20 Georgia 512.

CHAPTER SIX

1. Murray, *Letters from the United States, Cuba and Canada*, II, 37-38.
2. Calhoun, *History of the American Family*, II, 321, citing Underwood, "Women of the Confederacy."
3. Lyell, *Second Visit to the U.S.*, II, 264; Shryock, "Medical Practices in the Old South," in *South Atlantic Quarterly*, XXIX, p. 172.
4. Martineau, *Society in America*, II, 224; Augustus Longstreet Hull, *Annals of Athens* (Athens, 1906), p. 284.
5. Felton, *Early Life in Georgia*, pp. 29-34, 40-41; Calhoun, *History of the American Family*, pp. 317-21; Hull, *Annals of Athens*, p. 284; Hundley, *Social Relations*, p. 98.
6. Rupert B. Vance, *Human Geography of the South* (Chapel Hill, 1935), pp. 65-66, citing John P. Arthur, "Western North Carolina, 1730-1913," p. 256.
7. Burke, *Reminiscences of Georgia*, p. 21.
8. Ibid., p. 208.
9. Gilmer, *Sketches*, p. 166.
10. Steadman, *Southern Manufacturer*, pp. 69-70.
11. Burke, *Reminiscences of Georgia*, pp. 23-25.
12. Ralph B. Flanders, *Plantation Slavery in Georgia* (Chapel Hill, 1933), pp. 125-26.
13. MacKay-Stiles Letters and Papers.
14. United States, Original Mss. Returns of the Seventh Census (1850), Agriculture, Dade to Houston Counties, Georgia. (Hereafter referred to as U.S., Returns for Census.)
15. U.S., Returns for Census of 1860, Floyd to Murray.
16. U.S., Returns for Census of 1850, Dade to Houston.
17. U.S., Returns for Census of 1860, Floyd to Murray.
18. U.S., Returns for Census of 1850, Dade to Houston.
19. E. H. Manigault to Charles Manigault, Charleston, November 9, 1843, Manigault Letters and Papers.
20. Manigault Letters and Papers.
21. U.S., Returns for Census of 1850, Dade to Houston.
22. U.S., Returns for Census of 1860, Floyd to Murray.
23. U.S., Notes for Census of 1850, Dade to Houston.
24. U.S., Returns for Census of 1860, Floyd to Murray.
25. Frederick Law Olmsted, *The Cotton Kingdom* (New York, 1861), I, 232.
26. Hull, "Family Chestnut Tree," in *Alexander Letters*, p. 121.
27. Forrest, *Women of the South*, pp. 463-75.
28. Ibid., pp. 13-47.
29. Ibid., pp. 328-53.
30. Ibid., pp. 163-83.
31. Virginia G. Gray, "Activities of Southern Women, 1840-1860," in *South Atlantic Quarterly*, XXVII, p. 273.

32. Augusta *Evening Dispatch*, January 4, 1859.
33. Ibid., pp. 416-19, 423-24.
34. Milledgeville *Daily Federal Union*, November 13, 1859.
35. Sherwood, *Gazetteer*, 1837. 3rd ed., p. 267.
36. "A College for Teachers," in *Southern Ladies' Book*, vol. I, no. 5 (May 1840), pp. 257-58.
37. Sarah J. Hale, "A Profession for Ladies," in *So. Lit. Mes.*, II, pp. 571-72.
38. Augusta *Daily Chronicle and Sentinel*, September 29, 1849.
39. Savannah *Georgian*, May 25, 1831; Columbus *Enquirer*, December 14, 1833, May 17, 1834; Augusta *Daily Constitutionalist and Republic*, August 13, 1838; Augusta *Daily Chronicle and Sentinel*, September 18, 1849, October 11, 1849.
40. E. M. Coulter, "A Georgia Education Movement during the Eighteen Fifties," in *G.H.Q.*, IX, no. 1, p. 30.
41. Georgia, *Acts of the General Assembly*, Act of 1858, pp. 50-51; Fannie F. White to David L. Roath, n.p., February 4, 1852, Richmond County, Inferior Court Records: Poor School Letters and Papers.
42. Abbie Graham, *Ladies in Revolt* (New York, 1934), pp. 95-96.
43. Shryock, *Georgia and the Union in 1850*, pp. 80-81, 85-86; Hundley, *Social Relations*, p. 104; Felton, *Country Life*, p. 62; Booger, *Secondary Education*, pp. 152, 172-73, 293, 309.
44. Richard Arnold to John Stoddard, Savannah, July [n.d.], 1858, "Arnold Letters" in T.C., *Historical Papers*, series 18-19, p. 91.
45. Milledgeville *Federal Union*, September 15, 1855.
46. Burke, *Reminiscences of Georgia*, p. 225.
47. Julia [?] to Louisa Alexander, Washington, January 3, 1842, Alexander Letters and Papers.
48. Mary E. G. Harden to Marian E. Harden, Athens, May 28, 1857, Harden Letters.
49. Richmond County Academy, Minutes, December 6, 1816.
50. Georgia, *Acts of the General Assembly*, Act of 1852, p. 3.
51. Ibid., Act of 1857, p. 10.
52. Richmond County, Inferior Court Records; Poor School Letters and Papers, Poor School Account, 1860-1861.
53. Georgia, *Acts of the General Assembly*, Act of December 5, 1851, p. 337.
54. Richmond County Academy, Minutes, March 4, 1815, December 27, 1815, December 6, 1816, November 22, 1817.
55. Chapter Five of this book; C. C. Van Blarcom, "Rate Pie, among the Midwives of the South," in *Harper's Magazine*, CLX, pp. 322-32; Shryock, "Medical Practices in the Old South," in *South Atlantic Quarterly*, XXIX, pp. 171-76.
56. Paschal, *Ninety-Four Years*, passim.
57. Ibid., pp. 147-48.
58. Henry H. Cumming to Mrs. Emily H. Tubman, Augusta, May 22, 1845, Tubman Letters and Papers.

59. D. P. Hillhouse to George R. Gilman, n.p., February 4, 1851, Alexander Letters and Papers.
60. Park, "The Puritan in Georgia," in *G.H.Q.*, XIII, p. 356.
61. Savannah, *City Directory*, 1860, II, passim.
62. Coulter, *History of Georgia*, p. 256.
63. United States, *Report of the Eighth Census* (1860), *Manufacturing*.
64. Anna Barnsley's receipts for 1847, Barnsley Letters and Papers.
65. Augusta *Georgia Constitutionalist*, December 16, 1841.
66. Ibid., December 16, 1841.
67. Ibid., July 16, 1842.
68. Chapter Seven of this book.
69. Augusta *Daily Chronicle and Sentinel*, August 3, 1858.
70. E. H. Harden to Edward Harden, Savannah, November 21, 1844, Harden Letters and Papers.
71. Louisa M. Roath to David L. Roath, Gordon Springs, August 13 [1854], Roath Letters.
72. Richmond County, Inferior Court Records: Receipts for 1832.
73. Savannah *City Directory*, 1860, II, 9.
74. Andrews, *Reminiscences*, p. 96.
75. Kellogg, *Notes and Reflections*, pp. 36-37.
76. Sherwood, *Gazetteer, 1837*, p. 46.
77. Andrews, *Reminiscences*, p. 37.
78. Olmsted, *Journey in the Slaves States*, pp. 82-83.
79. Ibid., p. 507.
80. Hundley, *Social Relations*, p. 120.
81. F. L. Olmsted, *The Cotton Kingdom* (New York, 1861), II, 357, citing *DeBow's Review*, January, 1850.
82. *DeBow's Review*, X, pp. 680-82; XII, pp. 41-42; XXIV, pp. 382-83; Paul H. Buck, "The Poor Whites in the Antebellum South," in *American Historical Review*, XXIX, pp. 48-49.
83. William Gregg, *Essay on Domestic Industry* (Charleston, 1845), passim; Augusta *Chronicle and Sentinel*, December 31, 1844-February 6, 1845.
84. Gray, *Agriculture in the Southern States*, I, 486.
85. *DeBow's Review*, I, p. 232; VIII, pp. 39-45; X, pp. 182-85; XVIII, p. 792.
86. Steadman, *Southern Manufacturing*, passim; Broadus Mitchel, "Rise of the Cotton Mills in the South," in *Johns Hopkins University Studies*, vol. XXXIX, no. 2, pp. 139-40.
87. R. H. Shryock, "Early Industrial Revolution in the Empire State," in *G.H.Q.*, vol. XI, no. 2, pp. 111-14.
88. Ibid., United States, *Report of the Eighth Census* (1860), *Manufacturing*.
89. Gregg, *Essay on Domestic Industry*, p. 22.
90. Ingle, *Southern Sidelights*, p. 85.
91. White, *Statistics of Georgia*, pp. 112ff.
92. Olmsted, *Journey in the Slave States*, p. 459.

93. Augusta *Evening Dispatch*, March 4, 1859.
94. United States, *Compendium of the Seventh Census* (1850).
95. United States, *Report of the Eighth Census* (1860), *Manufacturing*.
96. Richmond County, Inferior Court Records: Poor School List, 1852, pp. 21-30.
97. Buckingham, *Slave States*, II, 112.
98. Joel Crawford to Thomas Butler King, Bleckley, December 18, 1844, in Augusta *Chronicle and Sentinel*, January 3, 1845, citing "Fort Gains Whig," ibid., June 23, 1849; *DeBow's Review*, XI, p. 319.
99. Lyell, *Second Visit to the U.S.*, p. 205; Flanders, *Plantation Slavery in Georgia*, p. 205.
100. Flanders, "Farish Carter, Forgotten Man of the Old South," in *G.H.Q.*, XV, p. 150.
101. Buckingham, *Slave States*, II, 113.
102. Ingle, *Southern Sidelights*, p. 79; Shryock, "Industrial Revolution," in *G.H.Q.*, vol. XI, no. 2, pp. 118-19.
103. Buckingham, *Slave States*, II, 113.
104. Shryock, "Industrial Revolution," in *G.H.Q.*, vol. XI, no. 2, pp. 116-17; Augusta *Daily Chronicle and Sentinel*, November 12, 1849, citing Muscogee *Democrat*; White, *Statistics of Georgia*, p. 512.
105. Ibid., pp. 189, 481
106. Ibid., p. 182.
107. Ibid., p. 575.
108. Ibid., p. 134.
109. Ibid., p. 189.
110. Ingle, *Southern Sidelights*, pp. 80-81.
111. Olmsted, *Journey in the Slave States*, p. 543.
112. White, *Statistics of Georgia*, p. 575.
113. Ingle, *Southern Sidelights*, p. 81.
114. United States, *Compendium of the Seventh Census* (1850).
115. United States, *Report of the Eighth Census* (1860), *Manufacturing*.

CHAPTER SEVEN

1. Sarah M. Grimké, *Letters on the Equality of the Sexes and the Condition of Women* (Boston, 1838), p. 118.
2. Jesse Mercer, "Have Females the Right to Speak in Church?" in C. D. Mallay, *Memoirs of Jesse Mercer* (New York, 1844), pp. 447-48.
3. Henry Wheeler, *One Thousand Questions and Answers Concerning the Methodist Episcopal Church* (New York, 1898), p. 77.
4. Ibid.
5. Ibid., pp. 77-78, citing "General Conference Journal of 1880," p. 353.
6. Felton, *Country Life*, pp. 64-65.

7. Ibid., p. 64.
8. Smith, "Plea for the Church," in P.E.C., *Jour. of Conv.*, 1829, I, 7-8.
9. Richard Knill, "The Missionary's Wife," in William M. Engles, ed., *A Series of Presbyterian Church Tracts* (Philadelphia, 1840), II, 4; D. D. Jones and W. H. Mills, eds., *History of the Presbyterian Church in South Carolina since 1850* (Columbia, 1926), pp. 435-37.
10. Smith, "Plea for the Church," in P.E.C., *Jour. of Conv.*, 1829, I, 7-9.
11. Sam Jones, *Sam Jones Own Book* (Cincinnati, 1887), p. 117.
12. Chapter Two of this book.
13. Smith, *A Hundred Years of Methodism*, p. 36; P.E.C., *Jour. of Conv.*, 1831, I, 5.
14. Savannah, *Census of 1848*, comp. Joseph Bancroft (Savannah, 1848), pp. 45-47. (Hereafter referred to as Savannah, *Census of 1848*.)
15. Ibid., p. 47; Baptist *Minutes of the Georgia Associations*, Double Branch, Lincoln County (Washington, Ga., 1839), pp. 3-4; P.E.C., *Jour. of Conv.*, 1827, 1828, I, 11.
16. Augusta *Evening Dispatch*, January 21, 1859.
17. Smith, *A Hundred Years of Methodism*, p. 24.
18. Mt. Zion *Missionary*, March 18, 1823.
19. Augusta *Daily Chronicle and Sentinel*, January 22, 1845.
20. Savannah *Daily Georgian*, January 7, 1836.
21. Savannah, *City Directory*, 1860, II, 188.
22. Savannah, *Census of 1848*, pp. 45-47.
23. Augusta *Daily Chronicle and Sentinel*, February 3, 1852.
24. Ibid., March 4, 1852; Augusta *Constitutionalist and Republic*, July 12, 1853.
25. Buckingham, *Slave States*, I, 126.
26. Ibid., p. 125.
27. Ibid., p. 150.
28. Stephen Elliott, *Sermons* (New York, 1867), pp. 131-32.
29. Isaiah 3:16-24.
30. Methodist, *Form of Discipline*, 1798 (Philadelphia, 1798), sec. VII, pp. 159-60.
31. Methodist, *Form of Discipline*, 1791 (Philadelphia, 1791), sec. XXIII, p. 29; *Doctrines and Discipline*, 1836 (New York, 1836), chap. II, sec. VI, pp. 87-88.
32. Ibid., 1856, chap. IX, sec. 1, p. 87.
33. Dow, "A Journey from Babylon to Jerusalem," in *History of Cosmopolite*, p. 477.
34. Smith, *Hundred Years of Methodism*, p. 28.
35. Ibid., p. 37.
36. *Mt. Zion Missionary*, January 13, 1823.
37. Dow, "A Journey from Babylon to Jerusalem," in *History of Cosmopolite*, p. 477.
38. Jones, *Anecdotes*, p. 231.

39. Henry Kollock, *Sermons* (Savannah, 1822), II, 342-52.
40. Ibid.; Smith, "Plea for the Church," in P.E.C., *Jour. of Conv.*, 1829, I, 7.
41. Burke, *Reminiscences of Georgia*, p. 41.
42. Sherwood, *Gazetteer*, 1837, 3rd ed. (Washington, Ga., 1837), p. 126.
43. Moses Waddel, *Memoirs of the Life of Miss Caroline Smelt* (New York, 1875), preface, p. iv.
44. Ibid., pp. 12-13.
45. Ibid., p. 17.
46. Ibid., p. 18.
47. Ibid., p. 23.
48. Ibid., pp. 38-39.
49. Ibid., pp. 128-31.
50. Monroe, Album.
51. Presbyterian Church, *Confession of Faith and Covenant of the Independent Presbyterian Church in Savannah, 1842* (Savannah, 1842), pp. 10-22.
52. "Arnold Letters," in T.C., *Historical Papers*, series 18-19, p. 75.

CHAPTER EIGHT

1. J. T. Adams, *Provincial Society* (New York, 1920), p. 108, citing "Diary of a Voyage from Rotterdam to Philadelphia."
2. Graham, *Ladies in Revolt*, pp. 67-71.
3. Thomas J. Wertenbaker, *The First Americans* (New York, 1929), pp. 48-86.
4. Ibid., pp. 22-42.
5. Adams, *Provincial Society*, p. 103.
6. William A. Dunning, *Studies in Southern History and Politics* (New York, 1914), p. 328. (Hereafter referred to as *Southern History and Politics*.)
7. Graham, *Ladies in Revolt*, passim.
8. Ibid., pp. 18-20, 54-64.
9. Schlesinger, *New Viewpoints*, p. 137.
10. Ibid.
11. Graham, *Ladies in Revolt*, pp. 76-82.
12. Schlesinger, *New Viewpoints*, p. 138.
13. Graham, *Ladies in Revolt*, p. 134.
14. Dunning, *Southern History and Politics*, p. 328.
15. V. L. Parrington, *The Romantic Revolution in America* (New York, 1927), p. 4.
16. W. S. Jenkins, *Pro-Slavery Thought in the Old South* (Chapel Hill, 1935), pp. 289, 292; Dodd, *The Cotton Kingdom*, pp. 48-68.
17. Thomas Dew, "Debate in the Virginia Legislature, 1831-1832," in *Political Register*, October 16, 1833 [Washington, 1833], II, pp. 769-822. (Hereafter referred to as "Debate in Va. Leg.," in *Political Register*); "An address on the

Influence of the Federative System of Government upon Literature and the Development of Character," in *So. Lit. Mes.*, II, pp. 261-82.

18. William Harper, "Memoir on Slavery," in J. D. B. DeBow, *Industrial Resources, etc., of the Southern and Western States* (New Orleans, 1852), II, pp. 205-38. (Hereafter referred to as *Industrial Resources*.)

19. Parrington, *The Romantic Revolution in America*, p. 91.

20. J. H. Hammond, "Slavery in the Light of Political Science," in E. N. Elliott, *Cotton is King and Pro-Slavery Arguments* (Augusta, 1860), pp. 629-88. (Hereafter referred to as *Pro-Slavery Arguments*); Jenkins, *Pro-Slavery Thought in the Old South*, p. 289.

21. Ibid., John C. Calhoun, *Works of John Calhoun*, ed. by Richard Cralle (New York, 1857), II, 631.

22. George Fitzhugh, *Cannibals All!* (Richmond, 1857), passim.

23. Dew, "Debate in Va. Leg.," in *Political Register*, II, pp. 484-85.

24. Fitzhugh, *Cannibals All!*, p. 43.

25. Dew, "Differences between the Sexes," in *So. Lit. Mes.*, I, pp. 493-95.

26. Harper, "Memoir on Slavery," in DeBow, *Industrial Resources*, II, p. 207.

27. George Fitzhugh, *Sociology for the South* (Richmond, 1854), pp. 214-17.

28. Ibid., pp. 230-31.

29. Harper, "Memoir on Slavery," in DeBow, *Industrial Resources*, II, p. 228.

30. Ibid., p. 220.

31. Hammond, "Slavery in the Light of Political Science," in *Pro-Slavery Argument*, pp. 645-46.

32. Olmsted, *Journey in the Slave States*, p. 508.

33. Ibid., p. 509.

34. Calhoun, *History of the American Family*, II, 326, citing Avery, "Dixie after the War," 23 footnote.

Bibliography

ORIGINAL SOURCES

Manuscripts

Government Records

Chatham County, Inferior Court Records:
  Wills.
Chatham County, Superior Court Records:
  Judgments.
  Minutes.
Richmond County, Inferior Court Records:
  Bastard Bonds.
  Minutes.
  Petitions and Orders.
  Poor School Letters and Papers.
  Poor School List.
  Retail Bonds.
  Writs.

Richmond County, Superior Court Records:
  Minutes.
  Writs.

United States, Original Census Returns.
  Agriculture. Georgia, Returns for the Seventh Census (1850), Dade to
  Houston Counties; Returns for the Eighth Census (1860), Floyd to Murray
  Counties. (Duke University)

Letters and Papers

Alexander, Adam Leopold, Washington, Georgia, Letters and Papers, 1785-1909. (Duke University)

Barnsley, Godfrey, Savannah, Georgia, Letters and Papers, 1828-1873. (Duke University)

Briggs, Isaac, Philadelphia, Letter, November 23, 1785. (Georgia Department of Archives, Atlanta)

Harden, Edward, Athens, Georgia, Letters and Papers, 1772-1930. (Duke University)

Kell, John McIntosh, Darian, Georgia, Letters, 1841-1865. (Duke University)

MacKay, Robert—Stiles, W. H., Savannah, Georgia, Letters and Papers, 1762-1899. (University of North Carolina)

Manigault, Louis, Charleston, S.C., and Savannah, Georgia, Letters and Papers, 1808-1883. (Duke University)

Mercer, Jesse, Macon, Georgia, Letter, March 5, 1805. (Duke University)

Niles, Alice E. (Andrews), Griffin, Georgia, Letters and Papers, 1859-1864. (Duke University)

Roath, David L., Augusta, Georgia, Letters and Papers, unclassified. (Office of Ordinary of Richmond County, Augusta, Georgia)

Tubman, Richard, Augusta, Georgia, Letters and Papers, 1753-1858. (Duke University)

West, George W., Cedartown, Georgia, Letters, 1806-1876. (Duke University)

Miscellaneous Manuscripts

Coombs, James Rowe, Recollections of a Twiggs County Planter. (Typed copy of MSS, Duke University)

Kellogg, Ebenezer, Notes and Reflections during a Journey from Williamstown to the Southern States in 1817-18[18]. (University of Georgia)

Monroe, Julia Blanche, Darian, Georgia, Album, 1853-1855. (Duke University)

Richmond County Academy, Minutes, 1783-1821. (Office of Mr. Warren Bothwell, Augusta, Georgia)

Printed Original Sources

Government Records

American Digest, Century Edition, 1658-1896. St. Paul, 1899.

Blackstone, William, *Commentaries on the Laws of England*, with analysis of contents by Thomas M. Cooley, ed. by James DeWitt Andrews, 4th ed., 2 vols., Chicago, 1899.

Cobb, Thomas R. R., *Digest of the Statute Laws of Georgia*, Athens, 1851.

Georgia, *Acts of the General Assembly*, 1802-1868.

_____, *Code of 1861*, comp. by R. H. Clark, T. R. R. Cobb, and D. Irwin. Atlanta, 1861.

_____, *Colonial Records*, ed. by Allen D. Chandler. 25 vols., Atlanta, 1904.

_____, Constitutions, in Walter McElreath, ed., *A Treatise on the Constitution of Georgia*. Atlanta, 1912.

_____, *Superior Court Decisions*. Part I, *Decisions rendered during the year 1842*. Augusta, 1843. Part II, *Decisions rendered during the year 1842-1843*. (DeRenne Collection, University of Georgia)

_____, *Supreme Court Decisions*, 1845-

Liberty County, *Records, Annals of Georgia*, comp. by Carolina Price, 2 vols., New York, 1928.

Prince, Oliver H., *Digest of the Laws of the State of Georgia*. Athens, 1837.

Savannah, *Census of 1848*, comp. by Joseph Bancroft, Savannah, 1848.

_____, *Census of 1860*, pub. by John M. Cooper, 2 vols., Savannah, 1860.

United States, *Census Reports*.

Wilkes County, *Records, Early Records of Georgia*, comp. by Grace Davidson, 2 vols., Macon, 1932.

Other Printed Original Sources

"Advice to Young Ladies," in *Southern Literary Messenger*, XX.

The Alexander Letters, ed. by Marion A. Boggs. Savannah, 1910.

Andrews, Garnett, *Reminiscences of an Old Georgia Lawyer*. Atlanta, 1870.

Baptist, *Minutes of the Georgia Association, Double Branch, Lincoln County*. Washington, Georgia, 1839.

"Benjamin Hawkins Letters, 1796-1806," in *Georgia Historical Collections*, IX. Savannah, 1916.

Bible, King James Version.

Bird, Powell W., "Physiological Incompatibility between the Sexes in Relation to Progeny," in *Savannah Journal of Medicine*, I. Savannah, 1859. (DeRenne Collection, University of Georgia)

Buckingham, J. S., *The Slave States of America*. 2 vols., London, 1842.

Burke, Emily P., *Reminiscences of Georgia*. [Oberlin, Ohio] 1850.

Butler, Pierce, *Statement Originally Prepared in Aid of his Professional Council*. [Philadelphia, 1850] (DeRenne Collection, University of Georgia)

Calhoun, John C., *Works of John C. Calhoun*, ed. by Richard Crallé. 6 vols., New York, 1857.

Chandler, Daniel, *An Address on Female Education*, delivered before the Demonsthenian and Phi Kappa societies on the day after commencement in the University of Georgia. Washington, Georgia, 1835.

Charlton, Robert M., *An Address*, delivered at the commencement of LaGrange Female College, July 20, 1853. Savannah, 1853. (DeRenne Collection, University of Georgia)

"A College for Teachers," in *Southern Ladies' Book*, Vol. I, No. 5 (May, 1840).

"Courtship Made Easy," in *Southern Literary Messenger*, XXV.

Dew, Thomas R., "An Address on the Influence of the Federative Republican System of Government upon Literature and the Development of Character," in *Southern Literary Messenger*, II.

_____, "Debate in the Virginia Legislature, 1831-1832," in *Political Register*, October 16, 1833, II. Washington, 1833.

_____, "Dissertation on the Characteristic Differences between the Sexes, and on the Position and Influence of Women in Society," in *Southern Literary Messenger*, I.

Dow, Lorenzo, *History of Cosmopolite, or the Writings of the Reverend Lorenzo Dow*. Philadelphia, 1855.

Elliott, Stephen, *Sermons*. New York, 1867.

"Eudora Unhooped," in *Southern Literary Messenger*, XXII.

Eve, Joseph A., "Review of Female and their Diseases by Charles D. Meigs, M.D.," in *Southern Medical and Surgical Journal*, New Series, IV. Augusta, 1848. (DeRenne Collection, University of Georgia)

Ewell, James, *The Medical Companion*. Philadelphia, 1817.

Felton, Rebecca L., *Country Life in Georgia in the Days of My Youth*. Atlanta, 1919.

"Female Education," in *Southern Literary Messenger*, VI.

Fitzhugh, George, *Cannibals All!* Richmond, 1857.

———, *Sociology for the South*. Richmond, 1854.

"Flirtation," in *Southern Literary Messenger*, XV.

Gilmer, George R., *Sketches of Some of the First Settlers of Upper Georgia of the Cherokees, and the Author*. New York, 1855.

Greensboro Female College, *Catalogue and Circular*, year ending June 23, 1853. Augusta, 1853. (DeRenne Collection, University of Georgia)

Gregg, William, *Essay on Domestic Industry*. Charleston, 1845.

Grimké, Sarah M., *Letters on the Equality of the Sexes and the Condition of Women*. Boston, 1829.

Hall, Bazil, *Travels in North America in the Years 1827-1828*. 3 vols., Edinburgh, Scotland, 1829.

Hammond, J. H., "Slavery in the Light of Political Science," in E. M. Elliott, *Cotton is King, and Pro-Slavery Arguments*. Augusta, 1860.

Harper, William, "Memoir on Slavery," in J. D. B. DeBow, *Industrial Resources, etc., of the Southern and Western States*, II, New Orleans, 1852.

"Hooped Dresses," in *Southern Literary Messenger*, XXII.

Hull, Augustus L., *Annals of Athens, Georgia*. Athens, 1906.

Hull, Mary Clifford, "Family Chestnut Tree," in *Alexander Letters*, edited by Marion A. Boggs. Savannah, 1910.

Hundley, D. R., *Social Relations in our Southern States*. New York, 1860.

Jennings, Samuel K., *The Married Lady's Companion, or the Poor Man's Friend*. Richmond, 1804.

Johnson, H. V., *Address*, at the commencement exercises of the Wesleyan Female College, July 14, 1853. [N.p.] 1853. (DeRenne Collection, University of Georgia)

Jones, Sam, *Anecdotes*. Chicago, 1888.

———, *Sam Jones' Own Book*. Cincinnati, 1887.

Kemble, Frances Anne, *Journal of a Residence on a Georgia Plantation*. New York, 1863.

———, *Records of Later Life*. 3 vols., London, 1882.

Kollock, Henry, *Sermons*. 4 vols., Savannah, 1822.

"Letters of Richard Arnold, M.D., 1808-1876," ed. by Richard H. Shryock, in Trinity College Historical Society, *Historical Papers*, series 18-19. Durham, 1925.

"A Letter to Teachers," in *Southern Ladies' Book*, Vol. II, No. 5 (November, 1840).

Lindsly, Harvey, "Observations on the Ill Health of American Women," in *Southern Literary Messenger*, V.

"The Literary Wife," in *Southern Literary Messenger*, XXXIII.

Lyell, Charles, *A Second Visit to the United States of North America*. 2 vols., New York, 1849.

Martineau, Harriet, *Society in America*. 3 vols., New York, 1837.

[Martyn, Benjamine] "An Impartial Inquiry into the State and Utility of the Province of Georgia," London, 1741. Reprint in *Georgia Historical Society Collections*, I, Savannah, 1840.

Mercer, Jesse, "Have Females the Right to Speak in Church?" in C. D. Mallay, *Memoirs of Jesse Mercer*. New York, 1844.

Merrick, Caroline E., *Old Times in Dixie Land*. New York, 1901.

Methodist, *Doctrines and Discipline*. New York, 1836; ibid., 1848; ibid., 1856.

————, *Form of Discipline*. Philadelphia, 1791; ibid., 1792; ibid., 1798.

Murray, Amelia M., *Letters from the United States, Cuba, and Canada*. 2 vols., New York, 1856.

Nesbit, Eugenius A., *Thoughts on the Beautiful*, an address delivered at the commencement of the Griffin Synodical Female College, June 1857, Griffin, Georgia.

————, "Views of Female Education and Character," in *Southern Ladies' Book*, Vol. I, No. 6 (June, 1840).

Olmsted, Frederick L., *The Cotton Kingdom*. 2 vols., New York, 1861.

————, *Journey in the Seaboard Slave States*. New York, 1865.

Paschal, George W., *Ninety-Four Years, or Agnes Paschal*. [Washington, D.C.] 1871.

Pencil, Mark [pseudo. for Mary], *The White Sulphur Papers or Life at the Springs of Western Virginia*. New York, 1839.

Pierce, George F., "The Georgia Female College—Its Origin, Plan, and Prospects," in *Southern Ladies' Book*, Vol. I, No. 2 (February 1840).

Pierce, L., "On Female Education," in *Southern Ladies' Book*, Vol. I, No. 3 (March, 1840).

Power, Tyrone, *Impressions of America, during the Years 1833, 1834, and 1835*. 2 vols., London, 1836. (DeRenne Collection, University of Georgia)

Presbyterian Church, *Confession of Faith and Covenant of the Independent Presbyterian Church in Savannah*. Savannah, 1842.

Sasnett, W. J., *Marriage*, an address delivered at the commencement of LaGrange Female College, LaGrange, Georgia, July 6, 1859. Atlanta, 1859. (DeRenne Collection, University of Georgia)

Savannah Sabbath School Teachers, "Circular," in Mt. Zion *Missionary*, July 29, 1822.

Sherwood, Adiel, *A Gazetteer of the State of Georgia, 1837*, 3rd ed., Washington, 1837.

_____, ibid., 1860, 4th ed., Atlanta, 1860.

Smith, Hugh, "A Plea for the Church of Georgia," in Protestant Episcopal Church, *Journal of the Proceedings of the Conventions in the Diocese of Georgia, 1823-1853*, Convention of 1829, I, Savannah, 1853.

Steadman, E., *The Southern Manufacturer*. Gallatin, Tennessee, 1858.

Stuart, James, *Three Years in North America*. 2 vols., Edinburgh, Scotland.

Shryock, R. H., ed., "Letters of Richard D. Arnold, M.D., 1808-1876," see "Letters of Richard D. Arnold . . ."

"To the Gentlemen of Georgia," in *Southern Ladies' Book*, Vol. I, No. 2 (August, 1840).

Washington Female Seminary, *Second Annual Catalogue*, 1840. Washington, Georgia, 1840. (DeRenne Collection, University of Georgia)

White, George, *Statistics of the State of Georgia*. Savannah, 1849.

Wilson, John Lyde, *The Code of Honor* or *Rules for the Government of Principals and Seconds in Duelling*. Charleston, 1858.

Wilson, John S., "Female Medical Education," in *Southern Medical and Surgical Journal*, X, New Series, Augusta, 1854. (DeRenne Collection, University of Georgia)

"Women of France," in *Southern Literary Messenger*, V.

"A Woman Worshipper in Trouble," in *Southern Literary Messenger*, XXIII.

NEWSPAPERS AND PERIODICALS

Athens *Southern Banner*, 1840, 1843, 1844, 1846.

Athens *Gazette*, 1814, 1815.

Atlanta *Journal*, March 17, 1929.

Augusta *Chronicle and Gazetteer of the State*, 1797, 1802, 1810.

Augusta *Daily Chronicle and Sentinel*, 1845, 1846, 1849, 1852, 1858, 1859.

Augusta *Daily Constitutionalist and Republic*, 1838, 1853.

Augusta *Daily Constitutionalist*, 1847, 1851, 1853, 1859.

Augusta *Georgia Constitutionalist*, 1841, 1842.

Augusta *Evening Dispatch*, 1859.

Columbus *Enquirer*, 1833, 1834.

Columbus *Sentinel and Herald*, 1838.

DeBow, J. D. B., ed., *The Commercial Review of the South and West*. 43 vols., New Orleans, 1846-1880.

Milledgeville *Daily Federal Union*, 1859.

Milledgeville *Georgia Journal*, 1824, 1825, 1838.

Milledgeville *Southern Recorder*, 1841.

Mt. Zion (Hancock County, Georgia) *The Missionary*, 1822, 1823.

Savannah *Daily Georgian*, 1831, 1836.

Savannah *Georgian*, 1831.

Savannah *Columbian Museum and Savannah Advertiser*, 1803.

Southern Literary Messenger. 38 vols., Richmond, 1834-1864.

Southern Ladies' Book, Vol. I, Nos. 2-6 (February-June, 1840), Vol. II, Nos. 1-5 (July-November, 1840), Macon, 1840.

SECONDARY SOURCES

Adams, J. T., *Provincial Society*. New York, 1920.

Bates, Irby C., "Chlorosis," in *Transactions of the Medical Association of the State of Alabama*. Montgomery, 1917.

Benson, Mary S., *Women in Eighteenth-Century America*. New York, 1935.

Bobbé, Dorothie, *Fanny Kemble*. New York, 1931.

Booger, Elbert W. G., *Secondary Education in Georgia, 1732-1858*. Philadelphia, 1933.

Brown, Isaac V., *Memoir of the Rev. Robert Finley*. New Brunswick, 1819.

Buck, Paul H., "The Poor Whites in the Ante-Bellum South," in *American Historical Review*, XXXI.

Calhoun, Arthur W., *A Social History of the American Family*. 3 vols., Cleveland, 1918.

Catt, Carrie Chapman and Nettie Rogers Schuler, *Woman Suffrage and Politics*. New York, 1923.

Clough, Paul W., *Diseases of the Blood*. New York, 1929.

Coulter, E. Merton, *College Life in the Old South*. New York, 1928.

_____, "A Georgia Education Movement during the Eighteen Hundred Fifties," in *Georgia Historical Quarterly*, IX.

_____, *A Short History of Georgia*. Chapel Hill, 1933.

Dodd, William E., *The Cotton Kingdom*. New Haven, 1919.

Driver, Leota S., *Fanny Kemble*. Chapel Hill, 1933.

Dunning, William A., *Studies in Southern History and Politics*. New York, 1914.

Flanders, Ralph B., "Farish Carter, a Forgotten Man of the Old South," in *Georgia Historical Quarterly*, XV.

_____, *Plantation Slavery in Georgia*. Chapel Hill, 1933.

Flisch, Julia A., "Common People of the Old South," in *American Historical Reports*, I, 1908.

Forrest, Mary, *Women of the South Distinguished in Literature*. New York, 1865.

Fox, Dixon R., *Ideas in Motion*. New York, 1935.

Fütterer, G., "Scrofulosis, Chlorosis, and Tuberculosis and their Treatment," in *Journal of the American Medical Association*, XXV.

Gamble, Thomas, *Savannah Duels and Duelist*. Savannah, 1923.

Graham, Abbie, *Ladies in Revolt*. New York, 1934.

Gray, L. C., *History of Agriculture in the Southern States to 1860*. 2 vols., Washington, 1933.

Gray, Virginia G., "Activities of Southern Women, 1840-1860," in *South Atlantic Quarterly*, XXVII.

Hale, Sarah J., "A Profession for Ladies," in *Southern Literary Messenger*, II.

Hecker, Eugene A., *A Short History of Women's Rights*. New York, 1911.

Howard, John T., *Our American Music*. New York, 1930.

Ingle, Edward, *Southern Sidelights*. New York, 1896.

Jenkins, William S., *Pro-Slavery Thought in the Old South*. Chapel Hill, 1935.

Jones, D. D. and W. H. Mills, eds., *History of the Presbyterian Church in South Carolina since 1850*. Columbia, 1926.

Knill, Richard, "The Missionary's Wife," in William M. Engle, ed., *A Series of Presbyterian Church Tracts*, II, Philadelphia, 1840.

Langdon-Davis, John, *A Short History of Women*. New York, 1927.

Lovell, Caroline C., *The Golden Isles of Georgia*. Boston, 1932.

Mallay, C. D., *Memoir of Jesse Mercer*. New York, 1844.

Mitchell, Broadus, "The Rise of Cotton Mills in the South," in *Johns Hopkins University Studies*, XXXIX, No. 2, Baltimore, 1921.

McCabe, Joseph, "How Christianity Has Treated Women," in S. D. Schmalhausen and V. F. Calverton, eds., *Women's Coming of Age*. New York, 1931.

Park, Orville A., comp., *The History of Georgia in the Eighteenth Century, as Recorded in the Reports of the Georgia Bar Association*. Reprint from the Annual Report of the Georgia Bar Association, June 1921. Macon, 1921.

Parrington, Vernon L., *The Romantic Revolution in America*. New York, 1927.

Peeples, H. C., "Women Under the Law," in *Report of the 31st Session of the Georgia Bar Association, 1914*. Macon, 1914.

Schlesinger, Arthur, *New Viewpoints in American History*. New York, 1928.

Shryock, R. H., "The Early Industrial Revolution in the Empire State," in *Georgia Historical Quarterly*, XI, No. 2.

_____, *Georgia and the Union in 1850*. Philadelphia, 1926.

_____, "Medical Practice in the Old South," in *South Atlantic Quarterly*, XXIX, Durham, 1930.

_____, "Sylvester Graham and the Popular Health Movement," in *Mississippi Valley Historical Review*, XVIII.

Smith, George G., *A Hundred Years of Methodism in Augusta, Georgia*. Augusta, 1898.

Spaeth, Sigman, *Read 'em and Weep*. Garden City, 1927.

Stanton, Theodore and Harriet S. Blatch, *Elizabeth Cady Stanton*. New York, 1922.

Staton, Kate E., comp., *Old Southern Songs of the Period of the Confederacy*: The Dixie Trophy Collection. New York, 1926.

Vance, Rupert B., *Human Geography of the South*. Chapel Hill, 1935.

Waddell, Moses, *Memoirs of the Life of Miss Caroline E. Smelt*. New York, 1857.

Wertenbaker, Thomas J., *The First Americans, 1607-1690*. New York, 1929.

Wheeler, Henry, *One Thousand Questions and Answers Concerning the Methodist Episcopal Church*. New York, 1898.

Woody, Thomas, *History of Women's Education in the United States*. 2 vols., New York, 1929.

Index

Scholarship in Women's History: Rediscovered and New

GERDA LERNER, Editor